BE A MASTER® OF SEX ENERGY

HYPNOTIZE YOUR PARTNER FOR LOVE AND GREAT SEX

Dr. Theodoros Kousouli

A Personal Empowerment Book

Kousouli Enterprises
Los Angeles, CA

Copyright © 2018 by Theodoros Kousouli D.C., CHt.

All rights reserved. No part of this book may be reproduced or utilized in any form or by any means, electronic or mechanical including photocopying, recording, or by any information storage and retrieval system, without permission in writing from the author and publisher, except for the inclusion of brief quotations in a review with proper credit cited.

The BE A MASTER® BOOK SERIES (http://www.BEAMASTER.com) trademarked brand and work is Copyright of Dr. Theodoros Kousouli.

The KOUSOULI® mark and the Kousouli® Method 4R Intervention health system are registered trademarks of Theodoros D. Kousouli D.C., CHt. and Kousouli Enterprises.

Heartfelt gratitude to the following for their contributions:
Cover and internal photography: Matthew A. Cooke
Editing & research / data assistance: Latasha Doyle
Book sketch illustrations: Valerie Woelk
Layout coordinator: Gustavo Martinez

ISBN: 978-0997328509   Softcover
ISBN: 978-0997328516   Epub
ISBN: 978-0997328523   Kindle

Library of Congress Control Number: 2016909170

Kousouli Enterprises
P.O. Box 360494
Los Angeles, CA 90036

Printed in the United States of America

CONTENTS

Disclaimers viii
Acknowledgements xi

Chapter 1: My Story 1

Chapter 2: Let's Talk About Sex 5
   2.1 Attitude Change 5
   2.2 Evaluate Your Values 6
   2.3 Following the Crowd 6
   2.4 Love - One Size Fits All? 7
   2.5 Releasing Your Inner Sexual Power 9

Chapter 3: The History of Sex 11
   3.1 Before Christ 11
   3.2 Medieval Era 15
   3.3 Past Lives and Sex Now 16
   3.4 Views of Sperm and Fertility 17
   3.5 Purpose of Circumcision 18
   3.6 Sexual Revolutions: Feminism and the GLBT (Gay, Lesbian, ...
       Bisexual,Transgendered) Uprising 19
   3.7 Opposing Views in Modern Times 20

Chapter 4: Breaking the Taboos of Desire 23
   4.1 Sex and the Church 24
   4.2 Spiritual Sex (The Chakras and Aura) 27
   4.3 Ego 39
   4.4 Pornography Addiction 40
   4.5 Prostitution 43
   4.6 Sex Sells 44
   4.7 Subliminal Messages Everywhere 45
   4.8 Hollywood Idols 46

Chapter 5: Battle of the Sexes 49
   5.1 Loss of Male Power 49

    5.2 The Problem with Being a Nice Guy 51
    5.3 Taking the Power Back 53
    5.4 Strong, Independent Women 54
    5.5 Using Sex as a Weapon 55
    5.6 The Hidden Forces That Guide Gender Roles 56

Chapter 6: The Psychology of Sex 59
    6.1 Defining Moments 59
    6.2 Love 60
    6.3 Sex and Lust 60
    6.4 Sex Transmutation 62
    6.5 Importance of Body Language 62
    6.6 Subconscious Desire 67
    6.7 Sex Styles Reflected in Clothing 68
    6.8 Hypnotizing Your Lover 70

Chapter 7: The Neural Wiring of Pleasure 77
    7.1 Oh, the Nerve! 77
    7.2 The Brain on Sex 78
    7.3 What Women (and Men) Want 80
    7.4 Debunking the Feminine Mystique 82
    7.5 Techniques for Female Pleasure 85
    7.6 The Power of Sacred Male Energy 94
    7.7 Techniques for Male Pleasure 96
    7.8 It Takes Two (Or More) to Tango 102
    7.9 Stimulating Sex Combinations for a Deeper Connection ... 104
    7.10 Energy Flow during Sexual Stimulation 112
    7.11 Enhancing the Mood 115
    7.12 Safety is Sexy 118

Chapter 8: Secret Sexual Chi 121
    8.1 Naturally Improve Your Sex Life 121
    8.2 Habitual Tips to Help Grow Your Natural Chi 126
    8.3 The Kousouli® Method Spinal Stretches (KSS®) for Improved
        Sexual Health 129

Chapter 9: Attracting the Right Frequency in Partners 139
    9.1 Understanding Your Sex Sign 139

    9.2 The Right Vibes 144
    9.3 The Right Attitude 145
    9.4 Attracting Lovers; Am I Ready? Are They? 146
    9.5 Sex, Money, and Men 154
    9.6 A Note on Gratitude 156
    9.7 Relationships Are Not Easy 156

Chapter 10: When Pleasure Becomes Pain **159**
    10.1 Spiritual, Emotional, and Physical Protection 159
    10.2 BDSM (Bondage, Domination, Sadism, and Masochism)
        and Demeaning Sexual Interactions 160
    10.3 Troubleshooting for Intentional Sex 160
    10.4 Pregnancy as a Result of Sex Without Intention 162
    10.5 When Energies Aren't in Sync 165
    10.6 Staying Together When You Shouldn't 166
    10.7 Nagging is Never OK 166
    10.8 Why Do People Cheat? 167
    10.9 Breakups Can Be Healthy 168

Chapter 11: Sexual Healing (Through the Kousouli® Method) **169**
    11.1 Healing Sexual Traumas with the Kousouli® Method 169
    11.2 Using the Kousouli® Method to Heal Your Heart 169
    11.3 The Kousouli® Method 4R Intervention System 176

Chapter 12: The Future of Sex, (Virtual Reality, Artificial Intelligence)
and Final Thoughts **183**
    12.1 Robot Sex 183
    12.2 Benefits of Artificial Intelligence 185
    12.3 Spirituality and the Advent of AI 186
    12.4 Mechanics of Sex 187
    12.5 Conclusion 188

About the Author **191**

References **193**

Be a Master® of Sex Energy

Life Changing Products · Books · Seminars · Empowerment Audios · Get on the Newsletter!
Connect with Dr. Kousouli, www.DrKousouli.com and on all Social Media Platforms
@DrKousouli #DrKousouli #KousouliMethod
You Will Also Enjoy Dr. Kousouli's Other Published Works Available Now from Major Retailers:

BE A MASTER® OF MAXIMUM HEALING
How to Lead a Healthy Life Without Limits
- Holistic Solutions for over 60 Diseases to Help You and Your Loved Ones Heal!

BE A MASTER® OF PSYCHIC ENERGY
Your Key to Truly Mastering Your Personal Power
- Uncover and Amplify Your Hidden Psychic Abilities to Change Your Life!

BE A MASTER® OF SUCCESS
Dr.Kousouli's 33 Master Secrets to Achieving Your Dreams
- Solid Success Principles You can Apply Right Now to Empower Your Life!

BE A MASTER® OF SELF IMAGE
Dr.Kousouli's 33 Master Secrets to Living Healthier, Happier and Hotter
- Simple Holistic Tips & Tricks for More Weight Loss and Body Benefit to You!

BE A MASTER® OF SELF LOVE
Dr.Kousouli's 33 Master Secrets to Loving Your Extraordinary Life
- Overcome Bullying, Abuse, Depression and Build Massive Self-Esteem & Self-Love!

BE A MASTER® OF YOUR REALITY
Authentically Manifest Your Desires
- Use the Law of Attraction to Radically Transform Your Life!

If you would like to share your story of how Dr. Kousouli's books, audios or seminars have impacted your life for the better, we would love to hear from you! (Messages are screened by staff and forwarded when appropriate.)

For A Free Gift from Dr. Theo Kousouli visit www.FreeGiftFromDrTheo.com

This book is dedicated to all the lovers; young and old, all sexes, past, present and future. For if you had not participated in your love, there would be no one and no thing.

*"We are like islands in the sea,
separate on the surface
but connected in the deep."*

~ William James

DISCLAIMER

In a land where being politically correct seems more 'right' than standing for the 'truth,' or more desired than expressing an honest opinion; it's sad that I must digress and add the following legal disclaimer to remind you the reader, that *you must think for yourself*.

This book is a collection of experience and research that forms my thoughts, opinions, and conclusions as a board certified Doctor of Chiropractic (D.C.) and Hypnotherapist (CHt); not a Doctor of Medicine (M.D.). The content herein is controversial as it presents an alternate view to the status quo. There are establishments who may disagree with certain contents of this book and would have preferred that this information never found your eyes. However, this book is not intended for them; it was written for the countless individuals yearning for better health and well-being amongst a society that has lost its way.

The writings in this book are based on my personal research, experience, interpretations and beliefs. Your personal beliefs will affect your ability to review this material, as you will put it through your own filters. I intend to guide you in developing your own ability to use your sexual energy in a healthy manner, and this book is a guide for you to grow, but is not by any means the final word on the subject.

I encourage you, the reader, to research, analyze and develop your own opinions on the subject matters discussed. As a holistic health care provider, I express the truth as I have come to know it. It is my duty to aid in the growth of my beloved patients, family, and friends with this love so they too may reach the heights of what their Creator made possible for them to be.

Theodoros Kousouli D.C., CHt.

LEGAL DISCLAIMER

This publication is for informational purposes only. The material presented herein denotes the views of the author as of the date of press. The material and ideas provided herein are believed to be truthful and complete, based on the author's best judgment and experience, formed from the available data at the time of publication. Because of the speed by which conditions and information change, the author reserves the right to amend and update his opinions at any time based upon the new data and circumstances. While every effort has been made to provide complete, accurate, current, and reliable information within this publication, no warranties of any kind are expressed or implied. The publisher, author, and all associated parties involved with this publication assume no responsibility for errors, inaccuracies, oversights or conflicting interpretation of the content herein. The author and publisher do not accept any responsibility for any liabilities resulting from the use of this information. Readers acknowledge that the author is not engaging in rendering guarantees of income or outcome of any kind in connection with using any methods, techniques, or information stated or implied. Any perceived results of the material's use can vary greatly per case and individual circumstance. Mention of any persons or companies in this book does not imply that they endorse this book, its content, or the author, and similarly the author does not endorse them. Any supposed slights of specific establishments, corporations, organizations, peoples, or persons are unintended.

You should consult your own chiropractor, acupuncturist, herbalist, naturopath, hypnotherapist or other holistic doctor(s) in combination with sound medical advice. Readers are cautioned to first consult with proper health professionals about their individual circumstances on any matter relating to their health and sexual well-being prior to taking any course of action. The author is not a licensed medical doctor or psychiatrist and the **information provided in this book should not be construed as personal, medical, or psychiatric advice or instruction.** All readers or users of the information herein, who fail to consult proper health experts, assume the risk of any and all injuries.

The contents of this book and the information herein have not been evaluated or approved by the Food and Drug Administration for the treatment or cure of any disease, disorder, syndrome, or ailment mentioned herein.

ACKNOWLEDGEMENTS

"A grateful mind is a great mind which eventually attracts to itself great things."
~Plato

I am in deep gratitude and admiration for the beautiful women I have been blessed to know personally and intimately. I have the inmost appreciation for their reflection of divine feminine energy. Our connection has helped me uncover sexual truths, dissolve inaccurate beliefs, and has unveiled specific understandings which have made me a better lover, man, and human being. A large part of this book is a reflection of their dedication to the movement forward in sexual consciousness.

Thank you to my parents for giving me life and allowing me the ability to learn from the path that I embarked on. Thank you to my siblings and close friends for their continued support and encouragement through the years. Thank you to my wonderful patients who allow me to share in their unfolding journey of healing and abundance; I am blessed and honored to be your mentor through challenging times. Your stories and experiences have helped me answer many of the questions and content that helped shape this book so I could help others with similar questions. Thank you to my mentors, past and present, which have molded my understanding of life and higher knowledge. Thank you to Latasha Doyle for her research and editing prowess to help me get this material out to the masses in time. Thank you to my illustrator Valerie Woelk with her many talents for bringing the book to life visually. I thank you, the reader, for wishing to expand your mind; by doing so you continue to help free mankind from the invisible bonds of its silent prison.

Lastly, but definitely not least, I thank the Almighty Creator of all things visible and invisible, great and small, explainable and unexplainable. I stand in awe of your pure magnificence as you lead and sustain me through your playground day by day.

This list deserves to be far longer than it reads. If I have forgotten your name in these writings of ink; kindly forgive me - and know that I am in gratitude to you from the depths of my heart.

Chapter 1:
My Story

"I don't know the question, but sex is definitely the answer."
~ Woody Allen

"You will go to Hell if you have sex outside of marriage," I heard once again, as my mother pointed her finger at my siblings and me. This was during one of her weekly Bible study groups she conducted at home for us - her children - and our friends. This line, among many other dogmas, was one of the only pieces of advice about sex passed down from my mother. It was a huge influence on my life, teaching me how to relate to the opposite sex and how to view my own sexuality as I grew up. My parents were the largest factors in my relationships and my view of self, something that would have to be addressed and healed as I reached adulthood.

My mother was a beautiful, model-esque daughter of a schoolteacher, her father's pride and joy. My maternal grandparents were very much involved in the Greek Orthodox Church, and my mother was raised to never talk about sexuality, and wasn't allowed to have a boyfriend until she was to be married. She was taught that sex was bad, and she would go to Hell if she had sex outside of marriage. My mother reached the age of 31 and began desperately seeking to find a solid, established man she could marry and start a family with. She met my father through an arrangement with a friend in class. My mother's friend, it turned out, was my future father's sister. When my mother met my father, he was a handsome Greek merchant marine "bad boy" who swept my mom off her feet. With a religious mother but a fairly non-religious father, my father was not raised with the stern dogma my mother was. He grew up in a more lenient family home, and left all the religious talk and teachings to my mother, who passed all of this down to us.

My father had wooed my mother, and within only one brief month of courtship, he had taken her as his wife, moved away from Greece, and brought her to America. In America, the hard reality of their infatuation began to settle, and the consequences of their hasty choices began to set in. My mother became very unhappy, as the American fairytale in her mind did not match the hard reality of her living situation in the United States. My father did not want my mother to become "Americanized," and thus shut her off from shopping malls, gossipy girlfriends, and the general materialistic culture of the

U.S. She had no car, no freedom, and she missed her family back in Greece. My father quickly found out he did not marry an independent, worldly woman, and instead found that she was fond of whining, nagging, and complaining. Their personalities, although originally appealing to each other, started to repel.

I grew up in an Eastern Orthodox family, in a very traditional Greek American home. When my mother and father came to the U.S. in the 1970's, my father became a restaurant owner, and my mother stayed home to take care of us (me and my twin younger siblings). I had what many would call one of the few "traditional families" in society - with the five of us living in one household and sharing meals together. My father was the cliché disciplinarian type, while my mother was the nurturer as well as the educator. Both of my parents strongly believed that my mother's place was in the home, while my father's place was in the workplace. My mother grew to resent my father for moving her away from Greece, and giving her no money or car to live her life. Because of their traditional beliefs, they stayed together simply because they were married with children. My parents always seemed to only connect with each other in one way: when they were arguing. My siblings and I always knew our parents loved us unconditionally, and each parent had their own strengths and weaknesses. Parents are, after all, only human, and can only do the best they can with the tools they have been given. When we were growing up, my siblings and I witnessed a lot of their arguments, and were raised in a fairly toxic environment thanks to all the fighting. When I left my parent's home and headed to college, I found that the way I was raised would affect my own experiences and how I interacted with the world.

Aside from the semi-parental dysfunction that I was raised in, my mother often force-fed my siblings and me her religious beliefs. From a young age, I was not allowed to express myself because of her influence, and thanks also to the surety that I would go to Hell if I even asked. My mother had full property of my thought process, and her voice was a power to be reckoned with. I felt that I wasn't allowed to ask questions about sex, or anything that she was directly against. In the end, what I learned about sex was passed down from public school interactions, sexual innuendo from movies, adult magazines, and from friends. My father left the "Birds and the Bees" talk to my mother, figuring that between what she taught us and what we'd learn naturally would be enough. However, being raised in such a traditional home, and seeing constantly fighting parents, affected how I began to think about love and sex between two people. This shaped my understanding that commitment and partnership can be painful and difficult. Being unable to express one's self naturally in their childhood home makes them feel ashamed to even have natural thoughts, so their "questions of self and true identity" get repressed. I know I am not alone in this, as many people have backgrounds similar to my own. Many more people have much more traumatic childhoods or original interactions with sexuality, such as physical abuse, rape, or incest, leading to an even harder process to overcome.

I look back on this now and am able to better evaluate the advice passed down to me over the years. This guidance is a mixture of traditions, personal beliefs, church dogma, and society's acceptance (or lack thereof) stemming from the time period they were sourced. What I realized, as I grew up and moved away from my mother's ineffable force, was that she and her religious programming were subconsciously guiding my interactions with others, when these things come organically from within. We are all social creatures on some level, and sex is a vital part of human nature. Why, then, does so much of what was passed down to me have the ability to affect my true nature? How was this healthy? Assessing these "original biases" I had growing up helped me come to terms with my identity, and I know it can help you, too.

What I have also learned through my adult years, and years in my professional practice, is that our personal and sexual relationships are more important to our overall health and wellbeing than we can entirely imagine. I provide the information in this book so that you can truly understand the power of the body, sexuality, and the Holy Spirit that created it. This book focuses on the physical reality of sex, but also the energy flow and spiritual power of sex, which is often weakly explained in sexual works. I wish for all who are touched by this vital information to wake up to the basic power of their minds and bodies. Sex is about more than just organs that create offspring, and is used to draw on universal consciousness that has incredible power - a power that is not explained in our society with the honesty and openness it deserves.

It is important to know that if the power that is instilled in the act of making love is not held in accordance with the highest vibration that made the world, it will revolt into something lesser than love, and attack the creator of the energy to deliver pain. It should also be noted that during sex without loving intention, a child may be created, and without loving energy and devotion to your partner, this child will also experience difficulties in life with parents who do not truly love one another. Many of us are products of marriages or pairings that do not reflect high vibrations of love, and we experience these ramifications throughout our lives, both in our family homes and in our own energies and future interactions. However, no matter what develops, we can grow if we decide to learn from the challenges we are faced with. The truth is that sexuality, as society promotes it, roots us in our human domain, keeping us from experiencing the bliss of the true sexual nature of male and female intertwined in divine consciousness. There are so many external influences telling a person how to have (or not have) sex, what they have to look like to attract a partner, and exactly what sex and love are defined as. In reality, none of these external forces control you, despite how much they push and pull. What rests inside each of us, our own innate energies and sexuality, will guide us and help us to engage with one another on a higher plane. When the powerful force of sexuality is used in line with the laws of the Universe, the results are nothing but astounding.

The topic of sex is far broader than the reach of this book, but the final word on sex is you and your experiences. Only you, your partner(s), your higher self, and God are in the bedroom with you. It's a healthy expression of love, and it is a good thing for the soul and psyche. Violent, negative, controlling emotions or low vibrations affect the act, actor(s), and health of all involved. If any of this hits home for you and you're looking to open up your sexual knowledge to satisfy yourself and your partner on a deeper level, this unique book will gift you the information needed to boost your connection to the next level. Let me provide you the resources and assets to love on the highest level humanly possible. I hope that the information in this book brings you more understanding of the spiritual nature and power you hold, as God force in human existence.

Chapter 2:
Let's Talk About Sex

*"Love is an ice cream sundae, with all the marvelous coverings.
Sex is the cherry on top."*
~ Jimmy Dean

Sex is an unspoken pillar of today's society, still taboo and controversial even in this modern age. Despite the fact that sex is a vital aspect of a healthy life, and the marker of a connected relationship, we tend to sweep it under the rug and never truly evaluate it. Social norms dictate that only very intimate friends and partners discuss their experiences, fantasies, or preferences. This "locked box" attitude towards sex means that many people repress their sexuality, tending towards what is considered safe and normal.

But who or what dictates what sex is safe or normal? If it is a private act, why do external forces have so much influence? So much of who we are as adults is rooted in the acceptance of our bodies, our passions, our spirits. The mass majority of people do not view sex as an outlet, an expression, and a detoxification process. When we deny our bodies and our spirits this most basic human instinct, to be a sexual being, we are essentially denying a major aspect of our physical and spiritual health.

2.1 Attitude Change

Most of what we know about sex depends on how we were raised, what society we live in and what religion we adhere to. The Law of Primacy states that what you were taught initially is what sticks the hardest, meaning that your biases and attitudes are a result of what you first learned in life. This makes it incredibly hard to change, but not impossible. What would happen if we changed our existing attitudes towards sex? How would we benefit if we all took a closer look at our sex lives - cleared the dust off, and really *looked* at our partners, our beliefs and ourselves without damning ourselves with judgment? What if you thought about your biases or tastes in sex and asked yourself: "Why do I think this way, who gave me this data, and why do I hold it as my truth?" While there may be some hesitance to break through the surface, the discomfort will not last long. Once you embrace this aspect of your health, your body, and your soul, you will find that the energy and effort flows freely. You will feel as if sex is truly a natural experience, an instinct that has been buried. For the purposes of this book, I ask that you tap in to your sexual identity, explore what makes you feel sexual, what doesn't, and delve into how you approach the act both with your body and your heart.

2.2 Evaluate Your Values

To get the full use out of this book, especially focus on your absolute beliefs about sexuality. When you think of sex, what is your immediate reaction? Arousal? Interest? Shame? Reticence? Is it a physical reaction, or an internal one? Would you find that you have grown up viewing sex in a particular way? Were you raised to believe sex was a private act, one that created children and doesn't warrant further explanation? Explore those assumptions, and reflect on how sex makes you feel.

Do you think sex is for recreation as well as procreation? What qualifies as "fun" for you? Consider how you feel after sex, and focus on which partners correlate to which experiences. Do you feel satisfied with your sex life or your sexual partner(s)? Do you feel your sexual experience is lacking, whether on your part or your lover's? What is your spiritual relation to sex? Do you desire a soulful connection or have you been seeking sex merely for pleasures of the flesh? Do you find yourself wanting a long-term partner but you are coming up short, or are you replacing an emptiness inside with sex?

Discovering your biases towards sex will help you move through this book, and develop a more positive approach to one of life's greatest pleasures and divine gifts.

2.3 Following the Crowd

So much of our sexual identity and experiences are composed of social constructs, realities that are only a reflection of the culture in which we live. When you look internally, and view sex within the parameters of your individual experience, those outside influences tend to have less of an impact on our behavior and emotions. We have all witnessed a great insurgence of sex and sexual identity within recent years, a changing tide in the psyche that represents the collective opinion on what is right or wrong, good or bad, normal or abnormal. This merely serves to show that, historically speaking, culture and society have weighed heavily on individuality and sexuality through the course of time.

What doesn't seem to have enough "pull" on sexuality in modern times is the reality that sex is both a physical and spiritual necessity. Human physicality requires touch and connection to others in order to thrive, but so does the soul. The energy created when two or more people engage in a physical expression of love cannot be replicated elsewhere. As we move away from sex as a natural and needed aspect of life, we are essentially denying the existence of the soul and its needs. By following the crowd, you are denying your individualism and energetic authenticity.

As time moves on, cultures change, and views on sexuality change as a result. If we focus on the influences that control our behavior, and realize there are strings that control the masses, we will be free to love as we want, and embrace our spiritual sexuality. What this book seeks to do is draw attention to the puppeteer - groupthink and social norms - that affect your individual experience with your body, your partner's body, and the sacred connection that occurs during sex.

2.4 Love - One Size Fits All?

Many societies and cultures, and especially religions, claim to know what love should look like and feel like, while rejecting all other options. The terrible consequence of this "one track mind" is that people who experience different types of love, sexuality, or desires tend to hide behind a façade of what external forces say is "normal." Society forces gay men and women to "come out" of the closet, hoping for acceptance. Transgender and transsexual individuals often hide their gender affinity from even their closest family. "Different love" is forced underground, literally, where swingers groups, polyamorous relationships, and BDSM (Bondage, Domination, Sadism, and Masochism) or dominant and submissive roles can thrive. Instead of accepting all love and all forms of consensual sex as equal in the eye of the Divine, these lovers must hide their true selves and their spirits suffer all the more from it. Some may argue that this is not Godly - this is human will exerting itself over God.

The reality may be that these people all experience love in the same way that heterosexual, monogamous couples do, but maybe that love takes a different path of expression. What if sex with multiple partners doesn't have to mean you're a slut or a "player;" open relationships don't have to mean you're afraid of commitment or a total sleaze. Having a threesome could be an intense, vibrational experience where love is shared equally three ways rather than just two (or however many ways you can dice it). The Divine in its true form recognizes these expressions of love for what they are, rather than what they look like.

Did you, the reader, stop there and say, "Whoa, that's a lot to take in and I am not too sure I agree with that"? If you found yourself thinking along those lines, consider the possibility that you are filtering your thoughts through your primary belief systems (religion, childhood experiences, adult interactions, etc.). You may have felt uncomfortable, a bit on edge. If so, then you have hit a place of resistance within your engrained thoughts – each reader will experience this in their own ways, whether now or later in the book. Perhaps, with further reading, you can understand the points being made. The high minded and emotionally mature will read with an open mind as the lesser minded will judge and possibly stop reading due to discomfort. Which are you?

If you are here to be open and willing to learn about love in all its forms, here are a few examples of the "different loves" that can be found all around the world, if only you are willing to see them with open eyes, minds and hearts without judgement:

Polyamory

A polyamorous relationship, meaning a long-term relationship between three or more people, is often viewed as unnatural and unsustainable. Think about the questions these individuals receive when they tell someone about their lifestyle: "How do you do that? Don't you get jealous? Do you have sex with one person every night? Do you have gay sex or just heterosexual sex? Does your family know?" All of these questions aligned with only one mentality: the heterosexual monogamous viewpoint. In reality, people who express their sexuality openly and safely, without a need for approval, tend to be happier and therefore healthier than their repressed counterparts. Who is to say you can't love more than one person equally, and without negative emotions and lower vibrational energies interfering in your pleasure?

Homosexual/Bisexual/Pansexual

For most of modern history, homosexuals have been actively hunted as "enemies" of society. Bisexuals (attracted to either females or males) and pansexuals (attracted to anyone regardless of sex or gender identity) represent a smaller population, but one that society feels needs to be labeled in order to be understood. Rather than just saying "I love anyone who can make me laugh," or "I love anyone who I feel safe with," people must label the person they love based on sex and gender roles. These individuals, willing to embrace their love, face incredibly difficult obstacles in life, but still manage to have fulfilling relationships and gratifying sexual experiences.

BDSM (Bondage, Domination, Sadism, and Masochism)/Dominant and Submissive

Recent "pop culture" like porn and especially erotic fiction like *Fifty Shades of Grey* have brought the BDSM lifestyle to the forefront. BDSM stands for "Bondage, Domination, Sadism and Masochism," and covers a wide range of sexual play. However, what most people are missing when they consume this sort of material is the reality of a real BDSM or Dom/

Sub relationship. Many of the people who live this life do not support the portrayal they have been given in the mass media. It's not just about "rough sex," or tying people up, or spanking men while wearing Dominatrix costumes. That is mistaking the trees for the forest; BDSM focuses on a very deep connection with one's partner or partners. Dominants focus on the needs and limits of their submissive(s), and while it seems they are the ones in power, the submissive gives the dominant a great gift: their trust. While outsiders may disagree with the approach, and there are a number of ways to allow this lifestyle to devolve into sectors of lower vibration, it is possible to "get it right." When individuals focus solely on each other, and trust each other implicitly, there is a connection that many people who engage in usual "vanilla" sex never manage to reach.

Of course, this list is short and concise. It does not cover every "flavor" of sexuality out there. What could be an entire book on different lifestyles and sexual preferences does not actually pertain to the topic of this book. We are merely here to evaluate why we label things that can be healthy and pleasurable for individuals. We also need to consider the dangers that are posed when you refuse to be the person you know you are. These lifestyles and their descriptions serve as a way to show you, the reader, that you can be a sexual person and have a healthy interaction with yourself and with others no matter what your sex life may look like.

Withholding Your Sexual Nature

When you withhold your sexual energies, only channeling them one way for fear of retaliation, rejection or some misinformed view of the afterlife, you're changing your vibrational dynamics, your essence, and risking your mental, emotional and spiritual health. The people who are able to accept their sexuality, embrace it and act upon it, release the positive energy in their interactions with their partners, transforming stagnant energy into positive flow. If you are open to all sex that is consensual and made in love for the other person or people, you allow higher levels of energy and spirit into your life. Who is to judge a person who acts and lives in love? Only other humans who do not understand love are capable of this judgment (not a loving God who created all).

2.5 Releasing Your Inner Sexual Power

Think about a time you were truly sexual. You gave yourself freely, your actions were uninhibited and you felt at one with the person (or persons) you were engaged with. What made this encounter so unique? What would you do to experience that every time you have sex? Look at how men are afraid to talk and express their desires, so instead they place their energy in hiding it behind a locked door with a porno magazine. So often our peers tell us, "Once you get married/have a baby/gain weight, it's all downhill from there and you never have sex." Or "Wives don't give their husbands blow jobs," or "You're a pervert if you like much younger girls/older men/ whatever." Look at how women try to act like what they see on TV or in porn. Women hold themselves accountable for their looks and how they are seen in the eyes of men (or competitive women) rather than focusing how they see themselves - as uniquely powerful, divine feminine beings. This is not always how things used to be. Women (and men) have both changed dramatically over time; let's examine the history of sex to evaluate this further.

Chapter 3:
The History of Sex

"It's been so long since I've had sex I've forgotten who ties up who."
~ Joan Rivers

It is arguable that the history of sex goes beyond the span of this book, including the first multi-celled organisms found on this planet, the dinosaurs, other planetary beings, the first humanoid species, and even, *yes*, your parents. For the purpose of brevity, however, this chapter will focus on the history of sexual experiences. This storied past goes back millennia, predating Christianity and Judaism, and spanning to the very first days of man. Going back over 6,000 years, we can see how sex has been a vital part of every major civilization, and has been a symbol of vibrancy and spiritual connection. When we move through the years, you will see a tangible digression from sexual acceptance and reverence to sexual repression and disdain. Sex has always been exploited, since the Dawn of Man, but it has never before been such a source of internal affliction and social sickness. By evaluating where we once were, and where we are now, it is possible to see how sex has been changed and molded over time into something it was never intended to be.

3.1 Before Christ

Mesopotamia

Contrary to some religions, the world has existed for an estimated 14 billion years, with civilized humans (as we are today) existing for only a blip in time - about 6,000 years. As long as the species has existed, there has been proof of sexuality. In Mesopotamia, the first true civilization in history dating back to nearly 5000 BCE, remnants of a strong sexual identity have been found. The Peor Cult, literally translated into "the cult of the phallus," was known throughout the region for their orgies, their loose norms and behaviors. Ishtar, the goddess of the Mesopotamians, was a very sexual figure. Young girls were encouraged to stand outside her temple and allow men to have sex with them, although virginity was demanded in a marriage contract.

Despite "traditional" marital roles between a man and a woman, many Mesopotamian men engaged in homosexual acts, and sex was viewed very openly and without judgment. Many art pieces have been found depicting various sex positions, and individuals were encouraged to act upon sexual impulses. Mesopotamia was a highly male-centered society, however, and women were not given the same freedoms with their sexuality, as they were told sex was for procreation.

Ancient Egypt

Fast-forward to Egyptian times, estimated to begin around 3000 BCE, and history tells a somewhat different story. The Egyptians were openly sexual, with many of their hieroglyphs and drawings indicating some sort of sexual act or intention. Egyptians, and especially the pharaohs, believed that ejaculation prior to death meant rebirth, or access to the afterlife. This spiritual connection to sex and life is a very important one to remember. Many sources find that homosexuality was somewhat common, but the person in the subordinate role was generally looked down upon in Egyptian society. What differs most in the accounts of ancient Egyptian sexuality is the role of the female. The female was a strong, independent character that provided sexual pleasure, the gift of offspring, and represented power in sexual interactions.

India

Moving to ancient India, you will already have an idea of the vibrant sexual lives of many Indians in the millennia prior to the Christian era. Of course, the *Kama Sutra* hails from India, providing dozens of sexual positions for partners to explore. The *Kama Sutra* is written in Sanskrit, but does not hail from ancient times (5000 BCE) - it is estimated to have been written between 400 BCE and 200 CE. In ancient India, Hindu texts like the *Vedas* lead anthropologists to believe that sex was viewed similarly to today's standards. These sacred texts indicate that marriage was a holy union between a man and a woman, and while sex was mutually pleasurable it was a private act intended to create children.

Ancient Persia and the Middle East

Moving on to Ancient Persia, 2200 BCE, we see the combination of Mesopotamian and Indian forces at hand. Persians worshipped Ishtar like the Mesopotamians, and believed that sex was a vital aspect of life, especially in creating life. However, the Persian Empire, which would later become the Middle East we know so well today, had a rich culture of homosexuality and what some may call sodomy. In Persia, homosexuality was commonplace, and often men would love one another freely. Whether in bathhouses or male brothels, or even in public, homosexuality was not viewed as a negative action or illness, as it is today by some. Young boys were often viewed as muses, and sexual intercourse with them was considered a transcendental experience, one that made the man closer to God. Transgenderism was not rare, and many male brothels featured young men playing a woman's role for paying customers.

Iran, around 1000 BCE, also had a deep culture involving same-sex relations outside of marriage. Marriage was viewed as a relationship between families and a way to bear and raise children in the community. Homosexuality was seen almost as courtship - men would give gifts to one another, or enjoy a teacher/student relationship. Military training and advancement was also a common source of these relationships, as well as general mentoring or apprenticeship for a future career. Homosexual relationships also were a way to make numerous social connections, and improve one's lot in life. These relationships were called "brotherhoods," indicating that sex was not the only dynamic found in these interactions. Yes, sex occurred, often in a loving and giving way - a way to show another man how to be sexual, or as a way to be closer to one another. These courtships lasted years, and were not exclusive to men. Women, too, had "sisterhoods," and would often propose a relationship with another by having a matchmaker of sorts deliver the proposal. These relationships had a code and a structure, indicating that they were commonplace and accepted.

Ancient Rome and Greece

Rome and Greece, probably two of the best-known sexual civilizations in history, mark a period in time where sex was free, widespread and came in many different forms. In Rome and Greece, between 1000 BCE and the beginning of the current era, pedastry was a common practice. This meant that adult men (erastes) had young male apprentices (eromenos) who also served as sexual partners. This was not viewed as sodomy, but instead a relationship between teacher and student, where knowledge in all its forms was passed down through their work and also through their relationship. Sperm was viewed as transference as well, passing down energy from teacher to apprentice. These apprenticeships were entirely commonplace, so much so that men were often married to women and still had sex with their students. Women were used as family orchestrators and community connections, rather than a source of sexuality and interaction.

The bathhouses in Rome and Greece were notorious through history for their open sexuality, where anyone was accepted into the fray, and nobody was judged for their behavior. The Roman pantheon of gods supported sexuality as an expression of divinity, an important distinction as many people today view their behaviors as depraved and unholy. Interestingly, Rome marks a period in time where sex was actually monitored by the state, or governing body. Chastity in women was considered a social concern, and brides were expected to be pure on their wedding nights. So too was incest considered immoral and unacceptable, and was avidly enforced. Rape and adultery were both illegal for Roman citizens, finally indicating a shift in the concept of consent and the structures of marriage. It is important to note however that homosexual interactions for men were not considered adultery. Greeks, as well as Romans, practiced anal sex frequently, and it was considered yet another area of exploration as a sexual being.

Greeks are often associated with the source of much of our current medical belief. Hippocrates, often referred to as "The Father of Medicine," viewed sex, and especially semen, as a balancing act to promote health in the body and to improve one's connection to God. The importance of food and general health balanced with sex was often emphasized, and many Greeks and Romans had foods they would not eat in order to balance their "humors," or bodily energies. In addition, Greeks and Romans are credited with much of the art that depicts female and male bodies. Appreciating the human form was commonplace and natural - never considered "indecent" or dirty.

One of the most important distinctions between many societies and the Ancient Greek and Roman civilizations is their relationship to "free love." Obviously this term is associated with the late 1960s and '70's, but these ancient empires practiced "polysexuality," polyamory and lacked a sexual structure. It didn't matter if it was two men together, two men and a woman, a woman and three men, or any combination therein. Sex was sex, and it was practiced openly and without retribution by the state.

The Roman view of sex was often depicted in terms of power - men who were "tops," who penetrated a man or woman, was considered the phallic energy. People who were "bottoms" were often seen as weak and valued somewhat less. In Ancient times we also see the development of the "butch" lesbian. The infamous Greek island of Lesbos, populated by women who ate, drank and fought like men, is believed to be the source of the term "lesbian." These women were seen as a unique breed compared to the traditional Roman woman, and were rumored to have the phallic power in their sexual relationships with other women and even boys.

China and East Asia

Ancient Asian cultures focused strongly on the power and energy transfers associated with sex. The infamous yin and yang symbol applies to ancient Chinese sexual interaction, documented heavily during the Chou Dynasty (770BC to 220BC). In this view, women represented a never-ending source of yin, and men contained only a limited source of yang. This meant that men's sexual force was to be monitored, and sexual intercourse with a woman meant she had to reach climax first, and often, in order for a man to "store up" enough energy to not exhaust his own.

Because of this unique reversal in power, women were often in homosexual relationships, as their energy and yin were never at risk during sex. Men rarely engaged in homosexual acts because it was dangerous for both parties - a loss in yang could result in illness and even death (as the Romans believed as well with loss of sperm). Fast forward to 220BC and on, sex became a controlled aspect of Confucian religion and lifestyle, and sexuality began to be seen as only between a man and a woman within the bedroom's confines. Japanese interactions were quite similar to the ancient Chinese. Sex was often considered an acceptable rite of passage, and many young men and women engaged in premarital sex prior to the dawn of the Christian era. The Japanese also held very strict interactions between man and wife, as marriage was a childbearing and rearing relationship. The Japanese also believed that all good things come in moderation - too much food, sleep or sex was (and is not) healthy. Therefore sex was to be an intentional act rather than a random or too-frequent occurrence. The Japanese also have a rich history of erotic images in their writings, indicating that sex was nearly an art and considered an important aspect of worship and experience.

3.2 Medieval Era

Once the Christian era began, the time period associated with the rise of Christ and his teachings, sex began to change rapidly and dramatically. By the medieval era, lasting from the 5th to the 15th century in Europe, sex had become a nearly unacceptable aspect of human nature. It was intended only for procreation, only within the confines of the marital bed, and the Church promoted the idea that God was monitoring a person's sexual interactions as well as their impure thoughts. This is the first time that God was considered a third party in the bedroom in a negative light. Other cultures and societies promoted the idea that connecting through sex was a way to reach a divine plane and share energies. That idea ceased to exist in this post-Christian era.

The medieval era also marks the beginning in the changing definitions of love, sex and marriage. Prior to this point, sex and marriage went hand-in-hand for purposes of procreation, but love and marriage were not synonyms as they are today. In medieval times, much emphasis was placed on "courtly love," the process by which you admire someone and wish to marry him or her. This is one of the first times in history where people held sex until marriage, and focused on the relationship more so than the tangible, physical aspects of love.

Sexual diversity also took a heavy blow during these times, resulting in the actual punishment of extramarital sex, homosexual sex and even non-missionary sex. Yes, parishioners in church were told that anything aside from missionary sex was a sin and would be punished accordingly. Any form of sex that was not intended for procreation was a sin in the eyes of God, including masturbation, "dry sex," homosexual sex, anal sex or sex without ejaculation. Homosexuality and sodomy were punishable by death, in such horrible ways as mutilation, hanging and burning at the stake. Such strict rules let many purists to avoid sex all together, aside from the intentions of creating a family. Better to be safe than sorry, after all.

Despite all this, there still existed unequal roles and rights for men and women. Women were expected to be virginal in this time period, and this epoch created the ingenious "chastity belt," literally locking a woman's sex organs away in order to prevent her from sullying herself before marriage. Men, however, were given codpieces on their daily clothing - bulges between the legs of pants in order to accentuate their virility and penis size. Men could sleep with prostitutes in brothels as a way to prevent adultery and "unnatural urges," but women who were prostitutes were considered criminals, and were often killed or imprisoned for their profession.

The hand of God, or more appropriately the hand of the Church, had an unprecedented amount of influence in the private lives of citizens in medieval Europe. Aside from strict rules like "No sex on Sundays," no oral sex and absolutely no lustful thoughts, churches provided people with written "Penitentials." These were books listing the number of sins an individual could commit, especially regarding sex, and gave recommendations for penance in order to avoid a future in Hell. No doubt, history has had quite a hand to play in the definition of sex over the centuries, and even now continues to evolve into a new era of discovery.

3.3 Past Lives and Sex Now

Do you find yourself pulled in a specific sexual direction, whether it is a homosexual urge, or a polyamorous inclination, or an absolute fear of divine retribution if you act upon any of your sexual urges? Have you attempted to attribute your needs, desires or biases on any event in your life and come up short? If you have no explanation for your sexuality, and find yourself confused and at sea with who you are, consider the influence of a past life. What if your spirit has been impressed upon by the life (or lives) it has lived prior to now? What if your eternal soul has spanned generations and eons, experiencing different sexual vibrations? Consider the possibility then, that in a past life, you held a different sexual orientation (a woman who enjoyed men, for example), but now you are a different person. You are still adjusting to your new sexual identity, even if you are a male, and you may still prefer men.

Consider the idea that you were first born in Ancient Rome or Greece, where sex was free and widely accepted in any form. Maybe you find yourself loving more than one person, or having multiple loving partners and find commitment to a single person difficult, compared to today's set norms. Our current society may tell you this is wrong or unnatural, but inside you do not feel the same. Could it be because your soul is wiser? What if your soul fell victim to the medieval ages, where the Church crushed sexual energies and spread fear more than love? You may experience extreme feelings of shame or reticence when it comes to sex, or an all-encompassing fear that you are going to Hell for your actions. Some metaphysical experts claim it is possible that you may have a latent past life that is shining through your current self, a soul that is older than your body's present physical conscious wisdom. This then begs the question: What is written in your spiritual DNA?

Many people have experienced the pain and loss that accompanies an unhealthy relationship, or a taboo one. When you love someone so much, even knowing that they're not a healthy match for you, you can't quite explain it away. Many past life regressions have shown people that their souls were once connected to this person in a past life, when things were different and they were other people. Your loved one has imprinted on the soul's "record," and that spans into this life as well, even if it is not the same as it once was. Our previous lives can connect us to our experience of sexuality, and influence how we behave, feel, and engage with others in an intimate capacity.

3.4 Views of Sperm and Fertility

This review of the history of sex is important because it exposes the spiritual and mystic nature of sex in general, something that is sorely lacking in today's culture. A very important aspect of these bygone eras is the idea surrounding the divine power of sexual organs and especially fluids. Sperm and female secretions have long held power and healing properties, and were revered as sacred in ancient times. Romans thought that ejaculating too frequently lessened a man's power, and could actually result in his premature death if a man experienced too much pleasure. Greek medicine considered sperm a vital "humor," an aspect of life that had to be kept in balance. Drinking sperm or performing oral sex was a way for a man to pass on his life force, wisdom and energy.

The ancient Asian cultures felt the same way as well, imparting the importance of moderation in sex because of the transference of energy that could be dangerous if not properly monitored. In some Asian cultures to this day, the emphasis of the man's yang, an easily expendable force, is still a major player in sex and power roles.

3.5 Purpose of Circumcision

Circumcision is one of the most debated religious rites in history. The source, of course, is Abrahamic religions like Christianity, Judaism and Islam that base the decision to remove a child's foreskin on a covenant made between God and Abraham. Genesis 17:9 says: "Every male among you shall be circumcised. You are to undergo circumcision, and it will be the sign of the covenant between me and you. For the generations to come every male among you who is eight days old must be circumcised… My covenant in your flesh is to be an everlasting covenant. Any uncircumcised male, who has not been circumcised in the flesh, will be cut off from his people; he has broken my covenant."

There is no reason stated for this ritual genital mutilation, aside from God requests a "covenant in your flesh." To this day, many Christians, Jews and Muslims practice circumcision, widely ranging in their implementation. Some boys get circumcised at 8 days old, as dictated in Genesis, some must wait until puberty, and many others at random times in their lives. There are also a few select African tribes that practice both male and female circumcision as part of their religious and spiritual beliefs. However, in the United States, it is often common practice to circumcise an infant boy despite religious beliefs.

Medical research has been done on the effects of circumcision, which dynamically changes a boy's anatomy. Foreskin is anatomically necessary for successful sexual functioning - it serves as a lubricant and a protectant for the tip of the penis. Removing the foreskin also desensitizes men, a phenomenon often documented by circumcised men who have a hard time reaching orgasm during sex. Myths surrounding foreskin and circumcision are still in play today, although science has debunked nearly all of these misunderstandings.

Circumcision is not done for health reasons, as often assumed, or to keep the boy's genitals clean and less prone to disease. During biblical times, the foreskin may have been a source of infection if kept unwashed, but during modern times this is not a problem. In reality, circumcision became mainstream when it was promoted widely in the beginning of the 19th century as a result of the Church's influence on medicine. Yes, the hand of God (Church) is at it again. Doctors believed that circumcising a boy would prevent them from unholy interactions, especially masturbation and lustful thoughts. Of course, this didn't work, but the popularity of circumcision has not slowed even in today's educated parenting world.

3.6 Sexual Revolutions: Feminism and the GLBT (Gay, Lesbian, Bisexual, Transgendered) Uprising

It would be remiss to not cover the rise of feminism in the late 1960's and early '70's as a major facet of sexuality in the modern world. While feminism was over a century old at the time, its "Second Wave" became a mark in history books synonymous with bra burnings, The Pill, abortion, and women entering the workforce en masse. In tandem with this movement was the self-ascribed "Sexual Revolution" associated with the same timeframe, made famous by the free love hippies so often portrayed in pop culture. This was a time of sexual exploration and an attempt to move society towards an accepting view of all types of sexuality. Of course, this brought the issues at hand to the masses, but not in the way it was expected. The Sexual Revolution turned many people against the open sexuality these people were trying to promote, making it seem like something only "hippies" were into, and something that educated, hardworking Americans would not engage in. This continued the close-minded attitude towards sex for some time.

Then came the gay revolution and the AIDS breakout of the 1980's. The start of the gay movement is accredited with the infamous Stonewall, NY riots of 1969, where gay men stood up to blatant prejudice by local police who raided a "gay bar." However, the forward momentum wouldn't gain traction until the late '70's and early '80's when more and more public figures began to come out and seek acceptance. The gay movement faced a huge hurdle in the 1980s when AIDS became front-page news, and many gay men and women had to fight the stigma associated with the disease. In 1993, President Clinton instituted "Don't Ask Don't Tell," essentially indicating that if a person didn't come out as openly gay, they could serve in the military. Major legislation protecting gay rights and promoting equality didn't start until 2000, with Vermont leading the way with their civil unions. Many people today are familiar with "Pride Parades," and the push towards same-sex marriage on a federal level. Prior to 1970, homosexuals had zero rights, and they still have a long way to go to social acceptance and equality.

Currently, another group is undergoing massive social change: the transgendered. These individuals differ from transvestites, who are people who simply enjoy (or prefer) dressing as the opposite sex. Transgender individuals feel that they were born in the wrong body, and seek surgical help to gain the proper sex organs and undergo hormone therapy. This is an incredibly traumatic experience, and one that is nearly always met with stigma and ridicule. The Internet and media have made the transgender movement quite a circus, providing so many platforms like reality shows and tabloids to criticize a person's private life.

Of course, many people in society assume that social movements created these numerous crusades towards equality in society, by the forward momentum of a subjugated group (women, homosexuals, transgender individuals). However, historians have come to understand that the Rockefeller Foundation (the richest company in America at the time) funded the push towards women in the workplace, knowing how it would benefit the bank industry. Families would be destabilized, and dependent on loans or banks for their daily financial interactions. In addition, this was ideal for "Big Business" because another half of the population would have a taxable income flowing through the federal government, giving more money to the corrupt system in place. Children would also be in school earlier, which allowed more influence over the information that they had access to and what they were "taught" (or programmed with) from an earlier age. Gloria Steinem, a leader and spokeswoman for the feminist movement, has even admitted that Miss Magazine, a forerunner in the feminist movement's public message, was funded by the CIA to encourage women to enter the job force. The Rockefeller Foundation, known by many to be a backer of the Federal Reserve (and thus the source of government money), essentially promoted women's liberation and other social movements knowing exactly how much it would change the nuclear family dynamics, and knowing that they would benefit tremendously in doing so. So many companies that promote or support social movements are, in general, found to be funded by these silent "special interest" partners like the Rockefeller Foundation with the sole intention of making the most money off of the American people as possible. While the feminist movement, the gay rights movement, and the transgender revolution are all worthy causes by themselves, the intentions and forces behind their success are obviously questionable at best.

3.7 Opposing Views in Modern Times

Today, we see a very different attitude towards sex in the public and private spheres. Especially in Western cultures, sex has become more than slightly taboo, especially if it differs from the "traditional" male/female relationship. Because of the influence the West has had on the majority of the developed world, this attitude has become widespread. With the wide reach of Christian and Islamic faiths, sex and religion have become antithetical to one another. What has happened, however, is not necessarily a change in people's personal sexual experience, but rather there has been a change in how they can express it. People who don't adhere to the male/female relationship norm often do not share their identities with anyone in their family or their social circle, and instead hide those desires or needs. Sometimes, people find outlets with similar people, or "tribes" who operate under the same conditions. This can be seen in the underground societies that give room for many groups to express themselves. There are BDSM and Dom/Sub "playrooms," swingers clubs, and pay-to-play elite access parties right under our noses; hidden in popular places or even in suburban homes, membership sex clubs, "Furry" conventions, with general access to any possible sort of fetish. The Internet has revolutionized sex and how people interact with their sexuality. While this is great in some regards, what it really illustrates is that people are forced to become "anonymous" through their online activity rather than be able to express themselves without fear of retribution.

Many may think that society is "cleansed," or less sexually inclined than we once were. What is really happening is that sexuality is being repressed, whether by governments, religions, social expectations or personal limits. Gay people come out and often lose the support of their loved ones; transgender individuals around the world commit suicide nearly daily; polyamorous partners cannot tell others of their "situation" for fear of government involvement. In reality, the only thing that has changed are the guiding hands that tell people what they can and cannot share about themselves.

The World Today

Throughout history, one thing is crystal clear. Without sex, none of us would be here today. Without sex, we would not have developed institutions of marriage or moral codes involving the treatment of women and our bodies. Our religions would be lacking in prose, and our bodies would not be our temples. Without sex, we would truly not be human, and humanity would have been extinguished long ago. It is not just an act of procreation; sex is an act of the soul, and a spiritual manifestation that connects each being to the next, each soul to another. Obviously, cultures and societies differ widely in their interpretations of sex. However, the universal truth is that sex is human, and humans are sexual entities. Why deny, hide, or shame this reality any longer? What benefit can be found in suppressing our sexual desires? How could such a natural and beautiful thing be immoral? Is it God or man who says so?

Consider the increasing presence of sex scandals, demoralizing and objectifying media, or pornography addiction. You can't change the channel without hearing about a politician caught in a hotel with their mistress (or mister). We only view people based on their weight or their outer beauty. Consider the sexualized nature of children's toys, mothers and older women (MILFs and cougars), and the rise in "Mommy Porn." Young girls are indoctrinated into how they should look, and value that above all else, and cougars are a mainstay of the younger male generation hoping to get laid.

The rise in books and movies like *Fifty Shades of Grey* indicate that less is going on inside the beds of married couples than previously thought. Consider that nearly half of all teenagers have had sexual intercourse before they're 17, and 1 in 4 people carry the Human Papilloma Virus (HPV). One in six women will be a victim of rape, and about 20% of all pregnancies are unwanted. All of this sums up one point: the direction in which sex is going is not a positive one. Our society holds sex in such low esteem that we have developed an incredibly unhealthy approach to it. We lock it away in a closet and wonder why it makes so much noise.

Chapter 4:
Breaking the Taboos of Desire

*"Taboos after all are only hangovers, the product of diseased minds,
you might say, of fearsome people who hadn't the courage to live
and who under the guise of morality and religion
have imposed these things upon us."*
~ Henry Miller

Why is sex such a taboo topic? Consider even your reaction to this book. Did you take it home, fully intending to read it in the privacy of your own home and never share it? Did you feel awkward checking it out? How can we provide nourishment to our souls and love one another deeply if we refuse to acknowledge one of the most basic human experiences? After evaluating your biases surrounding sex in the first chapter, you may have come to realize that your specific religion or belief system directly impacts your views on sexuality. While many attribute their beliefs and behaviors to an ascribed religion or deity, the reality is that many religions suppress sexuality and even harbor disdain for it. Human souls come from the one God and are of one source; when we misinterpret Biblical (or other holy) texts, we continue to draw the divide between a Higher Power and us. By allowing our man-made religions or social doctrines to dictate our behavior, we are essentially removing our inner divinity. In this respect it becomes clear that spirituality is Godly, but religion and its writings are filtering God's message through a human earthly ideal; thus is Man interpreting God, a less than 100% pure divinely direct message.

In the last chapter, we shed light on the history of sex, how it has morphed into something unacceptable and even dirty for the majority of people throughout time. Religions and social expectations have influenced individuals and their sexuality throughout history, and often not in a beneficial manner. Religion and institutions today continue to have the same effect- maneuvering individual experiences and spiritual needs away from the natural act of sex. By shaking this stigma - this guiding hand from our shoulders - we can awaken our spiritual sexuality in a healthy way. If we do not act in alignment with our authentic selves, we essentially deny our inner being. By claiming our sexuality as our own, as more than the physical duties of a Godly disciple, we can respect our body's needs and desires, and adopt a healthier overall view of a loving, joyous life. The takeaway from this chapter should be that sex and love are a spiritual (read: internal, deep, connecting) act, not an act that should be controlled by external forces.

4.1 Sex and the Church

Sex and the Church have long been antithetical to one another. Sex has been something assigned to a marital union between a man and a woman for procreation, and many religious texts provide strict rules for this aspect of human life.

Matthew 5:28: *"But I say unto you, that whosoever looketh on a woman to lust after her hath committed adultery with her already in his heart"*. This statement, when misinterpreted, brings on shame and disdain for accepting our sexual nature. While no woman wants to be ogled or cat-called, appreciating the female form is something that has been denoted through art and written history since the Dawn of Man. By interpreting this as a fundamental truth, rather than a guideline for a husband's wandering eye, Christianity has made men feel shamed in their sexual desires.

The Quran is guilty of this as well, claiming: *"Tell the believing men to lower their gaze, and protect their private parts. That is purer for them. Verily, Allah is all-aware of what they do"* (An-Nur 24:30). Nearly the same statement applies to women, but adding they should not "…show off their adornment except only that which is apparent," indicating that women should hide their bodies except around their family or husband. While this could be innocent enough, as encouragement to remain modest and give sex the proper honor it deserves, these excerpts have been infamously misinterpreted to squash Middle Eastern and Islamic sexuality, and to repress females within that society by covering them up with black overdress and veils (burqas).

Another important quote that shows the negative undertones associated with sex and Christianity is 1 Corinthians 6:13: *"Meats for the belly, and the belly for meats: but God shall destroy both it and them. Now the body [is] not for fornication, but for the Lord; and the Lord for the body."* This convoluted, and often abused, quote in the Bible indicates that God has created food for the nourishment of the body, but that "fornication," as the Bible refers to sex, is not meant for sustenance. Christians are called above the desires of the flesh, and are expected to accept Him in to their bodies rather than use their bodies for sexual purposes. While this could be a great argument against unhealthy sexual interactions with multiple partners or sex that doesn't reflect the holiness of the act, it is used to demonstrate "fornication" as a sin, and that sex affects your ability to interact with God as Christians see Him. In this interpretation, True Christians would not risk a place next to God for sins of the flesh.

As explained in the History of Sex chapter, the Church entirely took over the personal lives of the masses. The transition from sex as a spiritual and divine experience, as depicted in most ancient civilizations, to an immoral and ungodly behavior, has been well documented through time. It has become clear that the Church (or synagogue or mosque) has more of an influence on sexuality than any other single factor. While this book is not suggesting that you denounce your religion, the point needs to be made that this Godly relationship you have in the confines of your faith should also be translated into aspects of your life, especially in sex. Sex was once a divine tribute, a way to connect to the gods and to your holy energies. Religion has changed sex so much that in order to be godly, one must deny aspects of the divine or Godself! This is contradictory and unsafe for the soul, and for humanity as a whole.

Hypocrisy in Society and the Church

So much of established religion relies on directly controlling the lives of people who adhere to them. Consider the passages previously mentioned, which focus on controlling sexual interaction and very personal aspects of life. Also recall that circumcision has been deemed entirely unnecessary in medical and non-religious circles, but yet religion has the power to influence a major aspect of a young boy's life solely because "God demands it." Many people follow a specific religion, and while that is not inherently bad, as religion brings people closer to an understanding of God, there are many things that people "pick and choose" when it comes to living by the rules of their godly teachings. If you abide by one law in the Bible or Quran or other holy book, shouldn't you then abide by them all?

Rules we all break:

Luke 12:22: *"And he said to his disciples, 'Therefore I tell you, do not be anxious about your life, what you will eat, nor about your body, what you will put on.'"*

You heard it; don't worry about your life. Don't think about food or your body or your clothing either. But what is that most people do all day long? Think about what to buy at the next sale or what to eat for dinner.

Jeremiah 4:30: *"And you, O desolate one, what do you mean that you dress in scarlet, that you adorn yourself with ornaments of gold, that you enlarge your eyes with paint? In vain you beautify yourself. Your lovers despise you; they seek your life."*

Dressing well and beautifying yourself is a vain attempt to gain love, and spiritual writings view it as a sin. So how many young girls and women do you know who wear earrings, makeup, perfumes and such?

Matthew 6:1-7: *"Beware of practicing your righteousness before other people in order to be seen by them, for then you will have no reward from your Father who is in heaven... Thus, when you give to the needy, sound no trumpet before you, as the hypocrites do in the synagogues and in the streets, that they may be praised by others.... And when you pray, you must not be like the hypocrites. For they love to stand and pray in the synagogues and at the street corners, that they may be seen by others."*

How often do you "check in" to your church on social media, or put your volunteering efforts on a résumé? None of these things are bad on their own, but in the context of the Bible, we're all constantly sinning.

Ecclesiastes 5:10: *"He who loves money will not be satisfied with money, nor he who loves wealth with his income; this also is vanity."*

Who doesn't seek to earn money, or at least love having enough of it? Well, that's a sin too according to the Scriptures. However, to be fair, what is meant here is that the love of money, above all else, is a sin.

Deuteronomy 5:12-15: *"Six days you shall labor and do all your work, but the seventh day is a Sabbath to the Lord your God. On it you shall not do any work, you or your son or your daughter or your male servant or your female servant, or your ox or your donkey or any of your livestock, or the sojourner who is within your gates, that your male servant and your female servant may rest as well as you."*

Have you ever worked on the Sabbath? Has anyone you're related to ever worked on the Sabbath? What about the nurses and doctors and officials who work every day of the week to keep us safe? They surely are not going to Hell are they?

Quran 5:90-91: *"O you who believe, intoxicants, and gambling, and the altars of idols, and the games of chance are abominations of the devil; you shall avoid them, that you may succeed."*

Do you drink? Gamble or play the lottery? Give attention to celebrities or other idols? Nearly everyone does one all of these things at some point.

Among other biblical quotes can be found rules on not eating shellfish, not shaving your beard, or piercing or adorning any part of your body. In society today, it's rare that someone doesn't eat some form of shellfish, men cut their beards for work or personal grooming, and the majority of women have at least one piercing in each ear. In the Bible's Old Testament, it is written that Abraham was allowed by God to have sex with two women, his wife Sarah and his wife's slave Hagar, though we would view this as an unacceptable practice in today's world. Women are also decreed as only worth half of a man, and are not allowed to yield property in either the Bible or the Quran. For some reason, that doesn't seem to work in today's world. There is proof that society can advance beyond the control of religion, as it has already begun to do with Supreme Court rulings, laws and the increasing separation of church and state.

Yes, there are indeed quotes in the Bible and other major texts referring to abominations - men who lie with other men, women who commit adultery, and more. But if those commandments on sin are taken as Truth, why then are the other ones shown above not? Really, if we let these ancient texts fully control our lives, as they exist in today's world, we are not living a very modern or fulfilling life in the era we are now blessed to live.

If we as humans break any of these outdated decrees, are we truly damned to Hell? Should stoning, or torture, or exile be used to punish us for these transgressions? If a benevolent God truly loves us, and created us in His image, then why all the rules that would indicate differently? Why should we feel so ashamed of our true natures, and be unable to express ourselves in a way that does justice to the Divinity placed within us? What if, for argument's sake, it is found that religious figures, i.e. the Church, pastors, rabbis, imams, preachers, archbishops and the like, are really the ones to blame for this negative relationship between God and man? Keep in mind that The Bible and all other sacred texts were written with a human filter. Whatever God spoke through inspired holy thought has been passed through human minds and hands. Therefore, the perspective cannot be 100% truly divine if the one channeling the information has an individual bias. When we derive our basic interactions with things like sex on the interpretation of a human vessel, the person, area, culture or traditional reality from which God embodies his vessel, will determine the rules, regulations and importance of sex.

4.2 Spiritual Sex (The Chakras and Aura)

In direct contrast to the occasional brimstone and hellfire approach to sex with religion, the spiritual approach allows you to accept your body, your desires, your partner, and the sexual experience as a positive and beneficial one. Sex is a basic human instinct, but we can transcend that primal urge into something holy. The connection we experience with the right partner, the energy we feel, and the blissful releases all indicate that sex is composed of something greater than just animalistic behavior. Sex is meditative; it keeps you in the moment and present in your body and the pleasure of your mate. What society and outside forces do not tell you is that sex can allow us to rise about this plane, and to engage with one another in a place that is not beholden to the laws of man. What we all crave is unbound, spiritually connected sex.

When two partners have the intention of loving unconditionally, for creating and sharing a moment in time, they are expressing their Divinity. In a place that is freeing and unbound of any negative emotions, vibrations, frequencies, expectations, desires or manipulations, the individuals involved are connected to the Creator. Sex and love based in love for one another is considered the most holy of holy, and in whatever capacity or design, the lovers are blessed. The key here is whether the sex one engages in is actually based on a higher vibration, or if it is healthy. Can sex be positive if you engage in intercourse with one, two or even five people on the basis of intentional love? What if you engage in the same behaviors without vibrations of love? On a higher plane, where everyone shares their energies with one another, and the ego has no hold, people can reach the divinity within them.

White Tantric Sex

Tantric sex is one of the best ways to awaken the spiritual aspect of sex without focusing on just the act itself, or the resulting orgasm. Celebrities like Sting have made tantric sex famous, but really there are different subsets to Tantra. White Tantrism is a solo practice, something you use to get yourself ready for the "Big Game," so to speak. Individuals who practice White Tantric generally have a partner to sexually engage with. To prepare, Tantrists will meditate and focus on their breathing (alone) prior to intercourse. They center their energy in the chakras, and attempt to transmute the sexual urges and energy into the spirit and awareness. Pushing that energy into oneself allows Tantrists to approach their lover ready to mesh spiritually more so than physically. White Tantrists focus on a connection to God or the Divine, and allow their time alone to heal and energize them before entering a sacred realm with another or others.

Red Tantra

Red Tantra is what people think of most when they think of Tantric Sex. This is the sect of Tantra most often associated with marathon sex and withholding orgasm, as mainstream media interprets it. In reality, Red Tantra is a beautiful generation of synergy and a representation of the Divine in each partner. Essentially, your partners are all gods or goddesses, and by recognizing their Divine energy, you are recognizing God and the Divine on a higher plane of existence. To have a complete tantric experience, the chakras of each body must be aligned and connected. What most Western cultures do not comprehend is that both (or all partners) reach orgasm - multiple times. This includes men, who do not ejaculate until the full act is completed and both (or all) members have reached spiritual and physical fulfillment. Tantric sex has a lot to do with the differing chakras and their locations, so let's evaluate those a little bit.

Chakras

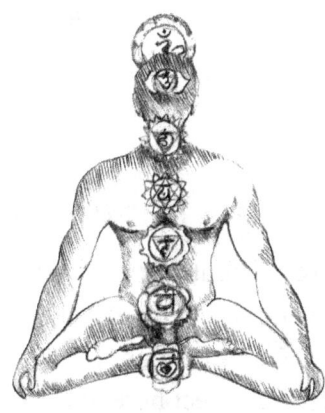

Chakras are a concept of traditional Indian medicine, where channels relate to the physical organs, and how chi is subdivided into energy that must be in balance in order to maintain health. The chakras reside over points of the spine as energy portals that interchange unseen spiritual information between our body, other's bodies, and our environment. The Kousouli® Method Master Chart (at the end of Chapter 11) shows the chakras, their positioning over the spine, and the relationship between the spiritual, mental, emotional, and physical aspects of health. This vital information can unlock one's sexual and personal power and is taught in seminars to interested participants. There are seven major chakras in the human body, each with their own energies that flow through them. Imagine you are sitting on the floor in lotus pose (sitting crossed-legged on the floor, spine straight). Imagine your chakras as pulsing lights from the bottom of your tailbone to the top of your head, all along your center. In order to be fully in balance, all seven of these lights must be lit. If you are meditating, as in White Tantra, the top 3 chakras closest to the heart, throat and head are pulsing the brightest. If you are practicing Red Tantra and engaging in spiritual sex with others, the bottom 4 are most likely the focus of your attention.

Muladhara: 1st Root Chakra (RED color) EARTH element

Root chakra at the base of the spine. It grounds us, and connects us to what is most important. Used in Red Tantric sex to keep us fully present. Located at the base of our spine; the coccyx, tailbone. Relates to the primitive life force energy, natural survival needs, grounding, assertiveness, aggression, adventure, impulsiveness, lustful passion, raw attraction, the need for feeling secure, and vitality. There is also a connection to the color red and primitive feelings, such as anger. Red in this chakra also is related to the power hormone testosterone, temperature increase, heat, hemoglobin production, and cell growth. This is important when setting the "mood" for sex - as the color red can affect someone with a more red aura to entice a much more lustful encounter.

Svadhisthana: 2nd Sacral Chakra - Spleen or Splenic (ORANGE color) WATER element

Lower abdominal chakra. It is the center of sexuality, and is used the most in Red Tantra. Located at the level of the genitals and reproductive systems, this chakra relates to primitive life, reproduction energy, raw emotions, primary interpersonal relationships, and emotional stability. Energy disharmony here can show up as a disturbance in the digestive and reproductive systems. Feelings of sexual or emotional repression may be linked to physical manifestations of diverticulitis, urinary trouble, fibroids, infertility, or cramping.

Manipura: 3rd Navel Chakra - Umbilical Solar Plexus (YELLOW color) FIRE element

This is your sense of self. This is a crucial aspect of Tantra, as you essentially delve into your ego and your identity to grasp the Divine and let it pulsate. Located at the navel under the breastbone, this chakra relates to power integration and life force management. Digestive system, pancreas, liver, stomach, adrenals, and the spleen connect here. It is the psychic energy battery, and storehouse for positive energy. This chakra links to the mind for processing negative feelings and is the area of your life force distribution. This is where your "gut reaction" comes from, and relates to your sexuality in that your truest desires and needs stem from this chakra being aligned.

Anahata: 4th Heart Chakra - Cardiac (GREEN color) AIR element

Heart chakra. This is your source of love, joy and peace. In sex and relationships, this is a key chakra. Open yourself up to love, in whichever form it may take. Located at the center of the chest, over the heart. By location, it separates the higher three chakras (5th, 6th, 7th) from the lower primitive three chakras (1st, 2nd, 3rd). Affects heart, lungs, upper chest, back, bronchial tubes, thymus, and immunity. This green chakra is the seat of higher emotions of true love, tenderness, compassion, honesty, and human connection. Many spiritual teachers claim that all of humanity is "plugged in" to each other through this chakra. This chakra is key in developing and maintaining intimate relationships, as it both attracts and sustains them.

Vishuddha: 5th Throat Chakra - Laryngeal (BLUE color) ETHER element

Throat chakra. This is the source of your inner and outer voice, and location of your inner truth. In a relationship setting, this is the chakra that needs be in balance; be who you are and don't be afraid to express yourself. Front and back of the throat; relates to the power of thought through communication, speech, expression, and self-identification. Some health connections with this chakra are metabolic rate, thyroid gland, vocal cords, eyes, ears, nose, mouth, and neck. Repression of this chakra is commonly seen in those who tend to be shy or scared to "speak up" in public to express themselves. Repressing the 5th chakra can lead to upper respiratory weakness, sore throat and susceptibility to head colds.

Anja: 6th Brow Chakra - Frontal Chakra 3rd eye (DEEP INDIGO color)

Third eye chakra. This houses your intuition, reason and wisdom. Practitioners of White Tantra are well versed in this chakra. This chakra is also important in reversing old negative patterns and beliefs associated with sex. Located between the eyebrows; relates to powers of mind and heightened self-awareness, psychic abilities, connection to physical and psychic eyes/vision. This energy is usually activated through a deeply focused and relaxed meditative state, and can prepare you for great Tantric sex, or just very soulful, connective sex.

Sahasrara: 7th Crown Chakra - Coronal (VIOLET color)

Crown chakra. This is where our bliss and our ability to connect spiritually stem from. Sexual experience lights up this chakra, as we recognize the Divine in ourselves and our oneness with each other and the Universe. Located on top of the head, designated for self-realization and enlightenment, knowingness; the seat of the soul. Associated also with perfection of mind, body, and spirit; connection to God, or The Source. The 7th chakra is usually depicted in religious iconography as a gold glowing disc or circle around the head. This energy is also usually activated through a deeply focused and relaxed meditative state.

The Importance of Color

Colors are used to reflect our personalities, moods, or subconscious states of being. Color vibrates on a specific level, depending on the shade, and can be used effectively to attract a mate, or seduce your current mate. Consider the importance of colors in your choice of bed sheets, flowers, or clothing and fashion apparel.

RED	Love, passion, sexual desire and activity, fast / quick speed, masculinity, strength, and stimulation. Wear red or use red sheets in bedroom décor to encourage sexual exploration. **Light Red or Pink:** Softness, tenderness, romance, caring, femininity, and emotional love. Wear pink to encourage gentle lovemaking. **Dark Red:** Anger, rage, lust, war, internal conflict, stifled aggravation, and impulse. These are not the best characteristics to encourage for a positive sexual experience.
ORANGE	Warmth, cheer, openness, freedom, creativity, enthusiasm, expression, kindness, celebration, sensual enjoyment, and zest for life. Wear this color to exude your inner energy, or paint a room or wall in order to stimulate it. **Dark Orange:** Materialism, insensitivity, overindulgence. Avoid this color in your sexual life.
VIOLET INDIGO	Spirit, divinity, compassion, transformation, renewal, meditative, electric, calming, and purifying. This color encourages a spiritual connection during sex, so use it liberally in clothing, sheets, décor and Feng shui or bagua settings. **Dark Violet/Indigo:** Slow movement, trickery, lowered potential. This is not encouraged for sexual encounters, so keep it light.
WHITE	Purity, spiritual energy, balance, positivity, enlightenment, divine inspiration, innocence, simplicity, and oneness. This clean, crisp color promotes a positive and spiritual connection with your partner. **Foggy, Off –White, or Grey**: Deceitful, depressive, apathetic. While white is considered "heavenly," muddled shades mean unconscious energy usually related to religious control or church dogma that interferes in your love and sex life.

BLACK	Mystery, stealth, secrets, death, and negativity. The void of life or light. Wearing black shields you from openness. Overuse of this color can unbalance the chakras and can breed hate, rage, seclusion, depression, stagnation, or fatigue. This is not ideal for a great relationship or sexual encounter. Consider how women often wear black lingerie for a new partner; it is a shield to protect them from vulnerable feelings while leaving things open to "mystery."
GREEN	Inner peace, harmony, healing energy, monetary wealth, honesty, hope, nurturing, safety, and connection. This is a great color to promote a mutual connection and a realistic, grounded relationship. **Earthy Green:** denotes grounding, nature, and connecting to Mother Earth. Can be great for exuding your natural spirit.
YELLOW	Joy, exuberance, cheer, happiness, logic, and optimism. This is a great color for brightening up your living space and showing your inner positive energy. This is also a strong attracting color, so wear it often when you feel like telling the world how happy you are. **Golden Yellow:** Authority, abundance, social power and status, absolute self-confidence, sun energy, luxurious, feeling like a winner. Can help a lot in attracting a lover.
BROWN	Practicality, stability, grounding, earth, elemental, solidity in relationship, and having a "down to earth" personality. While many people don't associate brown with sex or love, it is a strong color for grounding with a longtime lover. **Dark Brown:** Similar to Black.
BLUE/ TURQUOISE	Healing, miracle energy, cleansing, awe, increased intuition and sensitivity, intellect, insights, invention, water and purity. This is a great color for a room, especially for relaxation purposes. Wear blue to exude a balanced emotional state, healing energy, and static mood. **Dark Blue/Turquoise:** Depression, heaviness, sadness, longing, or feeling stuck. Avoid these when you are feeling less than great, as they will affect your energies.

The Chakras and Auric Field Energies

The seven chakras work like funnels, and generate energy in their individual areas of the body. The chakras spin in either a clockwise or counterclockwise rotation, depending on the energies that are present. Chakras can be opened or closed, and are healthiest when they are open and funneling energy. The collective energy moving through and from these chakras is known as your aura, and many living things and people have viewable auras if you are a sensitive "clairvoyant." You can make your aura more vivid by working on restoring energy to your chakras, and by sharing your energy with a lover. This is one of the most intimate parts of sex; the sharing and reciprocation of higher vibrational energies.

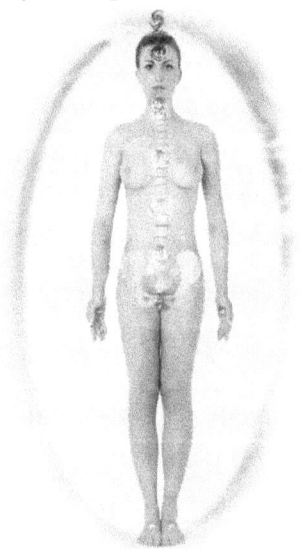
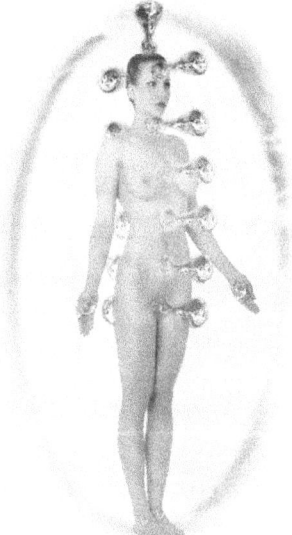

Energy Channels

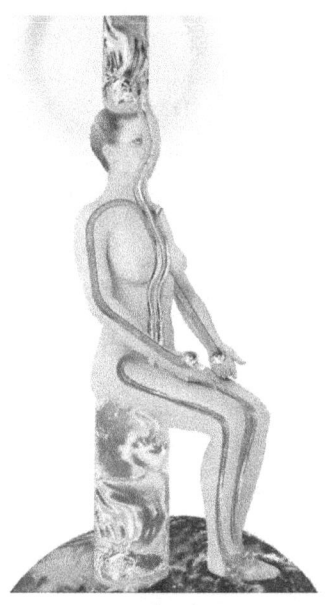

Energy moves in channels, or streams, throughout the body. Sometimes, people are sensitive enough to these energies that they can sense or even "pull" on them to heal a person. Injuries heal faster when these energy channels work properly, and many energy healers focus on sending the most energy to an afflicted area. Chinese medicine often refers to the energy meridian, which is located along the chakra-line of the spine. When spines are properly aligned and chakras open, energy flows freely, making a body, mind, and spirit healthy. During sex, these energy flows can be felt when you are incredibly tuned in to your partner, and if you have meditated before starting, you may be more open to actually feeling or seeing these pathways. Draw from one another, and feel the combination of the many types of energy you can share. Let's look at two major energy channels.

Cosmic Energy Channel

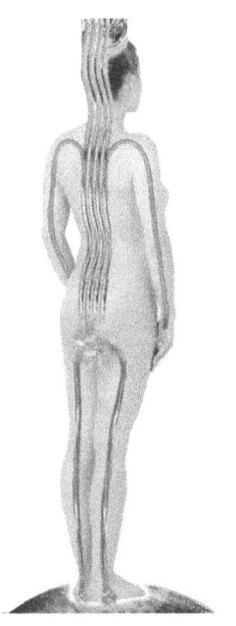

This energy comes from God, the heavens, the air, the ether, Universe, the sky, or whatever source you perceive. It is pictured as a radiant, electric blue energy entering through the top of the head at the chakra level. When people meditate, they experience this influx of cosmic energy, which cleanses the upper body channels and replenishes their energy stores. This cosmic energy flows down the back of the neck and spine, to the root chakra and then mixes with Earth energy, making a balanced and healthy body. This cosmic energy is what people receive when engaging in White Tantra or meditation, and they come to their partner(s) with a "full battery" ready to engage in divine love.

Earth (Gaea) Energy Channel

Mother Nature sends this energy through the leg channels and is represented by a reddish clay or red-greenish energy color. When people connect with nature, they feel invigorated and refreshed. This is because they activated a much-needed intake of Earth energy, which cleansed their leg channels and restored their "low batteries." Earth energy comes into the root chakra by way of the leg channels, mixes with cosmic energy at the root chakra, and flows forward and upward, bathing all the chakras on its way up. It then splits out the arm channels, out of the palms, and up out the crown chakra. The ideal situation is for Cosmic and Earth energies to mix well during sex, showing that you are connected both cosmically and physically with mind-bending sexual energy felt by both partners.

Other Energies

Palm chakra energy is one of the most important channels for energy transference, especially during sex. Located at the middle of the palm, this smaller chakra channels energy into creative endeavors, but also helps you give or receive energy every time you touch your lover. Arm, leg, and spinal channels help move energy throughout the body, whether to or from your chakras, or to or from your partner. Foot chakra energy stems from the middle arch of the foot, and takes in energy from Mother Earth. This is important during sex, as it keeps you grounded while you explore one another's space. The grounding cord (pictured in seated position) extends from the root chakra, and essentially removes negative or stagnant energy downward to be "recycled" by (Gaea) Earth.

The energy that we contain in the chakras and have flowing through our bodies erupts into the colorful auric field which is around each of us. Personal energy, whether well maintained or not, is constantly in fluctuation and affects our interactions with others. This is why some sensitive people can see or feel auras, and why you also feel drawn to another person without consciously knowing why.

For more information on healing with energy or developing your innate psychic abilities, you may see my previous book on the subject, "BE A MASTER® OF PSYCHIC ENERGY," and the content is taught in depth privately to interested practitioners at live seminar events. Details can be found at www.DrKousouli.com or www.KousouliMethod.com.

Relationships, Sex, and Auric Spaces

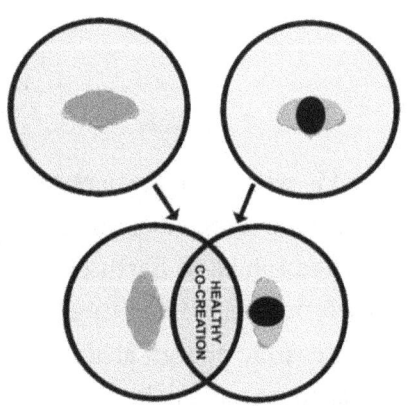

The first figure (Healthy Co-Creation) shows a female and male (viewed from above) separately, and then together, interacting where their auras cross. This shows a healthy positive co-creation for both the female and the male; neither invades the other's personal identity, auric space, or personal will. They each have plenty of their own identity and space to be comfortable, yet are still present within the relationship. This is positive, "normal," and healthy for all parties involved. When two or more people spend time in close proximity to each other, they share auric energy, reconstruct their reality and enter into co-creation. In any relationship, as long as both individuals hold on to their identity, power, and self-worth without giving over this power to another, they will remain able to appreciate both themselves and the other person. This is made evident when two people enter the infatuation stage of a relationship. Both are accepted for whom they are in their own power, and no one has yet to cross any personal boundaries or force the other to sacrifice auric energy, personal identity or space.

However, if the personal boundary is crossed there will be an imbalance, as shown in the second diagram (Unhealthy Co-Creation). When a partner becomes overbearing or seeks to change their partner, a conscious or subconscious agreement occurs where one person

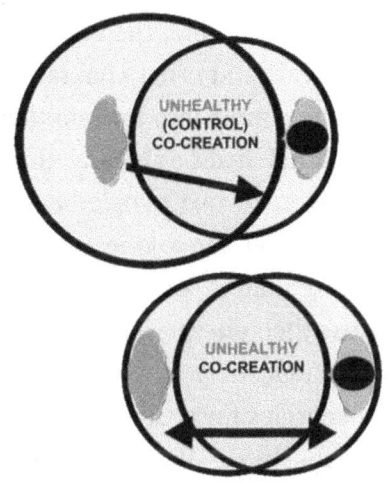

loses power and the other person gains it. The one who is submissive will be under control of the other's energy space, which holds the images, ideas, and desires of the overpowering partner. This new energy is foreign to the aura of the submissive person, and will either result in a lack of energy (depression) or a revolt (breakup/reclaiming of personal power). It takes a tremendous amount of energy to force another person to change, or to allow your energy to be drained. This results in disagreements, fights, and violent breakups. Breakups are inevitable when there is no healthy co-creation, because each person subconsciously wants their own space and identity back. The truth, however, is that this all happens by choice. The submissive individual, by his or her own free will, allows the exchange of power to occur. This could be a repetition of old incarnation (previous life) patterns, the soul's need to experience vulnerability in a relationship, a desire to overcome abuse and become an example for others, an attempt to strengthen personal aspects like loneliness or wealth, or to simply "try your luck" with a person you know isn't a match.

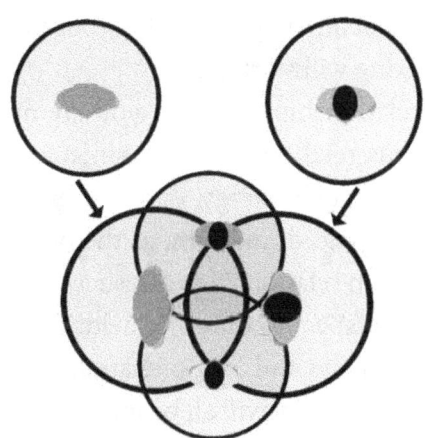

Loving, co-creative relationships occur only when each partner's personal auric space and identity is respected and allowed to be maintained by its original owner. Successful married couples that last always allow their partner to be themselves. Although they may interchange energy by compromising day to day for small things, they always retain their original energy as to not create a personal imbalance. They both cherish and respect each other for who they are as individuals, as well as who they are within the unit. We tend to be attracted to people we feel most similar to an auric or energy level. When auric spaces intersect, and are a good match, people feel the initial comfort that is hard to find with "just anyone." This sensation pulls us closer to the other person's reality, and partners become more entangled in each other's energy. These feelings can either be stronger (love at first sight), or can strengthen over time. This is how long term relationships form, and result in two people combining their root chakra energies (during sex), sometimes with the intention of creating another life with their energies.

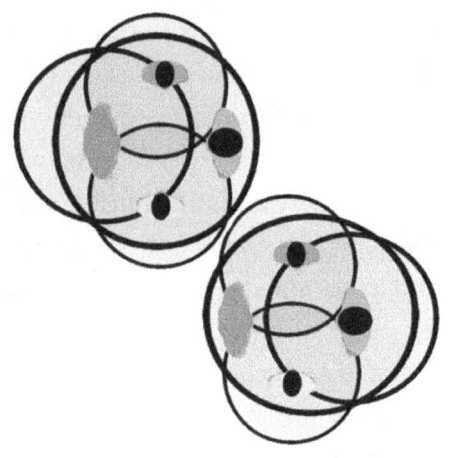

Even if a couple does not create life, the continued connection of the root, heart and other chakras will continue to intertwine the couple into one another's auric energies and personal realities. Many times, people comment on how alike two people become when they have been together for a long time (i.e. finishing each other's sentences or having same thoughts); this is because their energies have become nearly inseparable. Although these two people have combined and shared energies for so long, the mark of a truly healthy relationship is that each person maintains his or her own energy and auric identity. When one person holds more energy, or wants to change the dynamic (have a baby, move, or any other major life event), the other person will experience a give and take of energy. Most couples can overcome energy imbalances through mutual respect of their partner and both clear verbal and non-verbal communication. However, sometimes a breakup must occur. There will be a void or emptiness where the other person's auric field and energies once connected with yours. Eventually though, you will recall your energy and move forward by yourself or with another person whom you signal in. They will match your new level and individual reality and the process of energy mixing will start again.

It should also be noted that in a multiple person relationship (whether you are not committed, or whether you are in a healthy polyamorous relationship), the same auric and energy field rules apply. When one person takes too much energy, or requires too much of the other lovers, there will eventually be no energy to draw from, as the others will pull away or rebel. This is also how polyamorous or open relationships can succeed. If one or more people can interact in a healthy manner with respect to the auric fields of the others, who is to say that these people are not able to co-create and love one another? If they all share energy from their root, sacral and heart chakras, they will all be intrinsically connected. If they can combine that physical and spiritual connection to a healthy energy connection, it is possible that they can succeed just as well as a monogamous do.

Oh My God!

Finally, consider the worship and intention that is gifted to you and to your lover during sex, and especially during orgasm. Your spirits have connected, your minds have joined, and you are able to relax and trust someone else enough to be vulnerable. It is a holy act, one that often leaves you in awe afterwards. How many times have you become emotional after really, really great sex? Have you ever felt that your cup runneth over, and you find yourself fully satisfied and deeply connected to the person? This is a spiritual act, bordering on the religious. Keep in mind that sex is sometimes so good that during orgasm or climax, we tend to shout the words: "Oh my God!" This may be because we realize that a spiritual experience like this is the closest man will come to transcending religion and witnessing the power of their Creator, as a creator themselves.

Co-creation is a matter of what happens when two people combine their energy sources. The union of two people is a result of their ability to align themselves; satisfying soulful sex comes from maintaining a higher frequency of your own energy. When two people tend to their individual frequencies while coming together, they raise the energy within themselves and also outside of themselves. Whether sexual union or any other coming together of the minds occurs, that energy production is exponential and unstoppable when applied to creative manifesting. This is why it is said that when two people come together, they are under one mind and that God mind is there with them; a holy union.

> "For where two or three are gathered together in my name, there am I in the midst of them." ~ Matthew 18:20

Consider also every major corporation, municipality, or support group that has made large strides in the world; they have a boardroom where more than one mind unites and shares ideas and energy for creative manifesting.

4.3 Ego

Made famous by Freud is the power of the ego, id, and superego. The ego is the conscious, rational self, while the superego is concerned with social standards. The id is the center of pleasure. The id and ego are to blame when only the body is involved in sex, instead of the spiritual divinity and the power of God. Ego and id attach to lower vibrational energies, such as lust, jealousy, envy, mistrust, anger, fear, and revenge. When we engage sex under these conditions, Ego will bastardize the experience. Ego is heavily influenced by outside persuasions: our childhood, our society, or expectations from others. Rather than focusing on worshipping, loving, and entrusting our bodies and spirits to one another, social pressures have influenced our sexuality so much so that we have reached a plane where we only recognize the lower vibrations of energy associated with sex. We engage in unhealthy behaviors, treat sex like an end game, and do not focus on creating energy and sensing the higher vibrations associated with love and sex. Hollywood and international celebrities have become an unnatural obsession, and a symbol for what true beauty and sex appeal is. Plastic surgeons make a killing on this trend, helping men and women create their "ideal selves" based on what they see in a magazine. The United States and most of Europe have adapted a model of beauty that is so unattainable that women (and sometimes men) spend the majority of their lives wishing they were something they are not.

Because of this skewed view of the world, this unrealistic standard, we are drifting away from natural sex, and sex as it was intended to be. Sex is not meant to be only about the visuals, about how you look from a certain angle or how perfect your legs, lips, abs or breasts appear to your mate. Sex is intended to be a divine experience, a connection, and an expression of your humanity and also a release for sharing your inner energy. By focusing on the false idols, by placing importance in your appearance rather than your content, we have successfully moved sex from its holy origins into a place where it is devalued and essentially unrecognizable.

It has been estimated that at least 25% of males and females admit to fantasizing about sex with a celebrity. That number is probably even higher, but people may not even realize they're doing it as celebrities are so commonplace in our lives. Because of Hollywood's absolute infiltration into our daily lives, via movies and television, Internet gossip and social media, we have begun to hold ourselves to unattainable, unrealistic goals.

4.4 Pornography Addiction

Pornography addiction, prior to the mid-2000s, was nearly unheard of. With the advent of the Internet however, this compulsion began to reverberate through American, European and Asian societies. Psychology surveys estimate that 70% of men visit over twenty pornographic sites in a month, and Google traffic history indicates that more than 25% of all searches *per day* are for porn. While the majority of pornography users are men, the trend is on the rise for women, accounting for 1 in 7 views of total pornography online. The most shocking number, however, is the number of religious men that seek aid for pornography addiction. According to Promise Keepers, an organization designed to help men be Godly and Christ-like despite the temptations they are presented with daily, 50% of men who were surveyed said they had viewed porn despite their commitment to the program. Pastors.com and Focus on the Family have all done their own online, anonymous surveys with the same results - at least 50% of Christian men admit that pornography has become a problem in their daily lives. Similar studies have been done across religions and demographics, and "first world" countries with a strong Internet connection all report similar statistics.

Once again, the connections between religion and sex are directly correlated to an unhealthy manifestation of our passions and desires. Evaluating this trend, one can see that the stronger the belief, the stronger the "hand of God" (religious institution or Church) in a person's life, the more repressed and ashamed we begin to feel about our sexuality. If we are all made in God's image, as Christianity and many other religions suggest, why in the world would "He" create us as sexual entities, and then expect us to repress it? Addiction is always a sign of something vital lacking in human experience - trauma, abuse or dysfunction within a person's past, or the need to fill a void. Pornography addiction is no different - there is emptiness within, an inability to truly feel whole because a fundamental aspect of our humanity is being denied or mistreated.

If it is estimated that half of all men feel an urge to engage in pornography, it is because pornography is a silent, private partner that never needs justification or attention. It is easier to let our energies loose where they cannot be judged, rather than to expose ourselves to each other and open up about what we really need and want. The fact that so many men (and women) feel the need to release this energy on an inanimate, impersonal vessel shows that we truly have strayed from a holy, spiritual relationship with sex - and one another. By placing an immoral shadow over the act of sex, Christianity and religions have (possibly unintentionally) created a chasm between our bodies and our spirits.

There is another troubling aspect to the excessive pornography usage our society is facing. Alongside the emphasis placed on looks, celebrity trends, and unattainable beauty goals, pornography has created an unrealistic idea of what sex really is. Sex is not about screaming the loudest, or who can talk the dirtiest. It is not about different positions or blatant disregard of the female orgasm. Real sex is not about demeaning women, or who has the largest breasts or penis. Real life intercourse is not staged, well lit, and directed.

Individuals who view porn, and men in particular as the main consumers, develop biases towards this version of sex, and the real, authentic experience begins to feel somehow lacking in contrast to the "dolled-up" model performer on screen. If you view porn as a recreational addition to your sex life with a committed partner, there is novelty and mutual desire there. However, if you are comparing yourself, your partner, or your interaction to what you've seen on the screen, you are doing yourself a great disservice and maybe it's time to give it a break.

Pornography does not show the connection, the beauty, or the intensely transcendental event that sex can be. Instead of keeping score, erase the marks and start the game over. Focus on each other, on what feels good (not just what looks good), and embrace the synergy you feel with your lover. We are still instinctually driven to sexual behavior, but we are placing that effort into experiences and relationships that do not serve us. If we embrace our sexuality, and are allowed to express it freely, our spirits would be more connected to the act and we would not feel so drawn to a "false prophet" like pornography. We would want the real thing.

Whether a fantasy or reality, in the desiring of another person, your mind creates images that will put the universal gears of fulfillment into action. As you draw upon this creation, the other appropriate to your creation is brought to you through the law of attraction. If one desires another's wife or husband, the thought will manifest into creation, causing a rift between the attached person and their significant other. Thought creates reality. Because of this energy misuse, pornography is a blasphemy of mindful creation, creating a lesser vibration of love, called lust. And lust can indeed be a powerfully misused force.

Porn distorts sexual energy rather than allowing natural flow of sexuality and the flow between two people. Pornography objectifies the person, rather than relating to them and connecting. However, pornography is much more free and less judgmental in a lot of ways. Outside forces do not monitor what you view and search for in pornography. You are accepted as a sexual being. Pornography attracts more people who are engaging in sexual activities where their needs and emotions are being met. Society and religions often have rules that influence the vibrations you can put into the universe - you cannot meet your physical, emotional, and spiritual needs when so many forces are telling you to leave it alone.

Of course, porn is mostly targeted to men, with most videos focusing on men in a power role having sex with visually stimulating women. It should also be noted that rarely does pornography show women reaching orgasm, and instead focuses on "the money shot," the point where a man ejaculates and reaches full satisfaction. Most of these scenes are demeaning and devaluing of a true sexual interaction, but it is promoted to men as "how sex should be." In reality, porn isn't designed to help a man deal with his fantasies, heal him or create an open forum for sexual exploration.

At the end of the day, pornography triggers human primal urges to rake in tons of money. Pornography has surpassed the NFL, the NBA and the MLB as a moneymaking venture, generating $10 billion a year! The most interesting part is that big companies like General Motors, AOL Time Warner and Marriott earn massive profits from their low-key involvement in production and distribution of pornographic material. Sex is being used to generate income for these massive corporations; it's just part of business - supply and demand.

4.5 Prostitution

Prostitution, often referred to as the world's oldest profession, used to be a majorly accepted aspect of many cultures. Even up until the Mayflower left for the New World, brothels and prostitutes were a common fixture in European society. As people settled into the West, prostitution became no less common, but much more "nefarious" and hidden. Men who used prostitutes were very lonely and unable to afford/keep a wife, or were usually married or prominent figures in society who had a specific scratch nobody else could itch. Still today, prostitution fills this secret sexual role: a way to provide a sexual experience that people cannot access within their own relationships.

Prostitution is the *most* lucrative unregulated (black market) industry in the world, and in the U.S. brings in upwards of an estimated $300 million a year, while drugs are estimated to bring in "only" about $120 million. While there are a large number of sex rings that get busted every year, the sex industry is unstoppable. Now, there are underground clubs, the sex "trade," and even places like The Bunny Ranch in Nevada. Prostitutes come from a variety of backgrounds, and are generally from lower income families with someone else in the family working in the industry. The biggest concern with prostitution is that the women (and men) that are selling their bodies are not doing so by their own volition. As part of the sex trade, many women are promised work visas and permanent immigration papers if they work for a "company" for a given amount of time. Only after they sign a contract, or lose all contact with people who can help them, do they realize they are essentially being sold as prostitutes. This is nearly impossible to get out of, as these sex trafficking circles are wide reaching and very powerful. Women are often killed if they attempt to leave or alert the authorities, making this the darkest side of prostitution.

There are many people and legislators who believe that legalizing prostitution (and guns, drugs, etc.) will decrease the strength of sex traffickers, pimps, and reduce the excessive funding required to jail and prosecute "working women." There are plenty of arguments in support of and against legalizing prostitution, but consider for a moment the ramifications outside the legal aspect. What if a woman could sell her body legally, with the proper protection, and with access to the proper channels for support? Would a woman *want* to sell her body to make a living? If she does, should society let her? What if a person wants to use her services and exchange them for money? Do we allow that exchange of money to occur? What cost, aside from money, does society accrue at large if they allow that to happen? Take into account the spiritual and mental effects of prostitution and sex just for sex's sake. A woman selling her body gives strangers access to her energy, her reality, and (even if she doesn't know it) a piece of her soul. The person buying her services experiences this same exchange and vulnerability, with nothing more to show for it in the end than physical release. What is the price you pay for access to your soul when you have sex for money?

4.6 Sex Sells

Everyone knows the basic truth of advertising: Sex sells, and sells really well. As mentioned before, sex sells in obvious ways like in porn and sex industries, as well as in clothing and arenas involving physical appearance. The average American is bombarded with over 5,000 advertisements *daily*, and the majority of those have undercurrents of sex. Think of the clothing models that represent some idyllic form of social beauty and sex appeal. "Look like this, and men won't be able to keep their hands off of you," the billboards scream. Men's fashion ads focus on power and masculinity as their selling point, where women would be falling at your feet if only you sported this cologne or body spray. Beautiful women holding hamburgers in commercials sounds incredibly odd, but it is commonplace in fast food advertising. Car commercials ooze innuendo, using horsepower and comfort as euphemisms for male sexual prowess.

Through advertisements and marketing, men are told that the way to woo a woman is through jewelry, handbags, flowers, chocolates. Women absorb the message that men only want cars, beer, food, and beautiful ladies to complete their lives. We are taught that love is displayed through how much you can provide for your partner, not the traits and characteristics you have to offer as a human being. We are shown that the greatest symbol of love is a diamond, an over-priced pressurized carbon product of the Earth that has absolutely no bearing on the internal, soulful connection you have with the person you want to spend the rest of your life with.

DeBeers Diamond Cartel, nearly a century ago, sold us the idea that we can trade diamonds for love, and associate possessions with emotions. Before the 1930s, a diamond ring to symbolize an engagement was not the social custom. DeBeers, experiencing a decrease in diamond purchases, filled newspapers and billboards with propaganda. DeBeers is also credited for creating the "two months" salary rule when buying an engagement ring. Diamonds are intrinsically worthless, and the market has been falsely valued based on the flow of diamonds, the places where they are sourced, and the conflict zones that are exploited (think blood diamonds).

4.7 Subliminal Messages Everywhere

On the subject of propaganda, it is not excluded to only DeBeers and diamonds. What sells better than anything in the history of marketing and advertising? What did we say is the world's oldest profession? Sex. Everyone's in on the game. Even large corporations, with wholesome and entirely non-sexual products, like Coca-Cola, Disney, and others, have been accused of using sex to sell their products. You're probably shaking your head because you've never seen such a thing. That's just it - your eyes don't see it, but your brain does. This sort of hypnotic advertising is called subliminal messaging. What your eyes don't focus on, your brain retains.

Outlines of lettering designed to give just enough of an impression of a phallus, or the letters S-E-X. Photos with layouts that are similar to the female vagina, or the outline of a penis are placed just out of focus. Cola ads have sexual acts depicted in ice cubes; cartoon characters are seen with erections or near phallic structures. "S-E-X" is drawn in the sky using clouds or smoke in cartoons, and young boys are introduced to what the female body should look like, thanks to female super heroes portrayed as perfect specimens in comic books. Sex is everywhere, even when you're not looking. Even classics like *the Little Mermaid* and *Alice in Wonderland* have undertones of sexuality in their images.

Some may argue that the only reason we see these images on the sides of billboards, or in ads, or on TV is merely because we have sex on the brain and it's all we think about. But what if our minds are constantly attuned to sex because of this subliminal advertising? What if all we think about is sex because we're shown these subconscious images from such a young age? These undercurrents of sex and the images that we absorb are designed to keep us buying without really understanding why. Sex sells, even when you're not aware of it.

This undercurrent of sex and money, and the value placed on things and the acquisition of said things, manages to divert the masses in very important ways. Men and women work for money to be able to afford the makeup, clothing or car that will attract *any* mate, rather than attracting the *right* mate using their soulful existence to make a lasting connection for life. Politics are infused with sex scandals, distracting voters and citizens from the real issues involved in the actual processes of government. Money is made in sexualizing small girls in beauty pageants, promoting the focus on how they look and dress from a very young age. Instead of engaging in a flow of energy from human to human, we are placing our energy in inanimate objects and in areas that will never return the favor.

4.8 Hollywood Idols

Aside from subliminal and direct sexual messages, there is always the unique reality that is Hollywood. Hollywood sells us this picture perfect image of what love, beauty and sex are. Beauty is packaged in a very select few containers, and anything outside of the accepted varieties is considered too exotic to be beautiful. This is especially damaging to the spirit, which manifests the beauty of the body. By denying our outward appearance, we are denying our inner godliness.

On top of that, sex is merely smoke and mirrors thanks to Hollywood glamour. A little bit of drama, an excessive amount of romance, a classy and visually appealing sexual encounter, and it's Happily Ever After. Love and sex are not that cut and dry, and they are nowhere close to that superficial. Some of the best and most intense sexual encounters of your life will look nothing like it does in the movies. Awkward or fumbling, messy or short-lived, your love life will be more real and deeper than anything Hollywood can promise you.

Love, too, is poorly represented. It is not an unhealthy obsession, a dramatic interlude into a horrible breakup, a picture perfect story, or even a love story for the ages. What you will experience (and hopefully have) is so much more dynamic than what a scriptwriter, director or even the most talented of actors can provide. While nobody is telling you that you can't enjoy your "chick flicks" as a guilty pleasure, it is necessary to understand that this is not what life looks like. Real life is just so much better.

Rather than promoting love on a higher plane, Hollywood provides idols and images to lust after. Think of Madonna, and how she changed the idea of a celebrity and what a celebrity was for the masses. She became a sex symbol, and her songs touched on sexuality ("Like a Virgin," "Like a Prayer," etc.) to a point where people were immediately drawn into her image and what she projected rather than focusing on their own identities. The Law of Attraction dictates that what you vibrate will come to you as a match, and this environment of celebrity worship attracts only emptiness and false truths hidden behind the idea of love (in the form of lust, a lowered vibration). Marilyn Monroe, Heidi Klum, Nicole Kidman, and Beyoncé, just to name a few, are all examples of the sexual ideals that are perpetuated by the Hollywood mentality. People, especially women, absorb information on these personalities in hopes of being just like them and in hopes of reaching fulfillment as a "truly sexual woman." Obviously this aspect of marketing and moneymaking is directly targeted at women, and this prevents women from ever realizing that they are worthy all on their own and that a spiritual connection is much more important than a physical one.

We see even further influence that money has on sexuality when we look at social customs and traditions, like Halloween. Women dress sexy on Halloween because it's a night to be someone else entirely, or a "free pass" to show your uninhibited true colors without people knowing it's the real you. If you wish to see people unveil their repressed sexual tensions, Halloween is the best time to do so. Women are raised to think that men view this as sexy, and that to be viewed as worthy a woman needs to look and act a certain way. After all, nobody wants the Puritan Nurse, right?

Chapter 5:
Battle of the Sexes

"You see an awful lot of smart guys with dumb women but you hardly ever see a smart woman with a dumb guy."
~ Erica Jong

Where have all the real men gone? It is a question that single women have pondered for decades, while women have become an increasingly powerful figure in society. The rise of feminism, the increasing power of the GLBT movement, and the descent of the traditional male role are all very palpable currently in today's world. Women have been given anthems like, "I am Woman, hear me roar!" and songs like Aretha Franklin's 1967 song "R-E-S-P-E-C-T." Gay and lesbian rights activists have been shouting from the rooftops for decades, (justifiably) seeking equal rights and acceptance. However, fewer and fewer men are given a place of respect and dignity in today's Western culture.

5.1 Loss of Male Power

So much emphasis has been placed on accepting previously disrespected tenants of our culture that the traditional male role, commonly associated with power and capability, has fallen along the wayside. Marketing campaigns target working women and mothers, who can do it all while their husbands are depicted as incompetent, bumbling, and effectively useless. Women are hot commodities in high-end business roles, and seen as a necessary and valuable element to every industry. GLBT communities have also sought equal rights for marriage, and changed the landscape of a traditional, nuclear family forever.

Along with these changing trends in our collective landscape, men have become less and less of a vital role in families, workplaces, and communities at large. Single mothers are hailed as heroes, and fathers are often viewed as replaceable pieces. No one is particularly shocked when a man fails to achieve his duties as a father. Men are not needed for their income either, and many women have taken the role of breadwinner in the family. Sit next to a group of single women during Happy Hour, and you will hear many woeful tales: "All the good men are married or gay," "I can do more for myself than a man can do," "Men don't like the fact that I am very successful in my career," "Men don't want to hear that you make more money than them," "Men of today are weak. Where have all the *real* men gone?"

Just take a sample of advertisements as proof: men who cannot cope with a simple cold, men who place plungers and babies on the same wooden surface, men who can't tell the difference in paint colors, or the difference between their own children. Or better yet men are sold the idea that they can take back their lost power by buying the biggest lawnmower on the block, or having the car with the most horsepower. While obviously humorous, these commercials shed light on a cultural phenomenon that has made a mockery out of male power in order to build other groups (mostly women) up, and to make the big corporations even more money. Inevitably, this has swung into another extreme and torn down the male figure as a crucial aspect of society, leaving no room for actual equality.

When we think of a nuclear, traditional family, the instant image is of a married couple - man and wife - and their two or three kids eating around the dinner table, or playing outside together. The reality is that this visual is virtually a thing of the past, if it ever truly existed. Along with the changing economic climate placing women in the workplace rather than the home, the dynamics of a family have entirely changed. As mentioned before, men have become seen as a placeholder within the family, without true influence aside from the occasional disciplinarian. How many times have you heard a woman tell her children, "Your father is going to hear about this!"?

Because of the lowered perceived value of men in society, many social psychologists have studied this phenomenon. Through many studies performed, the focus was placed on changes associated with industrialization, longer work hours away from home, an ever-increasing global market, wars, and the revolutions of feminism and sexuality. Because of all of these factors, and arguably many more, the landscape of the nuclear family has been forever changed. Men work longer hours to support their families, more families get divorced now than ever, and many adult men today were raised in families with fathers who were away at war.

In addition, the past few generations have seen the rise in feminine power, and these male children were raised in an environment where their individual power was not as emphasized as it was in previous generations. Either boys were not familiar with their fathers from a very young age due to jobs or military drafts, or they were raised by women or influenced by the force of femininity. Without a father or male role model's guiding hand, these young boys would grow up being confused as to what their true role in life was. In today's world, it is hard for a man to rise up and say he has a voice and a right to a place in the world without coming off as chauvinistic or a misogynist. Men's power is taken away even more when they are forced to be subdued for the sake of social niceties.

On top of this changing landscape, men have become somewhat divided into masculine and feminine roles. Either men are a "man's man," or they're seen as a pushover or weak. Straight men who cry are teased, and men are rarely allowed to show their emotional range without immediately being labeled "gay." Society tells boys to "suck it up" when they get hurt, or tells them that *real* men don't share their feelings. The result is men who are not well rounded and who are not adjusted to the complexities of their individual self.

Through much of Europe in recent years, there has been a huge push to get fathers and men on equal social ground as women. Sweden allows fathers to take up to thirteen months off for paternal leave, while pushing citizens to accept a man's role in the home just as they have a woman's role in the workplace. Through the UK, there are efforts to create a true equality between men and women - focus has been placed on programs that allow men to be individuals rather than just a "group" that has little to no value. By embracing this, many men in Europe have discovered a more well-rounded, "caring masculinity" that allows them to openly care for their partners and families, work in whichever environment they please, and take care of themselves as needed. So much emphasis is placed in the United States on work/life balance for women and mothers, but rarely do people recognize the need for the same thing for men. Europe's model is enviable, and necessary in order to regain the family dynamic that America is sorely lacking.

5.2 The Problem with Being a Nice Guy

Instead of continuing this vicious social cycle of treating men like they are a step behind or under women and other groups, it's time to get men to take their power back. Your initial reaction may be hesitation, especially as a man who was raised by a very strong female or is married to a matriarch. However, social experiments and multiple studies show that women actually *enjoy* when men step up to the plate. There is an evolutionary mechanism at work there, whether a strong, independent woman wants to acknowledge it or not.

The number one problem facing men today is their inability to share their true selves for fear of rejection. This phenomenon applies to not only physical aspects men feel they lack (too skinny, big belly, going bald, funny nose, etc.) but also aspects of their personality they refuse to share. The most important thing a man can do is share who he really is and be entirely intimate with a partner. Show the side of you that you are most afraid of showing; that is the sign of true intimacy.

Men hide their true selves for a number of reasons: toxic shame, avoidance of confrontation, childhood dynamics continuing into adult and a general sense that they are not going to get any better partners. For men, shame is inbred in them from a very young age. Shame about their anatomy especially, and how it works. Think of a time when you laughed at a boy who experienced an erection in school - it happens to many men! Viewing pornography and being seen as "perverts" when men admire a pretty woman walking down the street is another source of shaming. Men internalizing this: Looking at women is bad, wanting to have sex with a woman this way is bad, etc. This means that a man will not share his sexual feelings or power with a woman out of fear of rejection or retaliation.

A lot of men are also afraid of confrontation because they don't want to come off as the aggressor. Men ignore their wives or girlfriends, even as they rant and rave about something their partner did wrong. Society has taught men that it's never OK to disrespect a woman, and that has trickled down into even having an evenly approached argument. They allow themselves to be disrespected out of fear and repeated indoctrination.

It is also a common assumption that "Men marry their mothers." Men do tend to flock to women with personalities similar to their mothers. In the case of men with very strong-willed mothers, this equates to a continuation of what they experienced as children. If men were very attached to their mothers growing up, or a boy catered to his mother frequently, odds are high that he will have that same dynamic in future partners. Unfortunately, psychologists have often found that people tend to gravitate towards people who contain the worst elements of their parental interactions. People who were abused by their parents tend to gravitate towards abusers, men with mothers who were distant or critical tend to marry women who are the same way, and so on.

Often, the problem for men is not finding *any* relationship. Men can generally make connections, have sexual partners and develop relationships easily enough. The problem with "nice guys" is that they cater to their partner more so than consider their own emotions and gut reactions. These men try to fix the relationship, or at least not cause problems (by keeping their mouths shut). They tend to believe that a safe relationship is the one that they have. To keep a relationship, "nice guys" will pretend to be something they're not. Think of all the times you or someone you know has changed for a woman. It happens all the time, but there is a way to break the cycle.

5.3 Taking the Power Back

This section can be summed up in one sentence: Be yourself. Unfortunately, it really is that simple *and* that difficult. There are a number of ways to improve this aspect of your life, some of them easier to implement than others. It will take time, and it will take a lot of work, but you can take some of that power back and become a strong-willed man who isn't afraid to demand what he wants in life, sex and relationships.

First off, men who are considered "nice guys" need to put themselves first. If you are in a relationship, or madly seeking a relationship, take a moment to reflect. Is the person you are with or admiring really somebody that fits your needs? Don't think about the other person aside from what they have to offer you for a moment. If not, it's time to move on or really work on seeing if the person you desire can acclimate to you, not the other way around.

After you've managed to take a look at your behavior in keeping or acquiring a relationship, you may realize that you're not ready for a relationship, or you need to end a poor one. From this clean slate, you can develop boundaries and standards for future relationships and interactions with partners. Did you hate it when your last partner yelled at you, but felt you couldn't say anything back? Did you feel like you had to always make your partner happy, or sacrifice your time because theirs was "more valuable" in some way? It's time to figure out what you're not willing to give up for another person. For some it's a career, a relationship with a friend, a pet, a hobby, or any number of things. Once you have a stronger sense of who you are and what you bring to the table, your partner will fit you better.

All of this leads up to the finale, of course, which is breaking old habits. Old habits do die hard, and this is probably the hardest step in rehabilitating the nice guy. While behavioral psychology may not be a topic of interest for you, the idea is simple. If you behave in a certain way with a specific trigger, work on removing the behavior or the trigger. For example, if you become withdrawn and quiet every time your partner has a bad day, work on removing your reaction to the trigger. Mix things up - go for a walk or do something on your own and allow your partner space so that their mood doesn't affect yours. Or maybe you grew up in a household where people insulted each other frequently when a confrontation arose. Instead of hurling insults at your beloved next time he or she disagrees with you, work on your reaction. This also works the other way. If you find yourself constantly drawn to partners with a specific behavior that you cannot stand (snapping, nagging, goading, etc.) try to ignore the behavior and focus on maintaining your own happiness. It's basic training, even for dogs. To get rid of a behavior, do not give it any power (attention). Once your partner realizes you will not acknowledge a certain behavior or reaction, the behavior will become extinct. This is all within reason of course. You're still going to have poor reactions to one of your triggers, and it will not be perfect. However, it will be the exception rather than the rule.

At the end of the day, "nice guys" are simply afraid that if they exert too much power they will be rejected or perceived as misogynists or, even worse, unlovable. Men, let this section serve as proof that you can and will find the love you deserve and are worthy of. All you need to do is look inward, and focus on the power you feel inside. Let your power and your intentions shine through, and you will find a partner who is perfectly suited to you, and you to your partner. Nothing less.

5.4 Strong, Independent Women

Women, you may have read the last few sections and done nothing but shake your head. It is hard to accept the concept that your status in society has surpassed a man's position, and that may be true in some arenas. However, in the personal arena, women have begun to run the show. How many times has a man been called "whipped" because he dotes after his girlfriend or wife? How often has a woman told a man to "man up" and deal with something? How many beat-up husbands think that if they keep their wife happy and deny their own needs, all will be well, i.e. the "Happy wife, happy life" fallacy. Women are very deserving of their increased lot in life, but they're receiving it at the cost of another. Men have become the proverbial rug on which to wipe your feet.

No one doubts that a strong, independent woman is sexy. Nothing is sexier to a man than a woman who has a strong sense of self and direction. However, men often cater to this powerful persona because society tells them that becoming her equal is not acceptable. Someone must yield the power in a relationship, and men who hold clout over women are misogynists or abusers. Women who yield power over their men are just strong and intelligent. See the difference? We cannot have equality if one group is sacrificing something at every turn. Women no doubt had the short end of the stick for millennia in most cultures. However, the tides have turned in most developed nations, and women are now at the top of the totem pole.

If equality is really something you seek, especially in sex, respect the opposite gender or the person with opposing energies. Women, treat men with the respect they are due.

Admire the sacred masculine energy, and explore your own feminine energy. Yin and yang are very important, but they are matching pieces of the same coin. If one is "more important" than the other, there is no balance. There is no love. Love one another as you do yourself, and your relationship and sexual experience will blossom accordingly.

5.5 Using Sex as a Weapon

It is no great secret that women hold their sexual power in high esteem. It is also no great secret that men let this happen. How many times have you, a man, been afraid to anger your partner because you knew she would withhold sex? Women also lord themselves over a man because of their gender; men are often accused of being perpetrators of domestic violence when it was, in fact, the woman. It is hard to get a jury to accept a male's version of the story. In addition, men are the ones who pay alimony when a wife leaves them, merely because he was the "bread winner." Men must also pay child support if a woman merely requests it of him. American laws have become so skewed to favor women that, in many cases, they hold power over men just based on their gender. Women also may use sexual acts as a way to overcome their past, or to get over a bad relationship/traumatic experience. "Working women" also prostitute themselves as a way to lower sex into merely a financial transaction as a way to show that they hold the power to control; women have what men want, and they can make them pay for it.

In a reversal of this status quo, men often use sex as a commodity to get what they want from women. Think of the cliché "creepy" boss, who promises to promote women if they perform sexual favors. Or consider the men who provide their latest lover with a nice new wardrobe or a car, just because they can. There are also plenty of examples of "trophy wives;" men marry women based on their looks knowing that they can provide for her financially enough to keep her around. Men who are in committed relationships but are found to be cheating often attempt to turn this around on their wife: "I cheated because we never have sex." While this may be entirely true, sex is not usually the only reason a man cheats. Using sex to gain power over others is a bad move. Men also pay women for sex in hopes of engaging in sex without repercussion, or to have an outlet for their specific desires while not needing to worry about the person they are actually having sex with. In all of these ways, and probably more, people take advantage of one another using sex.

The danger with these sexual tactics is twofold. Not only will you not receive the love and care you deserve and desire, but you will damage your personal energy. The energy that goes out comes back to a person; when you are putting out negative energy, it will come home to roost. Trying to hold up sex as a weapon will eventually make that weapon backfire. In addition, using sex as a weapon or a commodity means that you are not engaging with another in a positive way, and you are creating a deficit in your "karmic energy bank." Of course, the risks associated with negative energy are well documented, and by sending out poor intentions you are essentially opening the door for dis-ease and a number of other repercussions for your behavior.

5.6 The Hidden Forces That Guide Gender Roles

While male and female roles are delineated in some fashion by anatomy, chemistry, and all that makes us male or female, social norms dictate much of how people interact with one another. Little girls are drawn to pink not because their DNA tells them to be, but because other little girls love pink and their parents dress them in pink, etc. Girls learn from an early age that makeup and clothing make them beautiful because they see their mother doing the same thing. Little boys learn that they shouldn't cry, and that they should "take care of their mother" when their fathers are gone. These define gender roles much more strongly than biology, and while many people think that these are harmless enough and developed through years of tradition, the reality is much darker than that.

As mentioned previously in the History of Sex chapter, the Rockefeller Foundation and many of the banking business's big names funded the feminist movement, have encouraged the slow dissemination of the traditional family structure, and have strengthened the market to influence people to buy, buy, buy. More people working means more income tax that funnels through the banks, more separation in gender means more items that need to be purchased (think about men's body wash in "manly" packaging, but the contents are the same as women's), and more marketing propaganda means children become consumers earlier in life. So many products are geared towards women's sexuality. The makeup industry teaches young girls and women that makeup leads to sexiness. Corporations are geared towards sexualizing everyone - even children. Consider the toys that are out there for young girls; short "play" dresses, high heels, lipstick. All of these things are seen innocent by many, but the reality is that it trains young girls to see themselves as valued only by how they look to others.

By separating the nuclear family into working parents (who cannot spend time with their kids) and children who attend school all day (being programed by the state), the odds are much higher that the family will spend so much of their financial energy just to "get by" with their consumer needs that they will be easily indoctrinated into this system of marketing and banking without ever noticing how much they're providing to the Big Banks. This process has not stopped, and has only gotten stronger as time goes on. These external forces cannot remain external. Eventually they are internalized to the point where sex and how we interact with one another becomes nearly unrecognizable. How do we stop this insanity and wake up? We must think for ourselves, leading our lives with divine intuition and our innate power, while also understanding the outdated systems put in place around us by prior generations. Only by freely sharing new knowledge and data, discarding what no longer works, and implementing what does, can we free our minds and hearts into a more loving and peaceful planetary existence.

Chapter 6:
The Psychology of Sex

"If you love a flower, don't pick it up. Because if you pick it up it dies and it ceases to be what you love. So if you love a flower, let it be.
Love is not about possession. Love is about appreciation."
~ Osho

Hopefully, at least once in your life, you are able to experience the trifecta within one relationship: Lust, love and sex. While those may seem like interchangeable terms to you, there are nuanced differences that are incredibly important in understanding your sexual identity as a whole. While things may definitely begin as lust, turn into sex, and become love, there is often a signal that your body sends to another person, telling them your exact intentions. Body language is more than just a general indication of someone's feelings; it can also tell what your intentions are, and what exactly you're thinking. Let this section serve as a guide for enhancing your understanding of your inner motives and intentions when approaching a partner through lust, love or sex.

6.1 Defining Moments

The difference between lust and love is fairly basic, and it is a distinction that we make early on in our sexual development. We know that being extremely attracted to someone does not a life partner make. We also know that loving someone deeply may mean that the sex appeal and intense intercourse you once experienced wanes over time. There is a neurological reaction to lust - a non-specific, general drive towards mating, where hormones and neurons fire in an attempt to get you to mate at nearly any cost. Love, and long-term commitment, occurs when these hormones stabilize, and you enter the "Goldilocks zone" on a neuronal level.

It is believed that increased levels of dopamine result in intense focus on a new partner (lust). Over time and exposure to your partner, dopamine decreases, the lust recedes, and a long-term connection is made (love). When you love someone, interaction helps stabilize your brain's activity, while being away from him or her results in a hormone crash, something akin to homesickness when you miss your lover. The important distinction here is that lust is the immediate physical and mental reaction to a person, while love is the result of compatibility and connection that endures. The difference between all three is something slightly less detectable, and requires both social expectations and spiritual evaluation.

6.2 Love

While these are the biological explanations of complex human emotions, there are also other views to take into account. There is a "worldly definition" to love, which essentially boils down to love as a tender, deep, overwhelming *feeling* of affection and solicitude toward another person. Love is an intense *emotional* attachment or *feeling* for a person, place, or thing. Individuals experience a *feeling* of intense *desire* and *attraction* toward a person with whom one is disposed to make a pair. There is also expectation of romance, sexual passion and sexual intercourse.

On the other hand, there is the godly or spiritual definition. A quote from the Bible sums it up quite nicely:

> "Love suffers long and is kind; love does not envy; love does not parade itself, is not puffed up; it does not behave rudely. Love does not seek its own, is not provoked, thinks no evil; does not rejoice in iniquity, but rejoices in the truth. Love bears all things, believes all things, hopes all things, endures all things." (1 Cor 13:4-7)

Most importantly, love doesn't need to control others. Spiritual connection is dependent on an even playing field, where people meet in harmony to share energy and love. Interestingly, a study done in 2002 showed that 58% of men and 72% of women disagreed with the statement: "The best thing about love is sex." This further supports the idea that love and sex are entirely separate phenomenon.

6.3 Sex and Lust

Differences in lust and sex - one is physical, other is spiritual. Sex as an act and an experience greatly differs from lust. Lust is an emotion, a feeling, a drive. Sex is an action with an intention, and with divine ramifications.

It can be argued that lust is a vestigial component of our internal mechanism, leftover from the "Caveman Days." Lust is what drove us to reproduce in prehistoric times, and lust is what has continued the species through these millennia. Lust is a chemical and physical reaction to external stimuli - a beautiful woman, a sexual gesture, a well-muscled man. Lust can carry us for a significant amount of time before it wanes, leaving us looking for something else that triggers the same reaction.

If you find yourself using the terms of lust, love, and sex interchangeably, hopefully this section will help you understand they are very different indeed. Keep in mind that our definitions of sex, love and lust have entirely changed along our millennia as humans. In the past, marriage and love were not synonyms. Women were traded and exchanged to keep alliances, and to rear children and build community. 100 years ago in most Anglo-Saxon cultures, marriages were arranged. Even today in some cultures, arranged marriages still exist. If the definitions of love and marriage have been combined through time, it is understandable to see how love, sex and lust have become so inseparable as well.

Masturbation

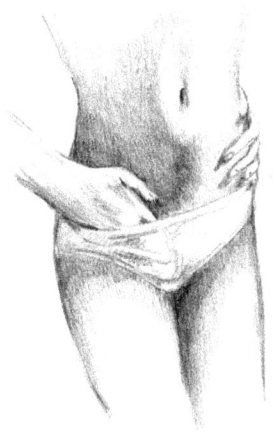

Masturbation has long been a subject of toxic shame for most people, especially men. Young boys are caught by their parents, or told terrifying tales that they will grow hairy palms or burn in Hell for their self-exploration. Girls are nearly never taught that they are even capable of such a thing, let alone actually encouraged to explore themselves. In reality, however, it is your intent during self-pleasure that sets your vibrations, making it an unhealthy or healthy act. Self-pleasure and self-exploration are not innately "bad" behaviors - they are a vital act in order to understand our own bodies, and understand the relationship our bodies have with another person during sex. Mutual masturbation in the presence of your partner can show them exactly how you like to be stimulated, and can lead to foreplay while exploring each other's bodies prior to intercourse.

To make sure that masturbation is a positive act, focus on the thoughts and alignment of your energies. Better yet, use your desire to masturbate to translate into increasing your stamina or performance for a future lover; not just doing the act to "get off." Many people also refrain from using their energy for masturbation as motivation to get other things done; essentially forcing that energy elsewhere in the body to achieve more. Often, people use thoughtless action in connection to random thoughts as they do in masturbation. Boredom, work stress, grief, lust; these emotions result in masturbation for useless temporary relief. Those thoughts/emotions are not in the highest vibration of self-expression and may be masking the real issue of a deeper pain that is not being dealt with (i.e. low self-esteem, loneliness or lack of social connection to others).

Use self-pleasure to align yourself through your sexuality; sexual energy in positive alignment is a healthy vibration if done properly. When you know what and how you like to be stimulated, you can share yourself with your partner for maximum pleasure while communicating confidently your wishes, thus creating a deeper bond.

6.4 Sex Transmutation

Sex transmutation, or the channeling of sexual energy into other efforts, has been touted by many people over time, including sports figures, inventors, artists, dancers, writers, and even millionaire money managers. Essentially, instead of spending all of your effort into acquiring an easy sexual outlet, store that energy and use it to enter a higher vibrational plane and to center your focus on something else desirable. When a young man frequently masturbates (as most teenage boys do), they are doing so with a future mate, or imaginary mate, in mind. The idea is similar to a man's exhaustible yang, his life force that is easily drained through his sexual experiences. Store the yang within the body for longer, and achieve greater things outside of the short-term sexual ecstasy experienced. Masturbating to release the sexual energy too often can be counterproductive and leave you spiritually, physically, and emotionally depleted. Sex transmutation with correct intention and application however, is a great way to have more phenomenal sex, as anyone who has gone on a "sex hiatus" with his or her partner will attest to. Withholding that energy means that you create a different connection with a partner, or develop a new skill, and generally increase your ability to perform in a number of arenas. There is something to valuing the yang principle, after all.

6.5 Importance of Body Language

Think of a time when you were inexplicably attracted to someone. While they may not have been your classic "type," or did not even seem like someone you'd have much in common with, you were just *drawn* to them. This doesn't mean you jumped right into bed with this person, but you found yourself aroused or more than slightly curious about what sex with that person would be like. For many, this sort of encounter is quite intense, as we rarely interact without words or emotions. This, friends, is the power of body language.

Body language is often so subconscious, so unintentional, that we don't recognize that we, or another person, are behaving a certain way. Take for instance the hip sway in women. Women, you will know how your hips sway more when you feel sexual, when you feel great in your outfit, or when you feel eyes on you when you walk by. You may not even intend to do this, and some women become embarrassed by their body's subconscious effort to attract a mate. Men, you've also probably noticed the way you stand taller, tighten your abs, with your shoulders back when you see an attractive woman. Your muscles tighten, and you hold your jaw tighter to create that chiseled effect women go crazy for. For most of you, this isn't even a conscious effort. The mind reacts to a sexual urge, and the body prepares.

Instead of hoping your body and mind communicate next time you're intrigued by your partner or a new prospect, we can train our body's behaviors to attract the other person. Without words, without even so much as an introduction, you can set the stage for your encounter. This is powerful, even if you're attempting to lure in someone entirely new, and it can also aid in bringing about a new approach to a comfortable, settled relationship as well.

Eyes

The importance of eye contact cannot be overstated. When you make eye contact with your lover, or a prospective lover, you are signaling your interest. Your eyes focus on them, and that tells them that you are receptive to what they are saying, you are connected, and you are interested. (Dilated pupils indicate sexual interest.) Making eye contact with strangers in a room also promotes your confidence, and others watching you will believe you are confident as well. Eye contact across a crowded room or at a longer distance gives a special charge, instantly making you sexier in the eyes of the other person. Consider holding eye contact for slightly longer than you may think is comfortable. In about 10 seconds of eye contact, you will have fully charged the other person's sex batteries, making you entirely irresistible.

Neurologists have long associated blinking as a sexual interest cue - you blink more when you want someone. Our bodies are designed to react like this, and you can replicate this by blinking more if you find someone attractive, and they will pick up the cue and mirror it back. In addition, playing coy with your eyes is also another trick you can use to draw in a mate, especially men. A woman can make eye contact with a man, move her eyes around the room or down to the floor, and back up again. Men view this as coquettish and flirty, and know you're interested in them making the first move.

Watch where your eyes wander when you're having a conversation with someone. Often our eyes migrate between a person's two eyes, their nose and their mouth. However, men often tend to trail a little further south, usually to the breasts of a woman or another woman in their periphery. Men are very visual creatures, as are some women. Just be aware that your eyes can speak volumes to others. They truly are windows to the soul.

Mouth

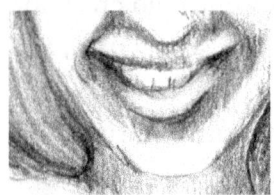

What's the most important thing you can do with your mouth to attract a mate? Smile! Smiling, aside from eye contact, is rated as the sexiest thing a man or woman can do to attract a stranger. Smiling shows you are happy, you are confident (people with poor teeth don't smile much), you are social and you probably have a good sense of humor. Genuine smiles are incredibly attractive and contagious, but subtle smiling differences are easily picked up - closed mouth smiles or fake smiles are read easily so try to avoid them if you're interested in another person.

Attract attention to your mouth. Studies have shown that pictures of women with larger-than-average lips were rated higher in attractiveness. Use lipstick to accentuate the color of your lips, or emphasize your pouty lip whenever possible. Moisten your lips with your tongue, or bite your lips, whatever you need to draw a potential partner's attention to your mouth. Subliminally, the lips on your face look rather similar to the lips a little further south, and attracting attention to your mouth sends signals to your partner that your sex is just as impressive. (Ladies, a word of caution if you choose to artificially enhance your beauty; overly injected lips or badly done plastic surgery, gives off the wrong impression to men. Instead of being viewed as sexy, males read this as a fake and desperate attempt to pass as something you are not.)

It is also commonplace for a person to watch their partner's mouth more when they are interested sexually. Next time you're talking to your lover or a potential mate, watch their eyes. If you want to tease your lover, place your finger or straws or anything near your mouth. You can also gently bite your finger between your teeth and enjoy the jolt of electricity it sends straight to the other person's sex antenna.

Chest

The chest is a powerful attraction tool in both males and females. Men, when they see an attractive candidate, will stand up straight and push their pectoral muscles out or bulge their biceps. This is an evolutionary cue telling the mate that the man is strong and can provide protection, something women still respond to. If you want to show your potential mate or current lover that you're interested in them, leave your chest open at the shoulders and face them.

If you bunch your shoulders or slouch, you're seen as defeated or uninterested. Lean forward, keep arms uncrossed, and push your chest out, focusing on straight posture. Women, play "peekaboo" with your cleavage. As a general rule, show a little cleavage, not too much - always leave something to the imagination. Men, like women, have huge imaginations. Wearing clothes that don't show much cleavage until you lean forward or press your chest against something is a great way to get attention; men enjoy waiting to see if they'll catch another glimpse. Subliminally, an open chest means your heart is open and available for love. A cute necklace and pendant dangling over the breastbone can accentuate the heart chakra and draw the eye.

Hands/Arms/Fingers

Hands and fingers are a very good way to attract a person visually and sensually. Hands and fingers are very closely associated with sexual acts, and also indicate mood very easily. Do keep your fingers and toes manicured well with a regular mani/pedi session? Men do love a well-kept woman, as this shows confidence in keeping yourself feminine and fertile. Women often talk with their hands, gesturing and moving through expressions. If a woman does this in a man's presence, it means she is trying to draw in his attention and keep it. Women also place their hands and fingers within touching distance, in order to test a partner and see if they will reach out and grab them. Men tend to hold their hands in stationary poses, generally displaying power.

If you are wondering what to do with your hands, here are a few recommendations: Avoid placing your hands under your chin, as that indicates boredom. Steepled or intertwined fingers generally indicate confidence. Play with straws, your hair, glasses, wine stems, anything that draws the eye and can be seen as a sexual expression. In addition, a man may use his hands to "steer" a woman, whether by the small of her back or by gently guiding her eyes with signaling motions toward his pelvis, by slightly tugging his belt. Ensuring that there is an electric charge by almost touching, but not quite doing it, helps to keep a woman attuned to the attention you pay to her body. If a woman grazes or touches your hand during conversation, this is a powerful sign that she is becoming tactile and may be ready for the next level of connection.

Hips/Legs/Feet

One of the best signs to tell if a person is into you is looking down. Are their feet pointed at you? If so, they are interested. When women or men cross their legs, watch which way they cross. If they cross towards the person sitting next to them, it is a sign that you are intriguing to them. Wide stances and both feet planted on the ground is usually a "green light;" the other person is ready and willing to get things moving.

When you're trying to attract a man, focus on crossing your legs at the thighs. This brings attention to your legs and, of course, your groin. Frequently crossing and uncrossing your legs will keep attention focused on the area as well. When you're trying to attract a female, focus on power stances. Either keep both feet planted firmly, slightly thrusting your hips forward, or try to convey confidence and ease with a laidback stance. Lean far back in a chair, extend your legs, and cross one over the other.

Walking with confidence and with the right hip structure is also a "call to arms" for a potential mate. If you stride leisurely through a crowded room with your hips squared (if you're a man) or hips swaying (if you're a woman), you will have more eyes on you than you can count. Taking strides and pausing for effect if you're a woman draws attention to your legs, your body, and the confidence with which you hold yourself.

Posture

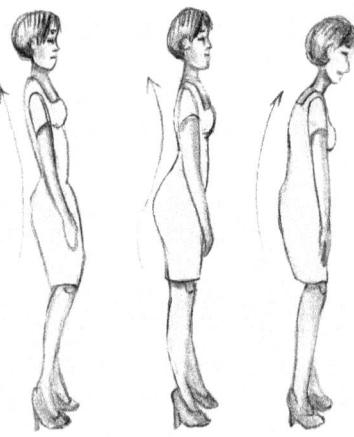

Enough cannot be said about the importance of posture for looking, feeling and attracting a mate. Keeping a straight healthy spine with relaxed shoulders indicates confidence, strong health, and a positive attitude to those around you. People who slouch too much over the span of years actually begin to be permanently hunched over with a deformity called kyphosis, which makes them look guarded, unhappy, older, less healthy, and much less confident in their lives. If you want to attract a mate, smile, stand tall when you enter a room, neck extended and head held high.

When you sit, don't slouch or melt into the chair you occupy; remain upright but comfortable. In addition to looking more confident, good posture makes your chest look more muscular if you're a man, and your stomach flatter. For women, it makes the breasts "perky," and the stomach flatter as well. Posture also has the ability to reflect the "Fake it Till You Make It" approach to body confidence. When you feel self-conscious and shy, straighten that spine and lift that chin up. Even if you make eye contact with no one, you are sending a powerful subliminal message that you are confident and capable, and people will be drawn to that. Need help? Just ask your chiropractor to teach you how to get back that power posture and sexy stride. Also, be *sure to view the powerful Kousouli® Method Spinal Stretches (KSS®) in Chapter 8, which will help you gain more posture confidence.*

6.6 Subconscious Desire

Body language is something we hear about often, and we understand some of the basics, especially when it comes to our careers and love life. However, what isn't entirely understood is the subliminal interaction we engage in on a daily basis, from power plays to relationships to our interactions with strangers. We also don't notice or have any control over our reaction to other people's body language. We may be happy and receptive to others, and meet a person with very closed off body language, which in turn shuts down our ability to carry on a conversation. We may find someone sexually attractive and try to engage with him or her, but by barely even glancing at his or her general stance we know that approaching him or her is not a good idea.

As humans, we also don't entirely notice how our bodies react when they detect sexual energy. Women don't even realize their hips start moving more, men don't notice that they stand up straighter or puff out their chests. Hair and clothes are straightened, and posture is immediately corrected. Hair is flipped, lips are bitten, our eyes dilate, and our breath gets shorter. Our bodies respond to the energy sensed, and they react automatically without ever really consulting the conscious brain. Not only do we change our body language when we feel someone watching, but we unknowingly behave in certain ways just to keep a person attracted. Women rub wine stems or suck on straws to simulate fellatio, men put their hands on their belt or near their pockets in order to draw attention to their virile organ.

When to Back Off

Unfortunately, there are just times when your manly or womanly appeal just does not hit the right target. The number one clue that you're not going to "get lucky" regards space. If you invade someone's space without him or her giving you the right "permission" cues, you may have to retreat and recoup with a different approach on another person. When someone is uncomfortable, you will often see people start to fidget or browse the area around them to look for an escape. Women especially will look down or away, while men tend to tune someone out and look around the room. Showing disinterest is much like a child hiding under a blanket to avoid a scary monster: Don't look at it, and it will go away. If you see someone start to tuck their chin to their chest and hunch a little, it means they are extremely uncomfortable, and you should back off (or step in, if you see a situation like this). To avoid this awkward situation, do not invade space (stay at least a foot or two away) until you get "interest" cues, like touching or shuffling towards you. You don't always have to be the initiator; let them come to you!

6.7 Sex Styles Reflected in Clothing

Obviously men and women are fundamentally different, but there are nuances within each gender that separate each person from the next. For example, some men feel best in jeans and a T-shirt, or some may pull off a more daring, trendy look. Men feel powerful in a suit and tie, and relaxed in exercise or sporting gear. Women, of course, are notorious in the wide variety of styles they frequently exhibit. Some women are most comfortable in jeans and a T shirt as well, but some may find themselves drawn to sexy, "skimpy" clothing. Others yet may like more traditional clothing, while others are drawn to edgier styles. Women can often range in their clothing just based on the day, and are very versatile. What a woman chooses to wear one day says a lot about her intentions and mood.

There are a variety of ways that clothing is used to illustrate a person's sexuality. Here a few examples, in order of the looks that convey the least sex appeal to the looks that scream "Do me!"

MEN

For men, looking sexy is not really a social expectation. For this reason, men are often sexual in whatever they feel most comfortable in. However, that doesn't mean that what they wear is appealing to the person they are attempting to attract. For example:

Sorry guys, but ladies don't go for a man who couldn't even wash his sweatpants before coming out in public. Keep the Cheeto-stained hoodie at home, brush your hair, and wear some pants. Women have their antennae set to always scan their perimeter for the highest male in the pack. The more you show yourself as successful and in demand, the better your chances are at attaining a mate. There are countless young physically attractive males who are dateless, left scratching their head in confusion. It's because they don't show themselves off as successful providers, which translates into difficulty in dating. The "baggy" look sends a subliminal, "Hello, I can't provide for you or a future family, I'm possibly homeless myself" message, which rates a big zero in the pre-programmed female mind.

The next step up from "slob" status is the man in jeans and fitted T- shirt. There is nothing wrong with wearing your favorite clothes when trying to get a date - you exude more confidence when you're comfortable. Just make sure your jeans aren't dirty, torn or ill-fitting, and that your shirt also accentuates something of your body. Whether it is your eye color, chest, slim waist or skin tone, play it up.

For women, the pinnacle of sexy is the famed "sharp-dressed man." There may be no other clothing on this earth that can attract a female more rapidly than a black suit and tie ensemble. However, if it is baggy, ill-fitting or not well put-together, it won't have the same panty-dropping effect. Make sure your suits are tailored or purchased to fit your body well, and that you keep it clean and pressed. Odds are, women will be looking at you more than twice showing off some very attentive body language.

WOMEN

Women are obviously the sex most affected by the need to reflect sexiness in their style. For men, almost anything a woman wears could be sexy if she manages to pull it off right. However, here are a few tips to get your wardrobe ready for attracting a mate, ladies.

The least sexy thing a woman could wear are clothes that make her appear older, larger or less vibrant than she is. If a woman wears baggy pants, baggy shirts, and has her hair in a sloppy bun, odds are she is not going to draw the attention of any men as this plays "too safe". Men like a slightly wild woman which can ride with the pack and shows high chances of survival. Men love women with a wide range who are down for anything; a gal who can dress down, but also dresses up well should the occasion call for it. Subconsciously this means that if the going gets tough, no matter the weather or danger, you will still be able to father his kids and his genes can live on.

A step up from the "frumpy" image is the comfortable second wardrobe option. Women have been given powerful bodies, and even comfortable clothing can be incredibly sexual. Tight fitting jeans or leggings, a loose but fitting shirt, and shoes or accessories that show off personal taste can be incredibly appealing.

The next category of style is the "casual professional" attire look that blends modesty and professionalism with feminine sexuality. What is sexier than a tight-fitting skirt, a button-up blouse that accentuates the cleavage, killer heels, and a brain and career to show that you're more than just a well-wrapped package?

The pinnacle of sexy in the eyes of many men is the sexually revealing style and appearance that shows the most skin and confidence on a woman. A woman dressed for a night out on the town in a small dress fitted to her body, "ravish me" pumps highlighting her legs, and makeup and accessories to accentuate her best features gives a woman an unprecedented advantage for finding a partner.

Of course, the best thing anyone (male or female) can wear is confidence. If you're underdressed or overdressed or somewhere in between, it doesn't matter - *if* you hold yourself like you know who you are and what you're doing. Men and women often admit that thing that most attracted them to their current or previous partners wasn't just how they looked - it was how they behaved.

6.8 Hypnotizing Your Lover

Power of the Mind

Consider how much power the mind has in regards to sex. How imagining our fantasies, focusing on the feeling of your partner's scent, or even their touch in a non-erogenous zone can help us reach climax. When you daydream about sex, your body becomes physically aroused. Our minds can make thoughts so real that we cannot distinguish the difference between fantasy and current reality (i.e. getting so deep into a movie you jump back when a scary scene frightens you). Your mind controls so much of your life, and your ability to be physically and spiritually present during sex is under your mind's control as well. What if we could use this knowledge to our advantage to put our lover into a hypnotic spell, or accentuate the love we're already in for a better, more intimate relationship together? Who would say no to that!?

With all this information out there on subliminal messages, is there a way to hypnotize your lover in a safe, honorable way that can help you excite your love life? Yes. Can you hypnotize a lover into the best orgasms they have ever had? Yes. Is it relatively easy when you know the methods? Yes, and I am about to let you know some of the basics you can use right now!

Note, however, that there is no way I can cram all the experience, skill, and know-how amassed over the years into just one book. Deeper mastery of these and other techniques must be meticulously practiced and understood on a deeper level. This is why the seminars and live instruction given are pertinent to success. However, these basic techniques will give you a kick start into nurturing a better love life. For those who wish to get more information and expand their understanding of their personal power and energy, they may attend the *live seminar events, by finding details at www.DrKousouli.com or www.KousouliMethod.com.*

Okay, first thing's first; in order to effectively hypnotize your partner, you have to understand what hypnosis is and what it is not.

Myths and Misconceptions about Hypnosis

Hypnosis, as a whole, is one of the most misunderstood practices in history, thanks to propaganda and mistruths in Hollywood films. Clinical hypnosis is safe, when performed by a qualified practitioner, whose intent is to help a patient heal their disruptive subconscious programming. I am going to help clear up some common misconceptions for you.

1. **Dr. Kousouli, I saw a hypnotist make someone do odd things; what is going on?**

The type of hypnosis used in an office session is very different, in delivery style and intention, than the hypnosis done in front of a large crowd or stage. Clinical hypnotherapy promotes health and well being, whereas stage hypnosis is done purely for entertainment value. In clinical hypnosis, you relax and focus on the sound of the hypnotist's voice while you are guided to remove stress, heal an addiction, toss a bad habit, or gain more self-confidence.

2. **Can hypnosis be used for brain washing? Does the hypnotist control my brain and mind?**

The hypnotist is actually a guide who helps you transcend the path to self-hypnosis. If you are unwilling to follow suggestions, unable to relax, or can't focus while the process is being conducted, there is no force that can hypnotize you. You still have free will, and it cannot be taken from you unless you give it over willingly. When hypnotizing a lover, you are guiding them to what they would already want do willfully but are currently not actively doing. Hypnotizing them toward a loving, sexually stimulating, and powerful connection is what they want if they are seeking to be with you. Hypnosis helps them (and you) get connected faster and on a deeper level.

3. **Can hypnosis be used to enslave me?**

Hypnosis can be used for positive intent as well as negative, but no one is permanently able to take your consciousness away from you. The intended process in a doctor's office is focused on helping you; teaching your mind to relax and let go of the negative stress or subconscious programs that no longer serve you. If you continuously watch negative television programming, your television acts as your hypnotist. The television programming will input negative thoughts (fears, violence, or other unacceptable behavior) into your mind over time because you allow it to, and by giving your focused attention to it. When you use hypnosis for the right reasons regularly with a relaxed open mind, you can literally change your life for the better. When it comes to building stronger relationships, as mentioned here in this book, hypnotizing your lover is a smart choice in securing a happier, loving connection with each other.

4. Do you forget everything that happened during a hypnosis session?

As I mentioned above, all that hypnosis does is teach your mind to relax and focus. If you do not remember anything from the session how in the world will your mind remember to utilize it when you need it? The body and mind always remember subconsciously; it is what we choose to recall consciously and what we retrieve from our stored memories that we use in our daily lives. You will not remember your session consciously if the hypnotist suggests you will not remember the session upon waking. In the technique described, we will provide subtle but powerful ways that make a difference for changing a lover's ways, though these techniques will be introduced while they remain awake.

5. Can I lie while under hypnosis?

You will have all thinking capabilities active. In fact you'll be more focused and more active because your mind is freer to create. It is your choice to "create" the truth or lie, even though it is never advisable to lie. The suggestions you make or are given will be more real or true to you depending on what you feel the 'truth' is.

6. Isn't Hypnosis against the basic principle of Christianity?

Seventh Day Adventists and Christian Scientists have religious doctrines that speak against using hypnosis, but not because it goes against Christianity. Rather, it is for possible traditional and political reasons. All Christians practice meditation through a modified form of self-hypnosis, or what some religions like to refer to as *prayer*, which helps them relax the mind towards asking God for divine intervention.

7. I've heard Hypnosis is very common in our day-to-day lives; how so?

Hypnosis is a natural process and all of us have experienced a form of it at some point of our lives. Road hypnosis is common for those who drive often on highways and suddenly find themselves at their destination in little or no time at all, wondering how they got there so quickly. Prior to bed every night, the body goes through a shutting down cycle referred to as sleep hypnosis. Some spouses claim their significant other unknowingly talks in his or her sleep, but seems very awake. Unresponsive teenagers, staring at the television with solid focus while mom is telling them dinner is ready, are the effect of television covert (concealed) hypnosis. Covert hypnosis is also the way you will instill the techniques mentioned in this chapter while your partner is intensely focused on you and your actions. A usual trait among hypnosis episodes is that time seems to have gone by quickly, or that time simply does not exist at all. Everyone at some point in his or her life has been in a self-induced hypnotic state without even knowing it. Clinical hypnosis refocuses and targets its use for positive changes in one's life.

Hypnosis works best when one fully uses their powers of imagination, concentration and intelligence while hypnotizing or being hypnotized. The following assumes that you, the hypnotist, have your lover's attention, and that you have bypassed their critical thinking state - which means they are in a relaxed and attentive state towards you; not in a combative, uptight or angry scenario which would inhibit focused attention to you in a positive way. In usual hypnosis practice, what is known as "pre-induction" occurs first. A hypnotic pre-induction is the process a hypnotist takes to establish relaxed conditions or the state required for hypnosis to actually occur (i.e. soft relaxing music or waterfall sounds in the background, while laying on a comfortable bed or couch). Then, he or she uses "induction" or induces, (instructive initiation), the subject into taking action through the use of hypnosis cues and triggers. Anchoring and repetition of hypnosis cues and triggers seals the desired action loops the subject is asked to execute. Let's look at some well-known terms associated with hypnosis.

Hypnotic Cue: Spoken word or an action that functions as a signal to someone to begin an action such as a performance.

Trigger: Anything that is anchored which produces an action.

Anchoring: To "anchor" our thoughts, trait, or piece of information to a reference point or placing something in association with something else. I.e. "The stuffed bear Jim got her at the carnival reminds her of her ex boyfriend's beard," "The blue shirt Andy is wearing reminds me of one I bought last summer," or "Her laugh reminds me of the Batman's Joker."

Action state: Something in motion or in the process of expressing itself. In hypnosis, it is the end-desired effect (i.e. When the hypnotist clapped his hands, the subject raised his hands as instructed).

Types of anchoring using hypnotic cues and triggers:

Hand or finger squeezing: Simply squeeze your lover's hand or select one or two fingers, like the ring finger or pinky. Gently squeeze, let go. Repeat again immediately. Squeeze, squeeze. Or you can do a three squeeze set. Squeeze, squeeze, squeeze. This combo, or code, is unique to you. You can replicate it at will when inputting hypnotic cues and triggers.

Stimulation of body points: Choose a sexy sensitive point on the body that you like on your lover. The collarbone, an earlobe, or hip ridges are excellent choices. Lightly touch, tap, or stroke the area. Just like above, set a sequence to it. Stroke, stroke. Tap, tap, pause, tap, or stroke, pause, stroke. Make up a short sequence and stick to it as your hypnotic cue/trigger.

Certain key positions: While in bed spooning with your lover, during sexual intercourse, or when you're arm in arm in love sitting on a park bench. Linking the position or positioning with hypnotic cues and triggers with the action state of activity taking place, will make your lover feel the same way whenever their hypnotic cue is triggered - even if they are not at that same place or position.

Spoken words: These are words that are specific to you and your partner, like pet names (doll, cutesy, baby, pup, etc.) that can be anchored to action states of being. They can be heard in normal daily conversations so that they can reactivate when heard.

Trigger phrases: "I adore you," "Love you always," or "You're the beat of my heart," "Baby just Imagine, feel, focus on," etc. Consider how powerful the words "I love you" are in relationships. Please note: Humanity is conditioned, especially women, to live for hearing that phrase. Do not abuse the phrase "I love you," use it loosely, or use it to manipulate others. The techniques in this book are powerful and do work, so please use them in the highest integrity for building relationships, not destroying them.

Music played: Use a specific song by dedicating it to your lover or having it in the background while setting an action state of being. Have you ever sat at a party or nightclub and then shouted, "This is my jam!" when you suddenly heard the DJ play your favorite song from years ago? That song's beat and melody are imprinted into your mind, mixed with feel-good feelings that awaken from within as soon as the song is played. The song triggered you, and instantly you changed your state of being. Your mind and body were essentially hypnotized by that song years ago, and the programming still affects your mood.

Eye signals or smiles: The way you look at your lover, blinking, staring, or smiling can be very hypnotic. Long after a breakup, many lovers remember, "I loved the way he or she looked at me and smiled."

Tantalize the senses: You can also combine food items like strawberries (taste) or perfumes/colognes (smell) to bring about a desired action or state of being in your lover. Every time they taste or smell the trigger(s), it will be you and your interaction with them that they will think of. You can pop a chocolate covered strawberry into your lover's mouth while they orgasm, or you can wear their favorite fragrance during hot sex. From then on every time they eat, see, or smell strawberries, or take a whiff of that fragrance, they will think of you.

When a hypnotic cue/trigger is intentionally paired with an action/state of being over a set period of time, the subconscious loop becomes programmed, the interaction automatically sets and can be easily triggered again in the future. The longer (and repeatedly) a cue/trigger is set, the deeper the conditioning.

For example, someone who now smokes habitually in a public party setting was, at one time, a nonsmoker. However, one day that nonsmoker introduced a cigarette to his or her mouth (cue/trigger) and mixed it with an emotional state of well-being when in the presence of their friends and peers who also smoked (active state of being). Even though their body rejected the action because it was new and harmful to them (by coughing), the repetition of the cue/trigger and the combination of peer group acceptance and well-being merged the two together, thus creating a feeling of "acceptance" every time a cigarette is smoked. This is a very effective and common hypnotic trance which tobacco and alcohol companies reply on for their business and even target customers through their feel-good ads. It works too well.

Now that you understand the basic terminology and how anchoring a hypnotic cue and trigger works, you may choose to hypnotize your lover. Assuming your lover is already in a highly focused and attentive state, the following are my five very basic steps to set a covert hypnotic trance:

1. Choose the hypnotic cue/trigger.
(I.e. stroking, squeezing, or tapping a part of the body using sounds, smells, or any of the cues and triggers mentioned previously - or simply create your own.)

2. Execute cue/trigger and link it to an action/state of being.
(i.e. Set the code or unique sequence as described in stimulation of body points. This

way, only that sequence will activate the action/ state of being, so it will only be when you do it; not activated by others.)

3. Introduce desired action/state of being.
(i.e. the desired feeling or end result you wish to link the cue/trigger with.[i.e.] a sex position, stimulation of an intense orgasm, romantic encounters together, etc. For more information on how to execute heavy states of sexual arousal, see the next chapter, Chapter 7 -The Neural Wiring of Pleasure.)

4. Expand the action state to develop a deeper anchored state through repetition with the hypnotic cue/trigger. Keep linking step 2 with step 3.

5. Maintain and strengthen the cue/trigger and action/state of being over time for a more permanent effect.
(i.e. Use the same cue/trigger sequence with action/state of being over a period of time to strengthen the cue/trigger's effects.)

Once you've established a specific pattern to your hypnotic cue/ trigger, you can maintain that cycle for as long as you are with your lover. The power of its effects comes from reinforcement over time. Even if months or years pass, those specific cues/triggers will bring your lover's mind back to that time when they were with you when the cue/trigger is activated – if the programming was originally strongly imprinted.

For example, the most common hypnotic cue/trigger and action state I am asked to teach is the hypnosis cue/trigger (squeeze) for orgasm (action state). When your lover is the height of orgasm, simply tap, squeeze or stroke a part of their body inconspicuously. At the first few tries, you will only prime your lover, but with time, if done correctly, you can simply be anywhere and activate the cue/trigger; they will have the same intense feeling come over them as if they were in the very act itself. Of course, you must use this one with caution.

If you'd like to learn more about hypnotism or how to master these specific skills and more, read BE A MASTER® OF PSYCHIC ENERGY, and consider attending a seminar. Details can be found at www.DrKousouli.com or www.KousouliMethod.com.

Now let's explore the physical aspects of neural pleasure which will be crucial in helping you connect step three for introducing the desired action and state of being.

Chapter 7:
The Neural Wiring of Pleasure

*"I know a man who gave up smoking, drinking, sex, and rich food.
He was healthy right up to the day he killed himself."*
~ Johnny Carson

Sex is a phenomenal example of the wonders of the human body. Men and women are literally designed for one another anatomically speaking, and the process of sex itself is fascinating. Aside from the aspect of physical penetration and climax, the body goes through so much more. The brain is so engaged with sex that it looks like a neuronal fireworks show in a person's head when they think about sex while in an MRI machine. Study after study has focused on the body's reaction to sex - the buildup, the act itself, and the aftermath. It has been found over time that hormones and neuronal connections are so entwined in sex that human chemistry is affected by the thought, act, and its resulting bodily reactions.

7.1 Oh, the Nerve!

Consider the tip of the penis and the button that is the clitoris; these areas of the body have hundreds of thousands of nerve endings that are responsible for the amazing orgasm. Without the spine and these nerves, there would be no orgasm, and most likely a lot less people on the planet. Sex would not be as enjoyable without these nerves that induce such great pleasure. The clitoris has over 8,000 nerve endings in its small surface area! Nerves carry impulses from the genitals to the brain, resulting in climax. It's important to understand how complex the body is, in order to understand just exactly how marvelous a phenomenon an orgasm truly is.

Nerves in the Genitals

- ✓ **Pudendal nerve: (S2 - S4)** Clitoris in women; scrotum and penis in men
- ✓ **Pelvic splanchnic nerves: (S2 - S4)** Rectum in men and women; vagina and cervix in women
- ✓ **Vagus Nerve: (Cranial nerve)** Only in women's cervix, uterus, vagina
- ✓ **Hypogastric nerve: (T10 - L2)** Uterus and cervix in women; prostate in men

Keeping all these nerve pathways open, clear and stress-free as a person ages are an important aspect of sexual health and maximum performance (and sensation) for both men and women. This is most significant when a couple wants to engage in higher level orgasms or decides to create new life and is looking to conceive a healthy child. If there is neural obstruction, stagnation or impairment of motion in the spine, particularly the lumbar and sacral regions (due to direct acute or chronic trauma, prescription drug use or emotional abuse), disease processes such as impotence, erectile dysfunction, nerve paralysis, painful menstrual cycles or loss of feeling (just to name a few) can materialize. To ensure proper function and health for top performance, see your chiropractor for a spinal examination and life empowering spinal adjustments regularly.

7.2 The Brain on Sex

Thanks to advancements in technology, scientists can actually see the areas of the brain associated with sex, relationships and love. When a person has sex, dopamine floods the reward centers of the brain because, well, sex feels good – and is good for you. This leads to an increased desire for *more* sex because your brain wants to feel that flood of feel-good dopamine again, which is why people "get horny." Dopamine receptors start to feel lonely without their favorite hormone, and the brain tells the body "We need more!" Also released during sex is oxytocin (affectionately named "the cuddle hormone"), a very potent hormone that is related to bonding and pain relief. This is why sex makes you feel "lighter than air" and really attached to your partner. Oxytocin is also incredibly important for people who have diseases or chronic pain; don't avoid having sex because it can actually help you feel better!

Chemicals in Sex

Cortisol is also a player in the brain sex game. It is associated with stress, and people with high cortisol levels tend to have anxiety or stress response issues. High levels of cortisol when engaging in sex have also been linked to less satisfaction and poor sexual performance (it's hard to get an erection or have an orgasm when you're stressed about something else). Sex can decrease cortisol, thankfully, by flooding the body with the feel-good hormones like oxytocin, dopamine, and serotonin. Serotonin, made popular by anti-depressant drugs, is why people feel so good after sex. The dopamine receptors are full, and the serotonin receptors are enjoying a nice influx of their own hormones as well. Vasopressin, also known as antidiuretic hormone (ADH), synergizes with the male hormone testosterone and triggers that age-old "Me man, she woman," beating-the-chest-with-your-fist behavior. Scientists believe this works similarly to oxytocin in women; it makes men much more likely to commit and feel protective of their mate. In these first stages of sex and love, the ventral tegmental area of the brain is activated, triggering the reward center and making you crave "more."

Chemicals in Love

All of the same hormones that affect sex also affect our ability to love or create long-term relationships. The orbitofrontal cortex of our brain is responsible for the pleasure centers, and is where most of the action starts when you meet someone. Oxytocin is the number one culprit here, as it is the "bonding" hormone. When you have sex with one person repeatedly, your oxytocin receptors essentially train your brain to need that one person for more influx of this amazing hormone. You tend to overlook things, like how they snore when they sleep or chew with their mouth open. You need and love that person. Then, as time moves on, your body has reached a more stable interaction with your hormones; you're not over-the-moon in love but you've created something much more comfortable. Oxytocin receptors start to wane a little, and this is when the honeymoon period ends. You're still committed to each other, but you also know that person isn't perfect either. This is also when dopamine and serotonin are not in full-flow either, as sex tends to be decreased as your body has reached its "feel-good" max. As dopamine and serotonin decrease, the body enters a plateau state, which is where you get more comfortable with seeing each other in sweats and no makeup, on the couch, eating ramen or passed out drooling on the bed. This is centered in the controlled areas of the brain like the ventral pallidum and raphe nucleus, where long-term goals and sustained activity and health are the motivating factor.

Chemicals in Breakups/Being Single

Of course breakups are no fun; no one enters a relationship saying, "I can't wait to break up with him/her." As we form a relationship with a person, whether sexual or personal or both, our bodies get used to that wash of hormones we feel when we are first connected (or in love) with a person. Dopamine, serotonin, and oxytocin are in full swing if you're having sex, and your cortisol is at the lowest levels it has been in a long time.

But then, you get comfortable and you realize maybe you two aren't the best match for one another. The hormone filter is lifted, and you don't feel so romantic towards one another anymore. Maybe the way he breathes makes you want to run screaming, or maybe the way she always bites her nails makes you want to cry. Finally, you decide you can't take anymore, and the two of you part ways. Even if your rational brain knows this is for the best, it still hurts. In fresh breakups, the nucleus accumbens has found to be most active - this area is concerned with love and pain. This is, in part, because your brain chemicals must now readjust to your new reality. The oxytocin, dopamine, and serotonin receptors are looking for their "next hit of the good stuff," and left out in the cold. When these receptors aren't filled, you're left feeling lonely, unsatisfied, and even depressed. Eventually, your receptors recover from the shock, and you move on. This also translates into why so many single people seem so desperate to find a mate. Their brain is signaling for them to fill up those hormone receptors; the reward centers of the brain are looking for more dopamine, the oxytocin receptors really want to cuddle, and the serotonin receptors just really want to feel happy. When these receptors aren't filled, it leads to an increase in cortisol, the stress hormone, which exacerbates the effects of your chemical shortage. You feel stressed because you're lonely, stressed because you want a mate, and stressed because you're depressed, and then you get more stressed just thinking about all of it. In general, hormones are very, very potent.

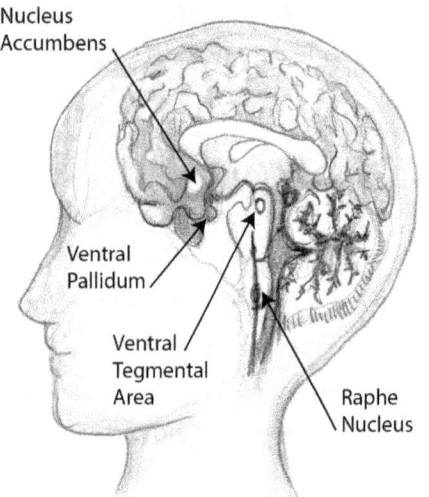

7.3 What Women (and Men) Want

There are many sayings like, "Men always marry their mothers," and "Women have bad relationships because they have daddy issues." Unfortunately, science has in fact proven that men and women are attracted to people who continue their caregiving patterns they experienced in childhood unless they break the loop in adulthood prior to choosing their partner, using powerful therapies like the *Kousouli® Method*, to change their belief structure and eradicate stagnant energy. A man with an overbearing mother is often drawn to an overbearing wife or long-term partner, and a woman is often drawn to men who are similar to her father. Depending on what a person wants out of a relationship or their life (marriage, children, etc.).

Studies have also indicated that, due to evolutionary processes, the "biological clock" begins ticking very quickly with very little warning. Women look for good genes, long-term stability, and a providing partner who would be a good parent. Because of their ancestral traits, women often do not pick a partner right away; they search through the possible candidates to pick the best one. Attraction really has nothing to do with higher thought processes. It is all about the initial emotional and subconscious reaction two people have towards one another's energy. This is why dating and relationships can take so long for some people and why it seems to be instant for others. What each of us is looking for or requires in a mate is different from what the next person requires.

For men looking for a mate, evolution once again rears its head. Men often mistake a pretty face for a great partner, and often find that the pretty face isn't enough to keep them with a person they don't actually like. Evolution has yet to adapt to the higher consciousness order, where beauty isn't synonymous with health or success. Men in today's world instead find that intelligence, health (mental and physical), and ability to invest in the relationship are more appealing than just striking physical looks. Yes, beauty is always the first thing someone notices, but evolution has not done men many favors. Look behind the face, and see what your mate has to offer you over the long term.

Humans are still very much working from primitive attraction factors instilled deep into our old DNA. Men respond to praise in a more primal way than women. When you tell a man that they are providing for you, or doing a great job during sex, they get a boost of testosterone that makes the desire to receive more praise even stronger. Essentially, men *need* to hear that they're doing a good job, and when you give them a little praise they will become even more attached and committed. That's a fact ladies! Compliments and appreciation go both ways.

It is also worth noting that thanks to our ancestral past, we are attracted to a specific body type. Heterosexual women are attracted to men with a taller height, lean build, muscle definition, and experience more attraction to men with visible physical skill (sports, running, etc.) as this shows health. This was also an indication that the man a woman chose would be able to take care of her in "the caveman days." Men are attracted to women with wider hips, larger breasts and more symmetrical features, as these were all once indicators of a woman's ability to procreate, as well as survive in harsh conditions. Pale, skinny, frail women were not ideal, as they would probably die while traveling or giving birth (ironically, this is the ideal in some Western cultures today). Of course, today these are not necessarily attractive to everyone, and the people we fall in love with do not always embody these traits. The reality is though that every human is engrained to have "a type." Next time you find yourself being drawn to a certain person or imagining a specific sexual fantasy, just admit that it's in your DNA.

Love and Marriage

Study upon study have found that the need to mate, to find love is an evolutionary mechanism designed to carry on the human race. It was also a way to extend our lives in our ancestral pasts; traveling in groups and having a protector was the best-case scenario for the survival of the race. Essentially, even now when we don't need to procreate, we need to find a mate. Today, we see this in women who feel the drive to find a man who can provide for her, even though women are fully capable of providing for themselves. It is a physical drive, usually driven by the reward centers of the brain that dopamine is most common in. Thanks to greatly improved technologies, MRI scans can show the areas of the brain that light up when someone is in love. When a person is deeply in love and in a committed, long-term relationship, the effects are nothing short of fireworks. Nearly every region of the brain lights up when a person talks about or views a picture of their beloved. Couples who were merely "dating" or hadn't fallen in love experienced a lot of activity in the pleasure centers of the brain, associated with sex, but nothing like the full-scale electricity seen in long-term lovers. In essence, these findings indicate that love truly is more powerful than sex on a biological level.

7.4 Debunking the Feminine Mystique

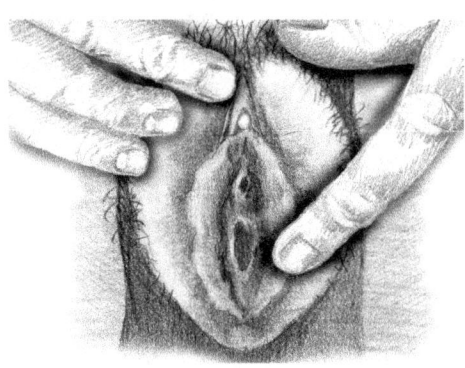

It is often a running joke with many women in our lives that men couldn't find the clitoris "if they had a map." Not only is this not true, but it is emasculating and condescending. While men may not, due to social influences, be entirely aware of the complexities of the female sex, many are willing to learn. This is another of those sexual myths to be busted, a barrier in sexual exploration that you can break down by merely *talking* to one another. When a woman trusts a man enough to share such a private area of her body and spirit, the man steps in to safeguard what she has entrusted to him. Trust one another, and share in the beauty of the act. Do not let external forces or pop culture enter this sacred realm.

There are many other ways that societal norms cloud our ability to interact with one another or even ourselves. For many women, their low self-confidence is a barrier to positive sexual interaction. They are often told by society and by peers that they need to look or act a certain way in order to be viewed as worthy, beautiful, or sexy. Women en masse have adopted this culture of insecurity, as if it is a healthy way to view themselves. Men, however, are wired much differently and the truth is that men believe that confidence is the sexiest thing a woman can wear. So put away the makeup, the lingerie, the diet pills and the self-loathing, ladies. Work on finding yourself beautiful just as you are, embrace what you have to offer rather than dwelling on what you seemingly lack. Men do respond to confidence and personality, and will overlook someone who relies heavily on outside support in order to function. This also translates into sex; women who know their bodies, know what pleases them, and who are not afraid to ask for it are incredibly desirable. Women who are inexperienced and shy may be endearing for a short time, but in order to really achieve sexual pleasure with a partner, they need to be open to exploring and learning their bodies well enough to communicate their needs to their lovers.

It is important to debunk the idea that women are not sexual creatures like men are. "Women don't like sex," or "Women only have sex because they have to," are entirely untrue and put up a wall between men and women. In reality, women have sexual impulses; they don't always want to cuddle, and sometimes they want to be on top. While their moods may differ, women want sex nearly as much as men do, if not more in some cases (i.e. when their "clock is ticking"). Women get horny, have sexy dreams, and sometimes just want sex for the sake of having sex. Their fantasies can include things as "outrageous" as submission or rape, role playing, quickies in public, or even taking the reins and being entirely in control of their partner for once. Under the façade of social and political correctness, we sometimes forget that deep down humans are still considered an animal species with raw, untamed desires and urges.

One of the biggest areas of concern for women is their vagina. Most women have never looked at this intimate area of their body, let alone explored it in depth. They are often concerned that it doesn't look "pretty enough," especially with pornography showing us a wide range of styling options for pubic hair. Women are also concerned with their fluids and the general state of affairs "down there." However, female secretions are not something women should be ashamed of. In fact, many women have learned to embrace this very exotic part of their bodies, as it is from a woman's womb that life springs. Today, it is commonly accepted that women also ejaculate, depending on their level of excitement and power of the orgasm. There is some debate on what this fluid is, ranging from female lubrication to urine, but many cultures have cherished this expulsion during sex as a "drink of life." Historically speaking, in many cultures female secretions (such as discharge and lubrication) as well as menstrual blood were once sacred liquids that were consumed in order to gain powers of life. Even Aristotle said that human life stems from the womb and menstrual blood. Islam's creation story even says that man was made "out of flowing blood." Today, the idea that these fluids hold power is immediately shirked in developed nations, and is often seen as unacceptable. However, some studies have found stem cells located in menstrual blood, which have amazing healing properties. Some empowered women have embraced this, and drink their secretions as well as their own menstrual blood, which provides these women with regenerative nourishment. All of this is to say: there is no shame to be found in the female body, only power and life.

Women are intricately made and uniquely built. Their bodies are designed for life and for pleasure, but many times it is hard to pleasure a woman when they themselves are unfamiliar with their bodies. A woman's body may seem complex and rather mysterious, especially if the woman is unfamiliar with the parts of her own sex during puberty. To allow a woman to experience the height of pleasure, both she and her partner(s) must understand her anatomy. Looking at the front of a naked woman's pelvis, there are three main parts that aid in pleasure: the labia, the vagina, and the clitoris. The labia, which is composed of inner and outer lips, protects the vagina and varies greatly in appearance from woman to woman. The labia is a necessary part of female anatomy, despite the fact that many women believe it is unappealing or unattractive. There are nerve centers in the inner and outer labia, making it a unique way to stimulate a woman before sex. The vagina, which is actually only the internal area, not the whole sex organ, is the canal that a penis (hand or vibrator) penetrates. A woman's vaginal canal lengthens as she becomes aroused, and will stretch up to an additional four to five inches in most women to accommodate the male penis (whose average erect length ranges from four to six inches).

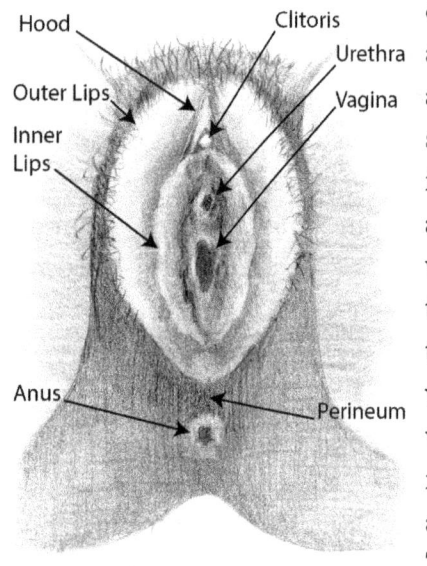

The front (top) side of the vagina, closest to the abdomen, is full of nerve endings. This is where you find the infamous G-spot, and where the most orgasmic stimulation will occur. On the northern end (top) of the vagina, you will find the clitoris. Of course, this famed nerve bundle will definitely send a woman into orgasm if stimulated properly. The tiny button-like area will literally "stand up," or increase in size, as a woman gets aroused. It is protected by the clitoral hood, but is easy to find once it becomes erect.

Hopefully the anatomy lesson helps you explore your own body or your partner's body. To aid you in this process of sexual discovery, keep in mind these next techniques are catered to the specific anatomy of a woman.

7.5 Techniques for Female Pleasure

You may or may not know that women can reach climax multiple times during a single sexual encounter. This refers back to Chinese ideas of yin, which is inexhaustible. Men, whose yang is easily drained, can only orgasm (with ejaculation) once before needing to rest and regain energy. If you are a man with a female partner(s), it would be in your (and her) best interest if you play this to her advantage. Foreplay before sex is incredibly important, and you can make a woman orgasm multiple times before actually having intercourse. Many sources and experts in the field of sex believe that stimulating a woman to orgasm at least three times during your lovemaking will not only make you a phenomenal lover, but it will also bring you closer together. With the instruction in this book you will be able to reach this goal much easier.

Stages of Orgasm

It is very important to understand not only the anatomy of a woman, but the process of sex and orgasm within their bodies. It is also important to note that orgasm literally involves every major region of the brain (in men and women). Areas like the amygdala, hippocampus, basal ganglia, cerebellum, the anterior cingulate, parietal and frontal cortices, insular, nucleus accumbens, the pituitary gland and the lower brainstem are all activated. In women, orgasm is marked by decreased activity in the amygdala and hippocampus. These are the fear and anxiety centers of the brain, which is why women who are too anxious or self-conscious have a harder time reaching orgasm. A relaxed mind and nervous system are key to achieving proper sensation from stimulation. Ask your chiropractor to help align and heal your lumbar spine with focused spinal treatment, particularly the L2 to L5 and sacral spinal areas.

Let it be clear: a woman can reach orgasm just as easily as a man if she is stimulated properly, but it usually takes longer if you are new partners, or the woman is inexperienced in her own bodily process. There are generally four steps to an orgasm for a woman, and these four steps can be repeated until a woman essentially is too exhausted to carry on (yin at its finest).

- ✓ Excitement is the first stage, where a woman's vagina becomes lubricated, her skin is sensitized thanks to increased blood flow, and her breasts and nipples ache.

- ✓ Plateau is a difficult stage to surpass, especially for new lovers. The female body has become "accustomed" to the new sensations, and if a new sensation is not thrown into the mix, it is near impossible for a woman to reach orgasm.
- ✓ Orgasm, the Holy Grail for women, is often a buildup of tension for a woman. The explosion happens rather unexpectedly, as the tension can build up for any amount of time depending on the type of stimulation being received. Muscles tense for a few seconds, and then she'll relax. This is when her clitoris and vagina are most sensitive, so slow down or retreat once she is appeased.
- ✓ Resolution is the stage where her body is relaxed and the "feel-good" chemicals in the brain are released. For women, this stage often is quickly followed by another Excitement phase, and the cycle starts over again. The orgasm is often described by women as a "roller coaster ride" full of ups and downs, twists, and turns.

Clitoral Stimulation

The clitoris is a bundle of nerves located at the entrance of the vagina. It has as many nerve endings in its small button-like area as a man does in the entire head of his penis. This makes a woman's clitoris very sensitive, and the most likely way she will reach orgasm. Women, if you are unfamiliar with your own body and wish to help your partner in your sexual adventures, it may be best for you to "test the waters" on your own. Pleasuring yourself will ultimately help you understand the pathways your body takes to climax, and you can guide your lover much easier when you're aware of this. Men (and female partners): when pleasuring your female lover, pay attention to her body language and vocalizations. This will tell you if she's overly sensitive, if you're at the right pace and pressure, or if she's close to climax. The clitoris is very easily over-stimulated, so start gently and then work your way up to the crescendo.

Note on Nipples

Many studies indicate that nipples, when manipulated properly, can stimulate a woman to orgasm almost as effectively as clitoral stimulation. While some women may not like their nipples played with (especially after having children), this is a very sensitive area that you should not forget about! And ladies, many men also have sensitive nipples which can bring them quickly to erection and stimulate their desire for sex. Remember that stimulating the penis along with both nipples at the same time drives most men wild.

Oral Sex for Her

One of the best ways to pleasure your female paramour and connect with her anatomy intimately is to "go down" on her. Cunnilingus, the fancy term for female oral sex, is a fantastic way to ensure your partner reaches orgasm. Of course, you can't just go down on her and hope you're doing it right - there is an art to it. Listen to your partner and ask her questions. If she is comfortable with you, that will help her more than any special tongue technique. Accepting that oral sex makes a woman feel especially vulnerable will help you provide the safety and comfort she must feel before she can reach climax.

After you've established a strong mental and emotional connection with your woman, follow the following techniques to make sure she sees stars and keeps coming back for more.

Main Course

Do yourself and your partner a favor, and enjoy the appetizers before you get to the main course. This, of course, means that you shouldn't just dive right for your partner's sexual demand for intercourse. Entice her, tease her, and kiss your way down to that most sensitive area. The more foreplay and excitement, the easier your job will be once you arrive at your destination. Note her erogenous zones, and pay attention to them with light touch or kiss throughout your lovemaking session. Earlobes, neck, sides of her back, collar bone area, inner upper arm, sides of her upper chest, hip crests, nipples, inner thighs, vagina, clitoris, perineum, ankles, feet, and toes all count as erogenous zones. Find the areas that drive your lady wild, and pay special attention to them.

Pay Your Dues at the Gate

Before using your tongue or fingers to enter your lover, kiss and lick around her labia (lips), and gently explore. Do not spread her lips open just yet, and do not penetrate her with your tongue. This will give her great pleasure and tease her at the same time. Just make sure you're moving at the pace she's indicating. If she is moving slowly against your mouth, move slowly. If she's about to claw at your back, move a little faster. Once you're ready, ask her to spread her lips open for you, giving her an extra jolt of energy to her clitoris. As you explore her labia with your tongue, keep moving your hands lightly teasing her skin with a soft touch around the inside of her thighs or side of her buttocks.

Give Her a Tongue, Hand, and Finger Fiesta

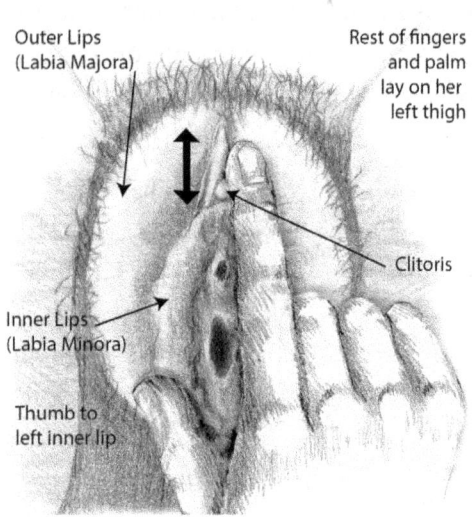

Let's look at powerful hand and finger positions that are highly effective in stimulating the clitoris. First, to gain access to the clitoris, also known as her "pearl of pleasure," you must gently pull back the curtains that conceal it. The outer, larger labia majora and inner less thick layer, the labia minora, are the folds of skin that protect and conceal the inner workings of the female reproduction system. As we go through this section of finger movements, keep in mind that you may also use your tongue (also referred to "cunnilingus", or "going down" on her) to stimulate the same areas pictured in the images. Use your fingers, mouth, lips, and or tongue to gently caress and move on the clitoris as shown. Start by gently activating her arousal with a single finger by teasing the clitoris with a slow simple up and down motion while ranging your pressure from soft to firm. As you do any movements, keep a close eye on her reaction so that you may adjust your movements and tempo as needed. If you see her moving in sync with your motions or starting to close her eyes, relax her jaw and mouth while letting out a slight moan, you're on the right track and ready to move onto the two finger V maneuver.

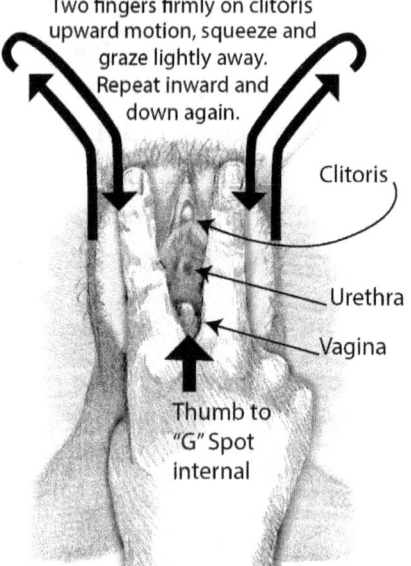

Introduce your middle finger by bringing it into a V shape as pictured, and continue the movement with a gentle up and then outward light graze before coming back inward and down on the clitoris. As you perform this in time you will start to see or feel a clear liquid at the entrance of the vagina which will signal her arousal and readiness for sexual intercourse. You may use your thumb to tease the entrance to her vagina and even enter her lightly. However, do not go into internal vaginal stimulation or intercourse too quickly. Extend the foreplay as much as possible, for it will only intensify her desire to be taken into full penetration. When she is aroused you may further your technique.

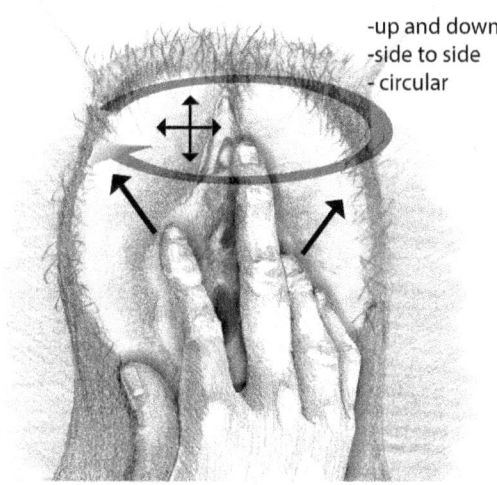

-up and down
-side to side
-circular

From the two finger V maneuver move into the three finger triple tease, where you now introduce your ring finger into the action. This takes some practice as you separate your index and ring fingers onto the labia minora while letting the middle finger take on the work of the previous index and middle fingers. As the middle finger creates a firm circular clockwise motion and then varies with up and down and the occasional left to right motions, the index and ring fingers massage the inner lips and further prepare the vagina for penetration. Be sure to always vary your motions and technique because her brain will start to become used to the sensations and the feeling's power will diminish. To combat overstimulation, you must change up the type of stimulation and its delivery constantly. Just like a roller coaster that whips you around a sudden corner unexpectedly, the same should apply to the sensations you are giving her. Too much of the same thing, no matter how exciting at first, can get boring, so keep it moving.

By now your lover will be ready for you to move her up the excitement ladder, and may have even had a light orgasm or two. Some women will need both clitoral and vaginal stimulation, which we will now discuss. Move your hand so that it is now upside down and position your body so that you can allow your hand's natural finger flexing position to "hook" or cradle the pelvis from the front of her groin. This will align your hand and fingers for the next maneuver, the four finger fantasy.

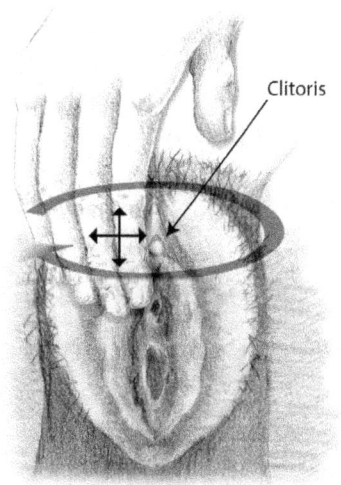

Clitoris

Take your index finger and place it on her inner left lip (labia minora). Insert your middle and ring fingers into her vaginal opening slowly, inward and up. You do not need to go too deep, 1-3 inches will suffice (review G-Spot illustration), while putting slight upward pressure during the insertion, and place your thumb onto the clitoris. You are now ready to double stimulate your lover and send

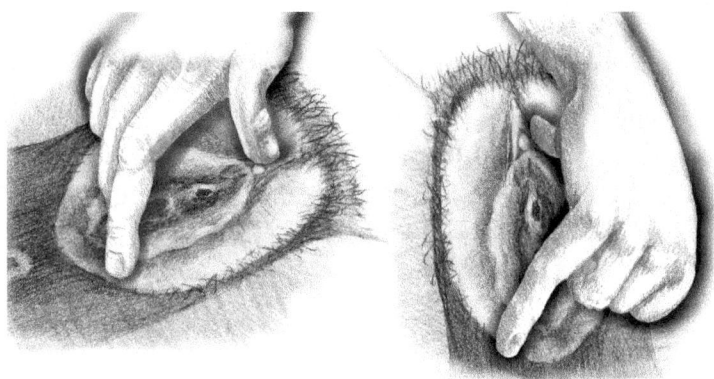

her through the roof. Alternate extending and contracting your ring and middle finger with your thumb. As the two fingers inside her vagina are used for stimulation, the clitoris will relax. Then do the opposite, where the clitoris will be stimulated by your thumb and the inner G-spot will relax. You can alternate and also stimulate both points together. Remember though, to keep your other hand and mouth very busy, stimulating other erogenous points of her body; i.e. nipples, inner thigh, neck, perineum, etc.

Oral Penetration

Once you have her "primed and ready," start flicking her clitoris gently with the tip of your tongue or sucking on it *very gently* unless she indicates a more excited approach. Being too rough with the clitoris right out of the gates may make her desensitized, and make your job much harder. After you've licked around the opening, rest the tip of your tongue at her opening and push, only a little at first. This is another way to tease her, and she will tighten more around your tongue. Then slowly (or quickly, depending on how much she's reacting) move your tongue deeper.

Hold Her Steady

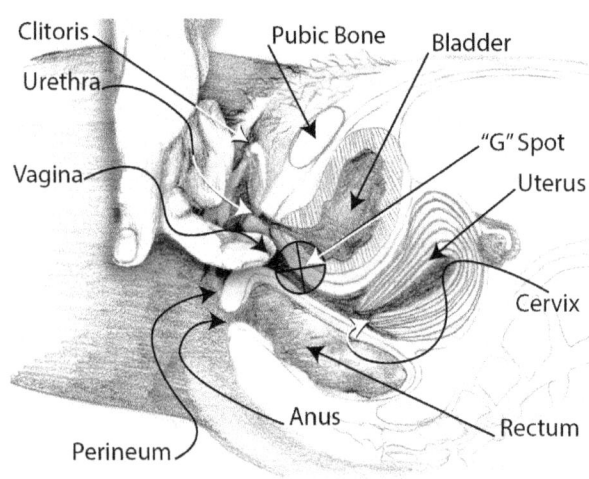

Your woman will let you know when she is getting closer to larger multiple orgasms. Her moans or breathing will have reached new levels, and she will most likely not be able to move. If you want to really send her over the edge, use one or both of your hands to trace her thighs, stomach, and labia area gently. Where before you were quickly pulsing your tongue in and out, move more slowly, with a pointed tongue that focuses more on the clitoris. When you're ready, move your hands to hold her labia wide, and begin quickening your strokes with a wider tongue all the way up her vagina (from the opening to the clitoris).

Double Team

If she needs more stimulation, insert one or more fingers to stimulate her G-spot and let your tongue rest on her clitoris. Move your tongue with the same rhythm of your fingers. When she begins to go rigid or vocalizes that she's about to come, really focus on her clitoris while providing as much stimulation as possible on the various parts of her body. Quicken your movements in and out, almost like you would use your penis during intercourse. Keep your hands and tongue in sync, and enjoy the fireworks. This double sensation will get her primed and ready for more orgasms, and she will most likely not be able to hold still. This is a sign that she's ready for the main course. And that's just the beginning; do everything correctly and she will hail you as her king, ruining her for all other men. But wait, there's more…

Penetration

Penetration, while rarely the source of a full-blown orgasm by itself, is a key tactic in pleasuring (and keeping) a woman. Without penetration, a woman's muscles will not clench in the same way, making it harder to reach climax.

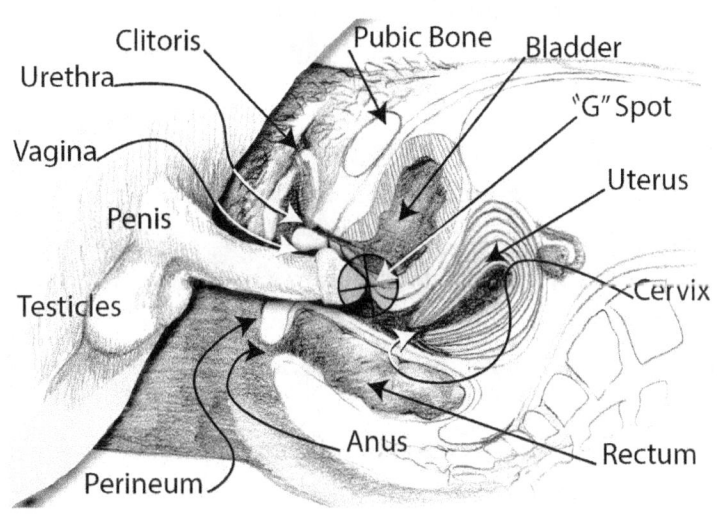

Penetration is also important for hitting the G-spot. It can be found when you insert a finger or two into the vagina, and feeling along the "top" wall - the area closest to the clitoris. Continue to move up until you find a rougher or raised area - that's the G spot. Some people say it's about two inches into the vagina, but it differs. For some women, it almost mimics a feeling of a full bladder if it's not manipulated properly, so be gentle and have her tell you what feels best.

Besides the G-spot, penetration activates the muscles and also increases the sensations. The pubococcygeus muscles, also known as the Kegel muscles, can be used during sex to grasp onto a man's penis as he exits the vaginal canal or to increase the sensation a woman feels. To maximize sensation, move from slow to fast and back to slow. The same speed will often not cause a woman to reach orgasm until you are stimulating her clitoris at varying speeds as well. For a blended orgasm, use both penetration and clitoral stimulation to send her flying. Also, change up how deep you enter her; some women have deeper canals, some women have shorter ones. Be gentle with her until you know her anatomy and her preferences.

Keeping Her Mind on Sex

Men's sexual pleasure stems nearly completely from visual and physical stimulation. Studies have shown that women become stimulated, and reach climax, more from their thoughts which are intimately connected with their emotions. The power of the brain is incredible, and also formidable, when it comes to this aspect of sexuality. In order to open a woman up to orgasm, you must work with her to get her thoughts laser focused on a sexual track towards climax. It's amazing what a woman's partner can do to eliminate stressors or distract her from unwanted thoughts that may pop up, like "Did I turn off the oven? Are the kids asleep? What if I don't get that promotion? Do I look fat in this position? Did I shave well? I just had tacos, I hope I don't fart." These are all things that can go through your female partner's head. Do your best to help her shut them down by keeping her too busy on stimulation so her mind doesn't wander.

- ✓ Keep her in the moment. Tell her what you're going to do to her body, or ask how good she feels. Talk a little nasty if she is comfortable with that, or just make sure she knows how into her and your lovemaking you really are.
- ✓ Spend a lot of time on foreplay. Many men treat foreplay as a necessary evil to get a woman's body ready for penetration. It's more than that. Treat this time as a way to get her to unwind, open up to you (literally and mentally), and focus on her body's sensations to make sex more fun.
- ✓ Remove all other distractions. Do not have sex after a fight over money, or when you're watching TV. Take away the cell phones, put the kiddies to bed, and focus on one another without the possibility that something (or someone) will interrupt you.

If you'd like to really amp up your game, and make sure she can only think about you and the great sex you're going to have, extend the foreplay over a day, a week, or however long it will be until you see each other again. By the time you walk through the door, or she sees you, she'll be unable to keep her hands (and body) off you.

- ✓ Compliment her looks and outfit, and let her see you admiring how good she looks. Vocalize your appreciation, without touching her or trying to make a move.
- ✓ Give her more "PG" physical contact. Hug her, place your hand on the small of her back, hold hands, kiss her softly, but do not grab the goods or try to tease her (yet).
- ✓ Tease her throughout the day. Shoot her a text or an email, reminding her how hot the sex was last night, or how you can't wait to get her out of her dress tonight. She'll be excited by your pleasure, and want to give you more. The more you activate a woman's hard-wired triggers of the emotional mind, her "likes" and her thoughts of being your one and only, the faster she will give herself over to you physically. Women want to be the queen or princess that is "taken" by a strong viable king. Yes, they love the fantasy, so give it to them.

Women are immensely beautiful and sensual creatures, but society has made something of a mockery of female sexuality. Women who don't look like models, or have perfectly flat tummies, may experience low self-esteem in a society full of "perceptual ideals". This is reflected in their sexual interactions, where they want to keep their clothes on, keep lights dim or only have sex in a dark room under the covers. For their partners, this is frustrating, unattractive and disappointing. Male partners find their female partners incredibly sexy in whatever form their bodies are, a fact that many women overlook. A warm shower together prior to sex can heighten arousal, relax tensions as you explore each other's body, and get your sex organs nice and tidy for your partner. When a woman feels less than the sex goddess she is, do your duty and immediately focus on applying the Three S's (Safe, Secure and Sexy) to get her in the mood:

- ✓ **Safe**. Make a woman feel safe by respecting her body, and by making her feel comfortable naked. Especially when you are new partners, building trust is incredibly important.
- ✓ **Secure**. Sometimes, all a woman needs to come out of her self-conscious shell is a little encouragement. Let her know how beautiful she is, how great her breasts or butt are, and vocalize how amazing she is during sex. Before you know it, the sex goddess will make an appearance.
- ✓ **Sexy**. By allowing a woman to embrace her sexuality, and by making it known that you find her irresistible, you are ensuring that she will be more carefree and expressive during sex. A woman who is open and confident in her own body can take herself and her partner to new heights of pleasure.

For many men, sex is a "one orgasm event," whereas most women can easily have multiple orgasms within a given encounter. While a man may feel slightly jealous that their female partner can experience more orgasms than he can, this provides a great opportunity for a man to highlight his lovemaking abilities. (Of note: the multiple male orgasm is very much a possibility. It can be achieved by mind training, willpower, and patience. This is an entirely other discussion which is covered in the seminar material.)

Overriding Triggers

The amygdala, a very important center in the brain, is responsible for a lot of the responses related to experience that humans exhibit. For example, if a person was frequently hit with a ruler as a child, he or she may subconsciously avoid rulers as an adult. If a man in a dark alley accosted a woman, she may feel fear whenever she walks by a dark alley. The important thing to note here is that this is a learned mechanism, one that you will have to override. This also applies to fighting as a couple, or overcoming insecurities with a new partner. Not everything is the same as it once was, and you have to be patient and willing to work through the triggers. Here are some tips:

- ✓ Make an agreement with each other that if you get uncomfortable you will immediately make it known to your partner in a relaxed and mature manner.
- ✓ Communicate with each other how you feel; good or bad.
- ✓ Share openly with your partner(s) any traumatic or abuse history that could trigger you to feel inappropriate and could hinder a positive experience together.
- ✓ Share honestly from the beginning your previous sexual partner status, STI/STD reports, and get tested together prior to regularly having sex if you are a new couple.
- ✓ Discuss and be clear on the intention of the relationship and your goals together. (i.e. sex only partner, or marriage minded, etc.)
- ✓ Never, ever hold onto negative thoughts or emotions. Transmute them into positive energy by working out or listening to music.
- ✓ Seek solo or couples therapy from a professional when needed.
- ✓ Write down the positive traits of your mate and why you love spending time together. Read this list any time you feel negativity about them creep into your thoughts.

7.6 The Power of Sacred Male Energy

Women's magazines and online publications are filled with tips on giving your man the hottest sex, how to spice things up, how to appear irresistible to men, and other such frippery just to sell magazines to the desperate. Sadly, these publications indicate that women are truly not engaging with their male partners, asking what they want, or asking how best to please them. It's amazing what can unfold when you just begin to *honestly and openly talk* to one another. It is also important for women to respect their male partners as an equal in the sexual act, rather than attempting to dominate or subdue them into whichever box they see fit. Women need to understand the Divine Masculine energy of the male, flow together with it and work on interlinking their own Divine Feminine energy during sex. This is something that has never been taught correctly to them from women's tabloid magazines.

As you read in the chapter on the history of sex, sperm has been considered a source of life and energy since the earliest beginnings of humanity. Sperm is designed to give life, make life and generate health. Many Asian cultures attribute male energy to the yang force, which is easily exhausted and needs to be retained in order to promote health and balance in a man's life. The many sages of Asian heritage claimed that male ejaculate (The Seed of Life) was one hundred times more powerful than blood. When a man has sex and reaches orgasm, he is giving away his energy, his chi, and can risk his own health if he does not regain it.

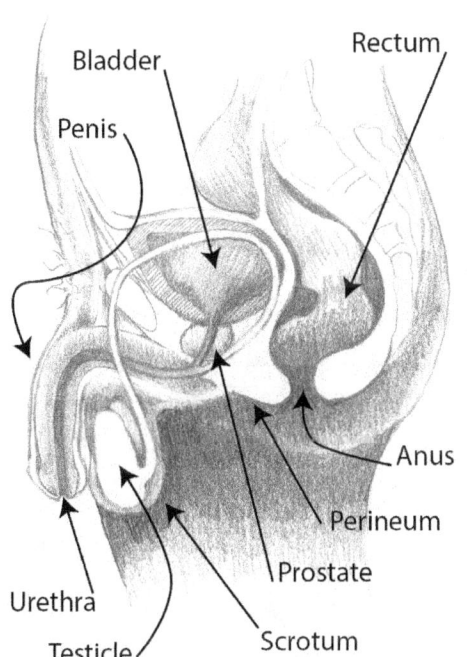

Many believe that the weakening state of men in today's world is associated with their inability to understand, express, or control themselves sexually. Men are essentially projecting their life force (physically and emotionally) into too many "empty" areas; this is why so many men have decreasing positions in their relationships, decreasing health, and general weakness.

When a man correctly holds onto or conserves his seed, he reserves his power and improves his health and happiness. This idea has been a large part of many cultures, specifically the Japanese who still adhere to this. Men often do not ejaculate during sex, focusing on pleasuring their wives without giving away their low stores of yang energy. As mentioned before in the section on Greek and Roman cultures, pedastry often centered on the "passing down" of knowledge and energy from teacher to student in the form of semen. A young boy would fellate his older teacher, and consume the semen in order to become a man. Even some undeveloped cultures in the world practice this today, including tribes in New Guinea.

The Seed was once considered a holy elixir that could pass down life and knowledge, and was often seen as a basic treatment for many ills. There are many scientifically based reasons to retain sperm. Within one teaspoon of male ejaculate, there are about 200 proteins, vitamins, and minerals. Spermine, one of the components in semen, has antioxidants and has been used in health drinks, skin cream, and more. In addition, women with committed sexual partners experience lower rates of depression, as semen has been found to contain both estrogen and prostaglandin, which are natural mood boosters.

Despite all this, the thought of consuming this very natural gift is, today, totally unacceptable in mainstream thinking. Now, a man's seed is seen as little more than a biological response to a physical action, and because of this there are increased rates of prostate disorders and cancer, erectile dysfunction, and other entire body system issues. Men who give their seed freely and without intent expend their life force on people or things that do not return that energy, nor care for the man on a higher vibration. Ejaculation without a mutually healthy and loving intention or love drains the man of his chi, his yang, creating an energy void.

7.7 Techniques for Male Pleasure

Men will often tell their lovers that they're pretty simple when it comes to sex: as long as it feels good, they're all for it. While this makes men slightly more easy to pleasure than a woman, there are nuances that can create a much more exciting experience for them and for you, their lover. First, it is incredibly important to understand a male's basic anatomy. The shaft, is the length of the penis, and where a man's partner will be focusing most of the action. The erect shaft's length greatly varies in size, "averaging" four to six inches in most men. The foreskin may be "trimmed" via circumcision, or may be left entirely intact. (Illustrations herein show the circumcised or erect penis without the foreskin shown or labeled.)

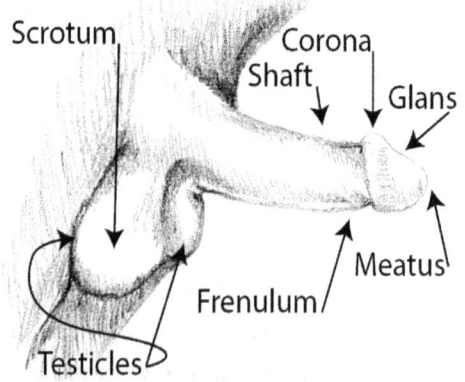

The scrotum, or ball sack, holds the testicles, which are the two glands (balls) that produce sperm. At the top, you have the head of the penis, which is very sensitive and full of nerve endings which are stimulated during oral sex and intercourse. Internally, there are the pubococcygeus

(PC) muscles and the prostate; the PC muscles contract and spasm during orgasm, and also allow a man's penis to move. These are just like the Kegel muscles a woman can use to tighten her vaginal walls during sex. The prostate gland contributes about 25 to 35 percent of the seminal fluid, and stimulating it can be a great way to bring a man to orgasm.

Precum, (a clear liquid that accumulates at the tip of the penis) also known as pre-ejaculate or pre-jizz, is produced by the bulbourethral gland, also called Cowper's gland and the glands of Littre which are mucus-secreting urethral glands. Precum actually contains fructose (sugar), which makes it taste sweet to your lover. While the odds of getting pregnant from precum are low, you should still wear a condom or use other birth control methods to prevent any small risk.

On the subject of semen, it should be noted here that ejaculation is something most men are proud of. Whether this is part of their youthful porn viewing experiences, or an evolutionary tactic to "spread their seed" literally, ejaculate is an important part of sex. The pre-ejaculate fluid that drops from the tip of the penis is a sign that man's body is geared to orgasm. The actual ejaculation is thicker in consistency, almost like white glue, and can taste different from man to man depending on many factors, mostly diet (i.e. meat eater or vegetarian).

There are many different studies out there that indicate a man can improve the taste of his semen (and therefore increase his odds of getting a blowjob regularly) by eating fruits like papaya, pineapple, and most fruit. These studies also recommend staying away from potent foods like garlic, asparagus, onions, alcohol, and more. For a man's partner, being unafraid of ejaculation is incredibly appealing. Part of the joy of sex is reveling in your partner's body. What better way to show that you worship your man and are intimately connected than to freely consume of his life giving fluids?

Stages of Orgasm

Exactly like women, although on a slightly different time scale, are the male stages of orgasm.

- ✓ Excitement is obviously noted by an erection. It is also marked by increased heart rate, sweat, and possible pre-ejaculate fluid at the end tip of the penis.
- ✓ Plateau is the state between excitement and orgasm, and is generally much shorter for men than women. When a couple draws out the plateau stage, it can actually make it harder for a man to reach climax later, but is also part of Tantric practice that allows men to orgasm multiple times without ejaculating.

- ✓ Orgasm is fairly obvious in men. It ends with ejaculate coming out of the head of the penis, tensed muscles, flushed skin, and more sweat. Brain imaging scans show brain waves are active nearly all over the brain, all muscles have more blood flow and contraction, and orgasm is incredibly intense. No wonder men like them so much!
- ✓ Resolution is the final stage where men relax entirely, their erection recedes, and they are unable to start the cycle again for a specific amount of time (depends on the individual's age, diet, and health habits). Men's heart rates lower, their breathing slows, they enter rest phase to reenergize and many times they fall asleep.

The Art of the Hand Job

While you may consider a "hand job" to be a youthful prerequisite to the Big Leagues, it is a very underestimated tool of pleasure for partners. And it shouldn't be considered a "job" at all. More like a fun way to start the party. Men manually pleasure women to get them prepared for sexual intercourse, so why should men be any different? Just because they get an erection and don't need much priming doesn't mean that it should be neglected. For the ultimate hand technique, play with grip pressure, speed, and always make sure to lubricate. You can use both hands to create constant coverage, pumping up and down with both hands or alternating hands while you move down the shaft. Brush your thumbs under the head, where the nerves are densest, and move from slow to fast to slow speeds. If your intention is to bring him to climax, watch and listen. Men often tense when they come close to orgasm, or will become more vocal. Tease him by slowing down, or help him reach the peak by continuing. Gently hold or caress his testicles to really give him goosebumps. When a man comes, he becomes sensitive like a woman does. Hold him gently and lighten the grip.

Kung-Fu Grip: Grip the penis with your four fingers and wrap your thumb to meet your fingers. You don't have to touch fingers to thumb if he has a large penis, but you can use your other hand if it helps. Go for it - don't be afraid you're going to hurt him. Simply ask him if your grip is too tight or if he would like it tighter.

Thumb It: Use your thumb when you move up and down his penis to stimulate the sensitive underside of his shaft/foreskin all the way up to the tip.

Tried and True: When you pump your closed fist over a man's penis, tighten over his shaft, down the base of his penis. Lift your hand or lighten your grip to shimmy back up to the top, and keep a very light hand over the head of the penis where the most sensitivity is. Twist your hand as you tighten the grip up again and move back down.

Oral Sex

It is rare to find a man who doesn't love a good fellatio (also known as fellation, a blowjob, BJ, giving oral, getting head, or sucking him off). "Rag magazine" surveys often indicate that men in committed relationships would change only one thing about their love life: the frequency of oral sex. It is also a misnomer in society that women don't give their long-term boyfriends or husbands blowjobs because they don't "want to"; many women enjoy oral sex just as much as men do. This is yet another inaccuracy about relationships and sex that people tend to leave unquestioned. Women who do enjoy performing oral sex on their male lovers are often seen as "dirty," but the truth is that a woman who can give great head is probably very in tune with her sexuality and her man's sexual needs. Great oral sex for men is more than just putting your mouth on it. There is finesse in the tongue, sheathing the teeth, and providing the right amount of suction.

When giving head to a male, make sure you cover your teeth with your lips and gently insert his penis into your mouth. Move slowly to ensure you lubricate the entire shaft before speeding things up (never allow teeth to touch the penis while thrusting). Move as deeply as you can, and slowly retreat. Focus on the head of his penis with your tongue, especially on the underside where your tongue rests. Swirl your tongue around the tip, and move back down the shaft, sucking gently as you retreat. Speed up after a few "pumps," and increase the suction. You can also use your hand to pump up and down as your mouth moves back towards the head; feel free to play with his testicles, nipples and perineum simultaneously if your end game is making him orgasm. This is an intimate act, so feel free to look up at your partner as you provide this intimate expression of your love.

The Original

This method of fellatio is one that everyone who wants to pleasure his or her male partner should have in his or her "sex repertoire." It is fairly basic, but it is the best. Put your mouth on the head of his penis (do this when he's soft for maximum effect), and then wrap your hands or fingers around the shaft (like in Kung-Fu Grip). Essentially you are mimicking the sensation of a vagina by providing your wet mouth and tight handgrip.

Move in sync with your hand and your mouth up and down his shaft, lubricating as you go so that your hand has less friction. Make sure to sheath your teeth behind your lips so you don't scratch him. Follow the signals he's giving you to increase your hand pressure or speed, and pretty soon he'll be calling your name.

Watergate

How better to investigate his oral fantasies than with Deep Throat? This involves either bypassing your gag reflex and pushing his penis down your throat, or almost swallowing his penis enough to relax your throat muscles. This takes some getting used to and needs practice, but the visual and physical sensations will drive him wild. The most important thing to remember is to be at the right angle. Your throat curves down, so if he has an entirely erect penis pointing towards the top of your head, it won't work. Turn upside down on the bed to double the effect: his penis will fit perfectly into your mouth and down your throat, and he will get to enjoy the view (important for men as they are very visual). This also works well for when he climaxes; he can easily pull out of your mouth and come on your chest or belly.

Importance of the Testicles

Two very underappreciated aspects of the male sex organ are the testes. While many men don't really consider them part of their sexual experience, they can be incorporated for a full "wow" factor. When you're having sex with, or performing oral sex on, your male partner, gently cup their testicles with one hand. If you don't do this often, it's sure to give them a nice surprise. If you have both hands free, gently caress his sack up to his shaft or back to his perineum. If you are performing oral sex, feel free to place each testicle delicately in your mouth and move your tongue. The importance of tenderness cannot be underestimated here. Much like the clitoris, too much stimulation can hurt, just for different reasons. Be gentle, sensual, go slow and make eye contact.

Play Ball

During oral sex, include the balls in your mouth coverage. Use the tip of your tongue to travel down his shaft and between his testicles, and then slowly encircle each testicle with your tongue. Once you've lubricated them, pop one or both into your mouth, sucking gently as you do so. This is commonly referred to as "tea bagging" or like dipping a tea bag into a cup. Be careful when you do this, as any fast movement of your tongue may cause him to jerk. Men are rather protective of their balls!

Groin Grooving (Kegel) Exercise .

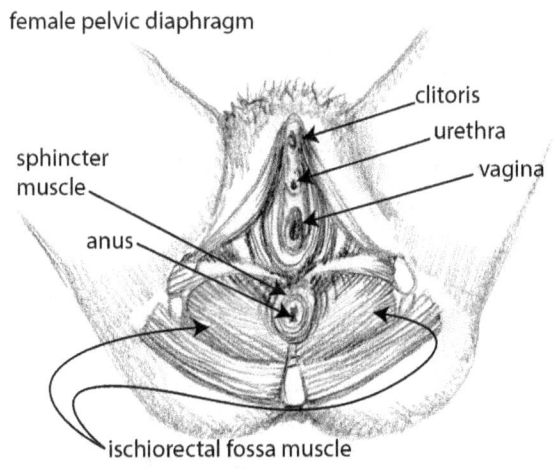

Kegel exercises help strengthen your pelvic floor muscles, and support your bladder, uterus, rectum and small intestine The muscles involved are the sphincter and ischiorectal fossa muscles, which control your bladder and rectum. Voluntarily strengthening and building this area by daily contractions can help intensify your orgasms. When your male partner penetrates you, that's just about as good as it gets in his mind. But there is something else you can do to really make him moan in delight. When he first enters you, relax your vaginal or anal muscles as much as possible in order to accommodate him. Then, as he begins to pull in and out, tighten your canal muscles (called the Kegel muscles) in order to grab on to him as he pulls out. This will feel a-ma-zing for both of you.

Vary the Party

Do not make the mistake of doing the same moves every time you perform oral sex. Variation of positions and stimulation is a key aspect of great sex, as you do build a tolerance to the routine. Nobody wants the same day in and day out, unless it's sex that is getting better and better.

When Things (Don't) Get Hard

Any man will know (but probably won't admit) that sometimes, erections just don't come naturally. This could be for a number of reasons; using any prescription or hard core drugs, work stress, and alcohol use being the most prominent. Women, of course, will take this as an insult to their beauty or their sexual prowess, which only makes the situation more difficult. If a man is too stressed, or his mind is elsewhere, he will have a harder time getting an erection just as a woman would have a harder time reaching climax. Rather than have an awkward meltdown, focus on continuing without giving it too much attention. Here are a few tips for resurrecting that lost erection, or enticing one out of your man:

- ✓ Shower him with praise; let him know he pleases you and that you find him incredibly sexy. Talk dirty to him. Get him to be in the moment by focusing on your words.
- ✓ Start giving him head. Even if he is soft, the sensations will feel great for him, and more blood flow to his penis will occur.
- ✓ Kiss him, give him a massage, and touch him all over. Use your hands and mouth to get him to focus on the sensations, rather than what's going on in his head. Get his mind on sex with you!
- ✓ Never insult him. While you may think it's funny, he certainly does not. Drawing more attention to it will make it much more difficult for him to get an erection now or in the future.
- ✓ Don't ask if he "has a problem" unless it becomes consistent. Then, only discuss it in terms of how best to improve it. Do not immediately assume he needs to pop a pill to get it up.
- ✓ Be sure your man is using the right condoms. One size does not fit all. Also, condoms remove proper sensation causing a loss of erection. Too much stimulation can also make a man lose an erection. Switch to "ribbed" condoms to get more sensation where it's needed most.
- ✓ Some men may need a lot of stimulation to keep an erection or ejaculate, so be sure to also stimulate other parts of his body during sex. Two or more areas stimulated together simultaneously should bring him to attention.
- ✓ Constrictive underwear and bicycling can cause erection issues due to constrictive blood flow to the penis. Switch to briefs and a wider bicycle seat.
- ✓ Ditch the drugs and alcohol which severely affect the brain and body's proper nerve signals. See your doctor if you are on any prescription drugs as common side effects are circulatory and sexual issues.

7.8 It Takes Two (Or More) to Tango

The Importance of Grooming

Traditionally, women have spent more time grooming and cleaning themselves for their partners. While the musky pheromone scent that is original to each person will at times suffice, human bodies need proper hygiene and care to enhance your partner's attraction.

For women, primping and preparing for sex is half the fun. To increase your feelings of sexuality, and feel good about your body, here are a few tips.

- ✓ Shave your bikini area to a desirable style, whether entirely naked or in a fun shape (Lightning bolt, heart, landing strip, etc.).
- ✓ Try a professional wax or laser. This will decrease discomfort when your pubic hair grows back, and will create a smooth, exciting landscape for your partner to work with.
- ✓ Clean your vagina with only water and a washcloth/sponge. Do not use "intimate" soaps, as they throw off your natural bacteria and flora. Vaginas are very capable of cleaning themselves without much help, though be sure the area is tidy and clean.
- ✓ Use natural healthy lotions after you shave. This will help your skin feel baby-smooth, and make your partner unable to keep his or her hands off of you.
- ✓ When comfortable with each other, have fun shaving, grooming, cleaning and washing off together in the shower. This usually leads to some real hot sex and you both will be refreshed and clean afterwards also!
- ✓ If planning on having anal sex, tend to proper cleanliness pre and post act.
- ✓ In today's modern society, men are beginning to realize that a little maintenance goes a long way. Instead of coming to your partner straight from a workout, or going days without shaving, take some time to "manscape," and see how much more your partner responds to your advances.
- ✓ Make sure you smell good. Shower if you need to, or just wipe the important parts with a washcloth super-clean before making a move.
- ✓ Trim your facial hair. Scruff can feel great on a woman's sensitive skin, but too much can chaff more than necessary.
- ✓ Trim "down there." Pubic hair is naturally coarse and grows wild in its natural habitat. Use scissors or your electric razor with length attachments to keep it to a manageable length.
- ✓ If you'd like to experience heightened sensation, try shaving your pubic hair entirely. Be very careful guys, as your skin down there is very thin. Your partner will appreciate the new view, and you'll love the extra inch or so of length you've "gained."

Half of the sexual experience is an internal one; we all have insecurities and concerns about our bodies prior to sex. By preparing our bodies and making them as appealing (to ourselves and our partners) as possible, we increase our confidence, and show our partner(s) that we are putting in the proper efforts. This mutual effort from both partners will increase your attraction to one another, and the new sensations that come with grooming will send your sex to new levels of pleasure.

There are plenty of books dedicated to Kama Sutra positions packaged with sexy couples having intercourse, but they give you little to no tangible useful applicable knowledge that you can use in your life right now. My intention with the following section is to show you how to transform your sexual life by making the information usable and practical so you too can be a sex god(ess) in your mate's eyes.

7.9 Stimulating Sex Combinations for a Deeper Connection

The following illustrations show combinations of positions that will give you the most "bang for your buck" so to speak. They are set strategically in a way to have you transition during sexual intercourse without losing the momentum and sparks. Nothing ruins the mood faster than having to figure out positioning strategy during the middle of an orgasm. The combinations aim to provide at least two stimulating positions per intercourse session. You may add more or do less, though these combos are recommended for best results.

Position: Eye to Eye

Description: This seated position allows for you to gaze into your lover's eyes and have plenty of skin-to-skin contact. Your third eye and root chakras are physically connected, and your energies are freely transferred. From this position the man can easily pick her up and rock her into the next lotus variation without losing a beat.

Pros: Intimacy, comfortable, skin-to-skin contact.

Cons: Less thrusting ability.

Power Meditation: Try to see yourself and your partner in a slow, lazy tide. Feel the motion, to and fro, and mimic that in your lovemaking. This position is a great way to meditate together and move into more active lovemaking.

Position: Eye to Eye (Lotus Variation)
Description: Seated on the floor, rather than on the edge of the bed, the man now is in lotus position as well. Once again, this allows your chakras to be in alignment and allows for easy, soft motions.
Pros: Intimacy, comfortable, skin-to skin contact. Easy transfer from Eye to Eye bed position onto the floor.
Cons: Less thrusting ability, less range of motion with man seated.

Power Meditation: Picture a forest of trees, rooted in the ground but still blowing in the breeze. Your root chakra is touching (or nearly touching) the ground at this point. Imagine that you are gaining energy from Mother Earth, Gaea, and that energy is spreading through your chakras and energy points. You are giving and receiving energy with your partner.

Position: Standing Bow
Description: Enter the woman from behind while she is bent at a nearly 90-degree angle. Have her support herself on her knees or against a wall or bed if needed.
Pros: Thrusting ability, depth of penetration.
Cons: No eye contact, not much skin contact.
Power Meditation: Imagine a waterfall, the power behind the water and the rushing sound it makes. Let that wash over you and imagine your orgasm taking over with the same force as the water.

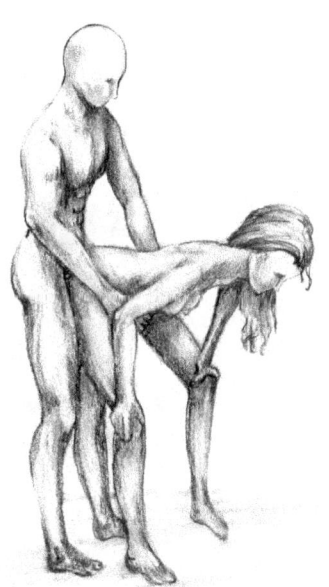

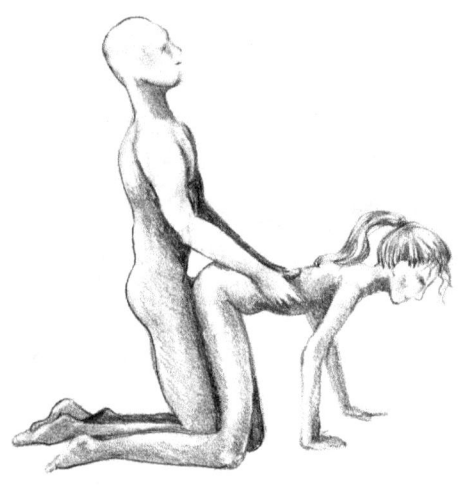

Position: Knee Worship
Description: This "resting" version of the Standing Bow takes the pressure off partners to stay standing. Simply bend at the knee and continue your lovemaking on the bed or floor.
Pros: Connection to Earth, thrusting power, depth, less weight to hold up.
Cons: No eye contact, possible rug burn.
Power Meditation: Imagine thunder clapping with every thrust, and the feeling of electricity right before lightning strikes during a storm. Every thrust results in more electricity between the two of you.

Position: Atlas Hugged
Description: On one knee, take your partner who is also on one knee. Use your other leg (bent at 90 degrees) to thrust and move your hips. Next, you may transition into the Ocean Motion position.
Pros: Skin-to-skin, eye-to-eye.
Cons: Low thrusting ability, hard to balance, difficult if partners are different in height.
Power Meditation: Imagine floating in water; only your slight movements direct you one way or another. You are at peace, your energy is renewed. Hug your partner and feel that serenity.

Position: Ocean Motion

Description: The woman lies under the man, but both partners match their thrusts and motions. Keep it slow or move it fast, whichever you prefer.

Pros: Skin contact, eye contact, ability to vary the speed and depth, female relaxed.

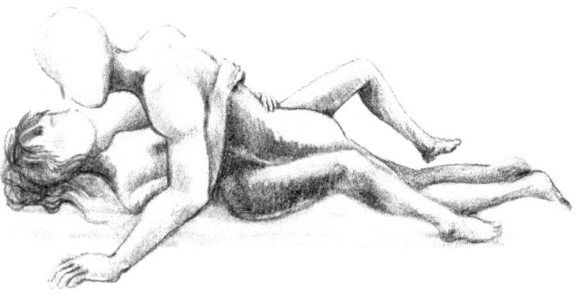

Cons: Man has to hold himself up and direct force.

Power Meditation: Imagine waves crashing on the shore; tide moves in slowly at first and then the waves get bigger. Imagine a large wave crashing on the shore repeatedly; feel that wave in your core.

Position: Corkscrew

Description: Moving directly from Ocean Motion, do not break contact, but simply lift the woman's leg over to her other side. Continue to make love with both her legs on one side and your leg in between.

Pros: Allows more muscle tension/tightness, can hit the G-spot, deeper thrusting.

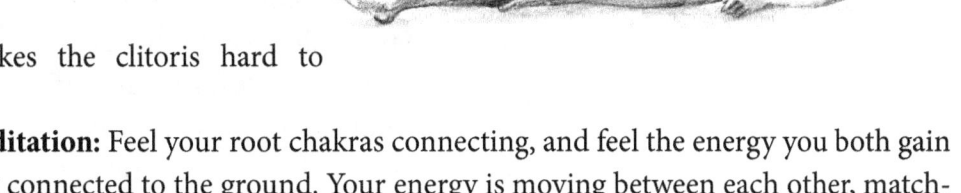

Cons: Makes the clitoris hard to reach.

Power Meditation: Feel your root chakras connecting, and feel the energy you both gain from being connected to the ground. Your energy is moving between each other, matching his thrusts.

Position: Breaststroke

Description: Continuing from the Corkscrew, the woman rotates so the man is now behind her but still inside her. The woman lies flat on her stomach, the man straddles both her legs, and takes her from behind.

Pros: Man has great thrust capacity, woman's channel is tighter, can be a lot of skin contact, man can gently tug on hair or stimulate her nipples.

Cons: No eye contact, no access to the clitoris.

Power Meditation: Picture yourself swimming underwater. You are weightless, you can move against the current with great power. Cut through the current, feel the water brushing over every part of you with great speed.

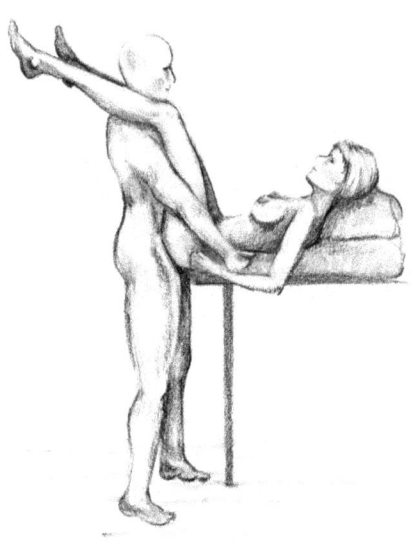

Position: Elevation

Description: On a high kitchen counter or desk, safely place your partner on the edge and put a pillow under her head for the proper angle. Enter her with her legs placed over your shoulders if she can, and hold her around the hips.

Pros: Exciting new position, deep penetration, moderate thrusting ability.

Cons: May require man to stand on his toes, woman may be uncomfortable on a hard surface.

Power Meditation: Picture yourself on a mountain or in a tall tree, and sense the thrill and the excitement at being so high. Feel the wind whipping around you and the intense sensations in your core as you feel crisp, clean, mountain fresh air, deep in your chest.

Position: Pyramid Play

Description: From the Elevation position, without losing connection, she wraps her legs around his shoulders and holds onto him as he moves her to the floor or in bed. Place her on a pile of pillows or blankets to slightly elevate her lower body. Keep her legs over your shoulders, and place your hands by her arms.

Pros: Very deep penetration, high thrusting ability, G-spot stimulation.

Cons: Man must be strong enough to safely transfer woman to floor. Requires some flexibility on the part of the woman.

Power Meditation: Imagine you're on a swing, and as you pump your legs higher you are building your strength. As you reach the apex of your swinging height, let go and realize you can fly. Releasing yourself from the swing, let your orgasm overtake you.

Position: Goddess Throne

Description: With the man lying on the bed, the woman straddles his leg and faces towards his feet. The woman then controls penis depth and the tempo of their lovemaking.

Pros: Female is in control, male gets great visuals, woman has the ability to stimulate clitoris while being penetrated for deeper orgasm.

Cons: Can't make eye contact, requires stamina from the woman.

Power Meditation: As you swing your hips and move up and down, imagine your root chakra is a tornado, tensed with energy and power. As you orgasm, feel that tornado of energy spread through your body, chakras, spine and into your partner.

Position: Escalator

Description: From Goddess Throne position and with the man still on bottom, have the woman turn to face him. The man will then lift his knees to about 45 degrees, or whatever is comfortable. The woman will shift up and down, using the man's legs as a guide and support.

Pros: Man can thrust a little, eye contact, more skin contact, woman still in control of depth and tempo.

Cons: Woman doesn't have full range of motion with man's legs propped up. Limited thrusting ability from male.

Power Meditation: In your head, feel the sensations in your muscles as your partner moves. Imagine those sensations as lightning, striking all over your body. As the lightning gets stronger, the thunder builds. Release your orgasm with a great clap of thunder as it overtakes you.

Position: Surfboard

Description: With the woman on top, the man moves his legs down from Escalator position and flat onto the bed or floor.

Pros: Female can thrust more, more friction on the clitoris, female in control.

Cons: Male cannot thrust, less speed with woman on top.

Power Meditation: With a gentle rocking motion or a fast, fluid movement, imagine yourself at the whim of the sea. You're floating, moving with the current, or trying to swim against it. Reach the crest of a wave as you swim against the current, and reach the crest of your climax.

Position: Queen's Sexy Sentry
Description: Standing tall (like a guardian protecting the royal gate), the male holds the woman as she climbs up and wraps her legs around. The man then holds her bottom and uses his arms to thrust her up and down.
Pros: Exciting change of pace, lots of thrust power, lots of skin contact, great show of virility.
Cons: Male strength and stamina must be high, lots of upper and lower body strength needed by both parties, can't last too long. Move into Two Trees Position.
Power Meditation: Climb a mountain, climb a tree, sprint through a valley. Feel your physical strength and picture yourself at one with the elements. You are the wind, the lightning, the water - you are strongly connected with Mother Nature's power and your orgasm is a manifestation of your strength.

Position: Two Trees Together
Description: From Queen's Sexy Sentry, as your stamina wears down, have the woman move one foot down to support herself on the ground. Arms can be moved down to the man's waist as well.
Pros: Easier to balance, longer lasting than Queen's Sexy Sentry, woman can help with thrusting.
Cons: Woman on her toes, can't get as deep with one leg down, lower thrusting ability.
Power Meditation: Imagine you are two trees forever rooted together, rustling in the breeze, a part of nature and sturdy, firmly in the ground. Feel the energy coming from the ground to your root chakra and spreading up to through your crown in orgasm.

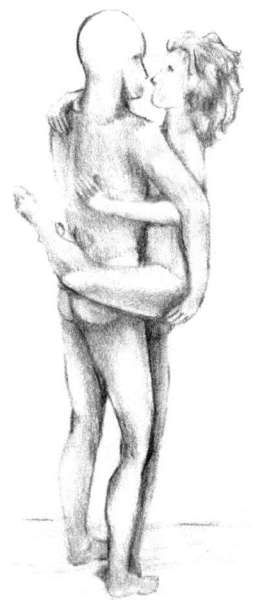

7.10 Energy Flow during Sexual Stimulation

"Dr. Kousouli, how can I get the most powerful orgasm?" you may ask. "Is it a special touch, movement, thought, position, being with a hot guy or girl of my dreams?" And I would reply that the power and intensity of the orgasm actually depends on you; the way you are thinking, your imagination, the way you feel about your partner, the way you control your breathing, and more than anything else, your focus on being fully present in the current moment's experience without resistance. Without a doubt, being able to be present with a clear mind allows you to channel your power and harness mind-blowing orgasms *time and time again*.

Let me explain… You are made up of powerful innate energy and since you are this cosmic infinite energy being, the way that your energy is directed by your conscious focused intention via thought will determine the effects of that focused energy and level of perceived awareness in the experience you're involved in at that time. If your thought energy is dispersed in other places in the universe (i.e. thinking about other people, wondering if you are doing things correctly, doubting the big contract at work will fall through, etc.), it will not serve you as much as when it is focused on the "right here and now," obviously.

To heighten sexual climax, knowing how to channel your life force energy is key. If you are lying down or sitting in a chair, close your eyes and imagine (yes, use your imagination) that you are pulling your greenish red clay colored Earth "Gaea" energy in from your feet chakras, into the leg channels and into your root chakra as picture in the image.

At the same time, envision Divine Cosmic energy being drawn in from the heavens into your crown chakra down through your third eye, into your throat, heart, through your solar plexus, into the sacral, plexus, and then combining with the root chakra energy from Mother Earth, Gaea, which you previously brought there. As movement of cosmic energy comes into the body, envision it pulsing brightly with waves of electric blue, which feel nothing short of amazing. With every breath, the pulse of light is electrifying every cell, tissue, and organ as it connects with each chakra. (Refer to the illustrations here, at the end of Chapter 4 and the Kousouli® Method Master Chart at the end of Chapter 11 for explanation of the channels and chakra locations.)

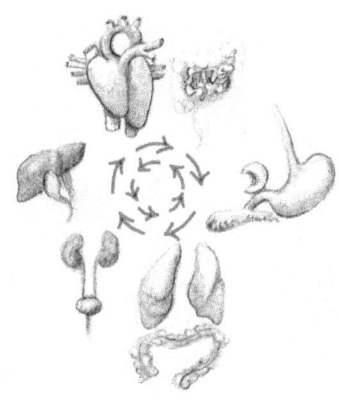

Vary your deep diaphragmatic breathing as you are simultaneously using your imagination through this process while being sexually stimulated. As climax draws near, hold your breath for as long as possible, quickly exhale and then quickly inhale deeply just as you orgasm and are about to cum.

You will find that holding your breath, quickly letting out the breath, or quickly inhaling a full deep breath while being sexually stimulated on your clitoris or G-spot, heightens orgasms. The oxygen high or low to your brain furthers the fireworks. For safety's sake; consult your doctor before trying this or any approach mentioned in this book; it's likely you may pass out.

As you build this energy, bring the energy up the spine to the crown and then down the front of your body, back toward the root chakra. With each breathe in and out, pump this energy continuously up the spine to the head and then down the front chakras towards the root chakra again.

Mix in the meditations during intercourse described with each position, and you will vary the feeling and power of each session's orgasm. This is very intense, and will take practice of course. However, if you do it all correctly, this method effectively provides orgasmic bliss.

All Together Now

Reaching climax together is one of the most sensual and intimate moments lovers can share. While this may seem nearly impossible if you are fast to reach climax and your lover takes more time, there are a few tricks that can help connect climax arrival time.

For men:
- ✓ Go slow, decreasing your odds reaching climax too fast
- ✓ Switch positions if it starts to feel "too good"
- ✓ Use a cock ring (purchased at your local sex shop) to restrict blood flow and allow longer thicker erections
- ✓ Use a non-ribbed condom which can lower incoming sensations

For women:

- ✓ Focus on the sensations, not how you look naked
- ✓ Communicate with your lover – tell them what a great job they are doing and encourage them to go faster, deeper or slow it down
- ✓ When you are getting close, let him know so he can come too

Using Pornographic Material as a Tool

Watching pornography together may be just the added spark you need to heat things up in the bedroom when sex has gone cold. This works well for couples who have been together for a while and are looking to add some new flavor into the relationship, but it should be used with caution. As mentioned in previous chapters, pornography can have some pretty intense consequences, both personally and spiritually. In order to use porn for good rather than evil, here are a few tips:

- ✓ Shop together online or in an adult movie store.
- ✓ Choose more "classy" films; you don't want to traumatize yourself with "Anal Academy #9" right out of the gates.
- ✓ Select movies that focus on lovemaking rather than money shots. Seek out directors and producers of adult movies who make sexually stimulating and respectful films without demeaning scenes to either sex. They do exist.
- ✓ Be open with each other about which movies appeal to you.
- ✓ When you push play, don't mirror the actors; sex should happen organically, not just because someone else is doing it.
- ✓ Don't compare your body to the performers'. "Smoke and mirror" techniques to create fantasy are used in adult movies just as they are in Hollywood movies - so don't believe the hype.
- ✓ It's ok if it doesn't work out; porn isn't a necessary sex aid.

Using porn to enhance your lovemaking can be a great idea, but it is not for everyone. Use with caution, and ensure that your lover is just as comfortable with it as you are before using it.

Anal Play

For some heterosexual couples, anal sex can be an exciting new avenue for exploration. For homosexual couples, it is obviously much more common. While society degrades this type of sex to being dirty or "illicit," it doesn't have to be. In a loving couple that's exploratory, this can be just one more notch in the intimacy post. Many couples include anal fingering as a way to add extra stimulation, especially for men as their "G-spot," their prostate, is located against the walls of the rectum.

The anus is composed of an external and internal sphincter, located between your "butt cheeks." The anus has half of the nerve endings found through the penis and the vagina, and most nerve endings are connected to the outside and interior of the anus. For men, anal sex also takes into play the prostate gland, which is highly sensitive when stimulated. However, with anal sex and anal play there are some concerns that are more relevant than with vaginal intercourse.

- ✓ **Keep clean.** Use the restroom well beforehand; wash both your penis/vagina and anal region. Do not move the penis from vagina to anus or anus to mouth as this is very unsanitary and will spread major bacteria. Colon cleansing is a good idea prior to having anal intercourse.
- ✓ **Be gentle.** The rectum is incredibly sensitive and has thin tissues which are not meant for heavy friction intercourse. If you tear these tissues, you could increase the odds of a really bad systemic infection.
- ✓ **Lubricate.** The anus and rectum do not have natural lubrication like the vagina does. Be generous with the lubrication, as it will decrease odds of chaffing or tearing, and make the motions smoother and more pleasurable.

Keep in mind that whatever you choose to do in the safety of your own sex life is your choice and no one else's. No matter what your sex looks like, it is the intention behind it that matters most.

7.11 Enhancing the Mood

Once you understand your partner's basic anatomy and how to drive them wild with just your body, you will likely become much more intimate with one another and attuned to your needs as a couple (or group). But sex goes beyond so much more than the mechanics. Sex is an experience, a connection, and a playground. Explore one another and engage fully in all of the senses. Encompassing the physical, the sensational and the spiritual aspects of sex will provide you with both mind-blowing climax and a deep-rooted connection.

To really enhance your sexual experience and feel closer to your partner, play with the senses. Of course, the act of sex is such a sensation in itself, but using some of the following tools will turn your great sex into legendary sex.

Touch

Use different tools, like a feather or a braided "whip," ice cubes, oils, etc. to touch your lover. Using handcuffs, ribbon, or ties for restraints can add an extra "wow" factor to your play. Focus on the sensations that you feel when your lover is holding you, and trace your fingers and lips around areas you don't usually pay attention to, like ears, eyes, nose, neck, hands, stomach, feet. Play with each other, tickle and tease. Dress in satin or silk, adding a dimension to your foreplay when you remove the clothing and feel it sliding from your hands and body. Use your long hair as another tool for tracing your lover's body, or use your beard to create friction and a rougher sensation. Giving your lover a bubble bath is erotic as well as gentle, and can make skin highly sensitive.

Withholding touch is also a powerful tool. By not touching your partner except for the parts that most count, you can induce a powerful orgasm when you finally get to touch one another. Preventing your partner from touching you can add a power element to your sex play, and make it even more intense for both parties when the touch finally occurs. Pausing while kissing or having sex to intensify the sensation can also make sex much more intimate, as you're taking a moment to relish in each other.

Taste

Have a tasty treat with your lover during foreplay or intercourse - feed them grapes, chocolate covered strawberries, share ice cream or whipped cream. Use peppermints or mouthwash immediately before kissing or biting to leave a tingling sensation wherever you kiss your partner. Indulge in lighter foods, and be messy. Feed your partner food without your hands, and don't be afraid to get creative. Many adult stores have exciting things like chocolate body paint and cotton candy underwear to really take your taste game to the next level.

Delight in the taste of your partner. There is no shame in enjoying the flavor specific to your lover's skin. Taste each other's fluids as well, and share with your partner how their tastes affect you. Men, keep in mind that the taste of your semen can change based on your diet. Eat a lot of papaya or pineapple to give your partner a nice yummy surprise when you cum. Ladies, use honey or spread chocolate onto his penis during fellatio to make it more delicious to you or put a little baking soda toothpaste in your mouth and lick his scrotum during head to send him into outer space!

Sound

Turn on classical music, intense instrumental tracks, or quiet lyrical songs. If you have a love song that has become "your song," turn it on to enhance the mood and ask your partner to dance. Engage in silent lovemaking, no talking or moans. Just breathe together, and allow your body to express your ecstasy rather than your voice. Especially listen to the sounds of your lovemaking - the creaking of a bed, the sound of skin against skin. It's erotic to be sensitized to sounds other than your voices.

In contrast, talk to each other - share your passion for the other person, or what you're feeling as you join together. This is place to share "I love you's" and express your gratitude or attraction to one another. "Dirty talk" does have its advantages, but attempt to make this a positive space where you focus on connecting spirit-to-spirit, rather than animal-to-animal.

Sight

Use blindfolds to remove the sense of sight, as this will heighten all other senses. Undress your partner in front of a mirror, or allow them to undress you. Perform a loving act in front of a mirror together. Make eye contact often. Dress in appealing colors for your partner, or in sheer lace or satin. Focus on where your bodies connect, and don't be shy - let your partner explore your body. Low lighting may be more forgiving, or allow you to loosen up a little without feeling self-conscious.

Focus on the sights: how her face becomes flushed when she's nearing climax, how his muscles bulge during this pose. Watch the area where you connect intimately, and marvel at how well you fit together. Look in each other's eyes and don't look away. Also, look at areas you've never considered before, like hands or feet. It's incredibly erotic to see the effects you have on one another. "The eyes are the window to the soul," as an English proverb declares, and how true that is. If you stare deeply into your lover's eyes while physically loving one another, you will experience a depth of spiritual connection you have not reached before. The encounter will most likely be one of the sexiest of your life.

Scent

Essential oils are a great way to add scent to your experience. Add 5-10 drops of lavender essential oil to a small spray bottle, mix with water, and spray around your room. The scent of lavender is calming and healing, and can make your sexual experience feel romantic and loving. Candles around the room can create a moonlit ambience, and can provide scents as well.

Your natural pheromone animal scent is the strongest sense tied to memory and emotion. If you're looking to entice your partner to romance, remind them of your presence by spraying a perfume or cologne you wore on your first day or leave your favorite shirt on your partner's pillow so they smell you when they lay down to sleep. Also smelling each other's distinct musk cues the other person to your sexual desire.

7.12 Safety is Sexy

While previous generations may have believed that pulling out a condom or asking your partner(s) if they're on the Pill would ruin the moment, modern times call for modern measures. Gonorrhea, Syphilis, Bacterial Vaginosis, Chlamydia / Lymphogranuloma Venereum (LGV), Genital Herpes, Human Papillomavirus, Hepatitis B and C, Scabies, Pubic Lice (also known as Crabs), Trichomoniasis, Yeast Infections, and HIV/AIDS are all out there lurking; the list isn't pretty. As a general rule, if after sex with a new partner you experience any "flu-like" symptoms like chills, fever, unusual tiredness, body aches and pains, or itching, painful urination, sores on your genitals, foul smelling penial or vaginal colored discharge, rashes and other unfamiliar signs, see a doctor immediately for testing. Always communicate clearly with your partner about previous sexual infections and diseases you have had. (You may also refer to my previous book, *BE A MASTER® OF MAXIMUM HEALING,* for holistic solutions that naturally boost your immune system.) Prior to becoming sexual with each other, you both should get tested to know where your health stands. It is very important to enter into the sexual union with clear conscious intent. Before engaging in sexual activity with your partner, make sure you always have a fresh, unexpired condom on hand as a "bare minimum" protection barrier. Not only does this decrease the odds of pregnancy, it decreases your chances of inheriting STIs and STDs if used correctly each time (Be sure to read contraception package for instructions and disclaimers). Entering your sexual domain with the intent to have mutually safe and exciting sex will create positive energy for the experience, and allow you to express your higher vibrations of love without worries.

To enhance your sexual experience with prophylactics, make sure you know your stuff when it comes to condoms and other protective options. Both participants must take personal responsibility to protect themselves and not leave all the responsibility of safety to one partner. The male should use a condom and the female should use her choice of contraceptive barrier as well (Progestin-only injections, hormonal implant, female condom, oral contraceptive pills, diaphragm, cervical cap, vaginal sponge, spermicide, or dissolving vaginal contraceptive films – be sure to research the pros and cons of each before trying). Some people are very allergic to latex, so make sure you have latex and polyurethane condoms on hand (or just polyurethane). For truly sensitive persons, there are "natural condoms" usually made out of lamb's bladder available as well (these only protect against pregnancy, not STI/STDs). There are different styles of condoms, too, which can aid in his and her pleasure. Ribbed condoms may help create more texture for the user and the partner being penetrated, as the design hits more nerve endings. Many men complain that condoms decrease their sensations, so pouched (looser tipped) condoms are beneficial as they allow more feeling around a man's sensitive "head." Ultrathin condoms, while they break much more easily, allows both partners to experience more sensations. For performing safe oral sex on a man, you could use a non-lubricated flavored latex condom, and have fun with one another without worrying about any negative consequences. To perform safe oral sex on your female partner, keep it clean by using a thin latex sheet separator, called a dental-dam. Even if you're not planning on having actual sexual intercourse with penetration, condoms can add a level of safety (and exploratory fun) to your play.

This chapter is devoted to doing; you have been provided a strong tool kit for sexual exploration. Use it. Some of the most intense parts about sex are the novelty, the intensity, and the mutual trust a couple shares together. There is vulnerability and dependence on one another, and a truly spiritual joining is one that pairs all of the senses, both internal and external. By involving all of your senses, you reach a heightened awareness of your body, you are in the moment, and it is an almost meditative state. All your focus is on the connection between you and your partner, and your energies are in sync. Hopefully this tool kit excites your senses and your body, awakening you to the full potential that sex has. Most importantly, know that sex is not just an act; it is a language and connection of the soul.

Chapter 8:
Secret Sexual Chi

"Sex is an emotion in motion."
~ Mae West

Consider the yin and yang, a symbol of combined yet opposing forces which, when placed together, make a whole. Two different energies merge to make one all-embracing synthesis. Is the yin and yang, representative of life forces, energies, and duality not also a symbol for sex? The yin is the archetype for internal forces, and in sex is the source of your innermost desires and sexual prowess that has yet to be tapped into. The yin also supports your core experience during sex, the private reality you behold. The yang, the model for your external sexual experiences, reflects your approach to the act, to your partner, and the outward manifestation of your libido. The yang also aids in your connection and energy flow between you and your lover. The two parts of the whole also symbolize your union in sex, or in a relationship; you are one part, and your paramour is the other. Together, you are one.

In order to fully experience your sexual capacity and your ability to love, you must understand the energies that you embody and how you share that with your lover(s). Inside us all lives our chi, our fundamental life force (that unseen energy that keeps your heart beating and lungs breathing). We are all familiar with the Circle of Life, which tells us that we all live and die, and that we are all connected. Chi is similar to this circle, as it is a constantly flowing cycle. We have energy that waxes and wanes, periods in our lives that come and go, and a daily experience of energy renewal and exhaustion. There are ways to maximize our chi, our life flow, through how we engage in our daily lives and how we treat our bodies. By maximizing our chi, we also maximize what we have to give to our lovers and how we express our spiritual selves with one another.

8.1 Naturally Improve Your Sex Life

The best way to improve your sex life is to treat your body like the temple it is. Do not put anything into your body that will cause it harm, including poor food, excessive alcoholic or sugary drinks, cigarettes, and so on. While this is sort of a blanket statement, the reality is that none of these things will benefit your health or your love life. Move towards cleansing and detoxifying your body in order to feel your energies rise and your capability as a lover improve.

Cleansing and Detoxification

Removing all of the aforementioned things from your daily life is much, much easier said than done. It is recommended that you start slowly, and allow yourself time to heal from this intense shakeup. The body will go through withdrawal symptoms especially if the patient is addicted to high glycemic carbohydrates, diet and caffeine drinks, smoking or drinking. The waste and toxins present in the body will leave the tissues and enter your blood system as they travel for neutralization and elimination. Therefore, patients will usually experience issues like: fever, nausea, headaches, chills, ulcers, skin rashes, thirst, increased urination, loss of appetite, eye pain, difficulty sleeping, extreme drowsiness and fatigue, diarrhea, muscle soreness, lack of motivation, and any already known problems usually become heightened briefly. Naturally, this does not aid in sexual encounters, hence give yourself sufficient recovery time. This detox side effect phenomenon is termed a "healing crisis" and generally lasts for a 1 to 2 week period after starting a detox. Although it may not seem like it at first, this is a good thing as it means the body has begun doing it's clean up of toxins and is removing impurities.

Detoxing Your Daily Beauty Regimen

Most if not all health problems are from one of two things: Not ENOUGH of a nutrient or substance the body needs, or TOO MUCH of what the body doesn't need. Let's discuss some hazards in the home that when removed and substituted with healthier choices will improve total health and raise one's natural chi.

- ✓ **Toothpaste and mouthwash** should contain no toxic fluoride. Remember that dental hygiene is very important to your sexual interactions, so maintain great oral health with natural products.

- ✓ **Colognes and perfumes** should be made of natural botanical oils, not commercial store brands made in a lab. One of the best scents you can wear is your own; your own brand will attract more people than any store bought concoction.

- ✓ **Shampoos and conditioners** should not contain parabens, or laurel sulfates! Your hair stays healthier and cleaner longer with all natural shampoo, allowing you to attract lovers with your shiny locks.

- ✓ **Shower filters** help remove chlorine and toxins contained in city water. Change them every 6 months, and enjoy healthier, more hydrated skin that is soft to the touch.
- ✓ **Do not chew gum** that has aspartames, saccharin, or phenylketonurics like Phenylalanine. Most gum also has toxins: BHT, propylgallate, acesulfame K, Red 40 Lake, Blue 1 Lake, and maltitol, which have all been linked to dis-ease and cancers. If you want to attract a mate with healthy fresh breath, chew on natural gum or mints.
- ✓ **Detergents** have chemicals that may cause all types of skin ailments, itching, color changes, and even cancers when exposure is long. Buy natural detergents. Unscented ones or ones that are scented with your own homemade natural floral scent collection is best for enticing people. Nothing smells worse than fake floral fabric softener on a potential mate.
- ✓ **Makeup** is often made from petroleum products and ground up animal matter. Avoid the potentially cancer-causing, skin-irritating chemical compounds and use all natural makeup and facial cleansers. Your skin will radiate and you will look and feel great.

Eating for Sexual Health

Consider what you eat on a daily basis. Do the foods you give your body help you provide energy and sustenance, or are they merely flavor fillers? Processed foods and high carbohydrate diets may taste great, but they provide very little in the way of benefits for your body. Not only will you gain weight eating poor foods, but also you will not build healthy muscle, keep your organs healthy or be fit for a great sex life.

A well-balanced diet such as the Mediterranean diet consists of vegetables and fruits, legumes, nuts, cereals, fish, and minimal amounts of alcohol. This diet differs from some others in that natural fats of the monounsaturated and saturated variety are encouraged. Eating a well-proportioned daily diet using all of those ingredients and balancing a healthy fat intake (like olive oil) will really help you improve your overall body function. For optimal "sexiness," avoid red meat, dairy and vegetable oils. Cut out all junk food and anything artificially sweetened. This includes soft drinks, ice cream, candies, diet or normal pastries, and processed cereals. For them to be digested and absorbed by the body, they depend on other food items you intake because they are deficient in enzymes. Hence, avoid empty calorie foods because they completely degrade your metabolism. It is also highly recommended that you stay away from food items that your body hints you are allergic to. Typical allergic reactions your body gives you are: coughing, mucus or phlegm production, sneezing, difficulty breathing or swallowing, skin rashes, face swelling, watery eyes, and fever.

Of course, changing your approach to food doesn't happen overnight, and neither will your transformation into a healthy, delicious sex god or goddess. Here a few tips to kick start your program:

- Buy and prepare food that can be mixed and matched. It helps when you can just piece together a meal from different parts that all "go together."
- Protein and monounsaturated fatty acids will help you feel satisfied and prevent you from binging on junk food when you get hungry.
- Spice up your life; add unique flavors to your new meals and play with mixtures and seasonings.
- Processed food is a no-no. Think of how unsexy you feel after eating it, and you can prevent yourself from caving in.
- You can never eat too many vegetables, and don't forget to eat a lot of fruit.
- Focus on why you chose this new food regimen: to be as healthy and sexy as possible.

The Chi of Food

Eat living enzymes found in vegetables and fruits. The best thing for your chi is to eat whole, raw (living) foods. Eating vegetables and fruits is ideal, as they are still alive, and have the proper enzymes and proteins that help your body the most. When cooking your vegetables, make sure to steam them lightly - do not heat them into mush or you will not gain any benefits.

Avoid eating pork or beef. We've all seen the documentaries on the horrible realities of the meat packing industry. Animals live in squalor and die in pain, and that energy is transferred into the meat you consume, which affects your chi. Seafood can be a great replacement for red meat, but avoid squid, shrimp and shellfish. Focus on oysters, catfish, herring, haddock, sockeye salmon, tilapia and codfish. The fresher the water is, the healthier the fish. Focus on fresh wild caught fish, rather than farmed frozen options for optimal chi.

Drink lots of water. Drinking enough water can be one of the biggest changes you make to your sugar drink lifestyle. Hydrated individuals can balance their chi much more easily, as the blood and water in the body are what conduct chi. Drinking more water can help you detoxify your body, and move your body into prime sexual ability. Remember, people can live nearly three weeks without food, but never more than a week without water. Water is vital to your chi.

Load up on antioxidants. Antioxidants like vitamins C and E promote health and youthfulness by fighting and preventing disease. What is more desirable than a young, healthy body when seeking to improve your sex life? For optimal health eat: blueberries, tomatoes, broccoli, leafy green vegetables, and oranges for Vitamin C. Vitamin E sources: Leafy green vegetables such as spinach, chard, collard greens, kale, etc. Eating these foods as close to raw as possible will help increase your chi.

Do not over eat. The source of inner power integration is in the area of the solar plexus. Not only is chi present, but you also have a chakra here. Overeating overloads the body's resources for food metabolism, and redirects blood to the gut instead of the muscles causing you to tire quickly. Avoid heavy oily and fried foods as this brings acidity to the body, causing the body to lose chi adjusting itself back to homeostasis. Plus overeating bloats your stomach and makes you less able to engage with another person on a physical or spiritual level. As a rule, don't eat after 7pm daily so your body can start its process for sleep preparation.

Eat more super foods. Super foods are super sexy! Eat omega-3s, which can be found in foods like sardines, mackerel, herring, wild-caught salmon, walnuts, flaxseeds, and soybeans. Quinoa, also a super food, is very high in protein, selenium, vitamin E, and zinc. Blueberries have phytoflavonoids, vitamin C, antioxidants, and potassium - plus they're a strong anti-inflammatory food, which helps reduce occurrence of cancer and heart disease. Eating beans and green leafy vegetables are vital because they provide protein, phytochemicals, fiber, antioxidants; they increase oxygen levels in the blood and can help lower cholesterol. All of these foods are high in chi considering they are fresh (as can be), which increases your own personal life force and sexual stamina for better performance!

Eat anti-inflammatory foods high in chi and supplement correctly. The best known healthy anti-inflammatory foods are: cauliflower, cabbage, chard, rhubarb, collards, sweet potato, green beans, broccoli, yams, Japanese pumpkin, spinach, fennel bulb, onion, avocado, apple, blueberries, blackberries, black currants, guava, mulberries, raspberries, kumquat, pomegranate, cherries, pineapple, almonds, hazelnuts, walnuts, mung beans, split peas, flax seeds, lentils, sunflower seeds, pumpkin seeds, and soy beans. Supplement these highly anti-inflammatory foods with oils like: rice bran oil, grape seed oil, olive oil, and walnut oil. The best anti-inflammatory herbs are: ginger, basil, cloves, parsley, rosemary, cilantro, oregano, cinnamon, mint, and turmeric. If you need to subsidize your intake, there are omega-3, flaxseed oil, or fish oil supplements. These supplements can be found in a liquid or capsule form, and you should be taking at least 2-3 grams per day. Because they are so high in chi, you will be increasing your life force exponentially when you consume them.

Chlorophyll is a pigment in plants, and is also a drink used to stimulate our lungs, blood, and intestines. Chlorophyll can halt foul mouth odor, slow down growth of putrefactive gut bacteria, impede bacterial growth in the body, prevent gum diseases, and even accelerate wound healing! It is a great addition to your new sexy regimen, as it will help you be healthier in a number of respects.

Enjoy one another. As mentioned in the chapter prior, natural bodily fluids were once considered God-given gifts of health, and consumed to enhance the body and mind. Consume freely the gifts your partner gives you, especially during sex. This means female secretions as well as male ejaculate. Not only will this intimate act bring you much closer, but it can also help you improve your health as well.

Hopefully this section serves to prove just how vital a good diet is to sex. Some may say that they are two entirely separate issues, but it is clear to see that they are two sides of the same coin. A bad diet affects your mood, which affects your approach to others and to sex. Poor nutrition results in physical problems, which decrease the likelihood that you will attract a partner or perform well during sex. Finally, an unhealthy relationship with food makes you obese, which will definitely affect your overall ability to be happy in life and relationships.

8.2 Habitual Tips to Help Grow Your Natural Chi

In order to be able to efficiently send, receive, and regulate energy flow for any activity, you need to have an ample supply of living energy in your body. Once you've managed to acquire optimal energy from your diet, there are a few other things you can do to improve your overall energy and chi.

- ✓ **Get chiropractic adjustments regularly.** <u>This cannot be overstated. Strong sexual power and performance comes from a well-functioning nervous system.</u> Spinal adjustments will improve your respiration and oxygen intake, thus contributing to your spinal chi. Assuring your nerves are working as they should will also help with your sexual sensations, allowing you to fully embrace the experience.

- ✓ **Master emotional stability.** Understand that part of your chi is giving and receiving energy. When you feel depleted, forgive others and relax any resistance to rebuild your chi and energy, and help others rebuild also. This is a great partner experience; focusing on sharing one another's unconditional love energy and feel how full you feel after a sexual or non-sexual healing session.

- ✓ **Breathe fresh air deeply for good chi.** If you live in a populated, polluted city, fresh air may be hard to come by. Work on providing as much fresh air to your body as possible, and buy air purifiers for areas where you spend the majority of your day. Aside from the quality of the air you breathe, focus on how you breathe. If you breathe in shallowly, you are not fully relaxing nor getting the distressing benefits that a deep breath give you. Clean air and deep diaphragmatic breathing will ground and de-stress you.

- ✓ **Get proper sleep every night.** Supplements like L-Tryptophan, L-Theanine, GABA, B Vitamins - B2, B3, B6, B12, Magnesium, Choline Bitartrate, Inositol, Vinpocetine, Melatonin, Galantamine, *5-hydroxytryptophan* (5-HTP), DMAE and Ginkgo-Biloba can help with a restful night's sleep. But you know what helps even more? An orgasm. Engage in playful or intense, meaningful sex with your partner(s), exchange your love and energy vibrations, and sleep the restful sleep that can only come after climax.

- ✓ **Meditate.** Meditation is incredibly important to increasing your chi. When you meditate, you focus on your inner self, and attempt to not let the stresses of the day penetrate through your concentration. This is a great activity to engage in twice a day; once in the morning to set your intention and mood for the day, and once at night before bed to clear your space of anything that doesn't need to tag along into the next day. Many people who practice White Tantra also meditate before engaging in sex with their partner, in order to bring maximum energy to the bedroom.

- ✓ **Be aware of your energy exit points.** Chi is believed to exit the body through the hair ends, the forehead, the throat, the palms, the fingertips, blood loss, menstruation, and semen secretion through the penis. When you have sex with someone and feel depleted, this could be because an uneven energy exchange took place. Focus on sharing energy, rather than just giving or taking.

- ✓ **Learn sexual restraint when applicable.** Sexual transference is an incredibly powerful tool for improving your life force. Of course, sex is a beautiful and necessary thing, but by withholding from excessive sexual activity (masturbation, casual sex, etc.), you actually increase your chi. A key sexual experience would provide an equally energetic individual who promotes the sharing of energy. Your sacral and root chakras are especially benefited from transferring sexual energy until it has a proper outlet.

✓ **Connect with the Earth - get naked.** There are few things more raw and real than undressing when you're alone or with a partner(s). The body you possess is a gift and a Divine tool with which to express your love. If you want to increase your chi, your life force, just marvel in the wonder that is the human body. Nothing connects you to the spirit more than connecting to the means by which energy is shared.

✓ **Exercise is vital for chi flow.** The catch with our life energy is that it is a constant cycle; every day we gain energy from sleep, deplete it with our activities, and then regain it through sleep again when our soul goes "home" on the other side to reboot. We use up food energies and pass the rest as waste to the Earth, and consume more just to start it all over again. Life is a cycle. To increase your chi cycle, and improve the overall energy flow through your body, it is necessary to exercise. If you want to bring well-balanced chakras and brimming chi to your sexual partner(s), keep exercising.

Benefits of regular exercise include:
- Increased chi energy, blood flow, and alertness
- Reduced risk of various forms of cancer
- Builds healthy muscles, bones and joints
- Decreased risk of obesity
- Lowered blood pressure
- Increased muscle strength and flexibility
- Combats osteoporosis
- Increased oxygen and alkalinity throughout the body
- Psychological improvements (reduction of depression, anxiety, etc.)
- Increases mood and helps keep lifestyle active

Essentially, accommodating any or all of these adjustments will greatly improve your overall life, but have a direct impact on your sexual chi. If you do not focus on the flow of energy into and out of your body, you will not understand the process by which sexual chi

8.3 The Kousouli® Method Spinal Stretches (KSS®) for Improved Sexual Health

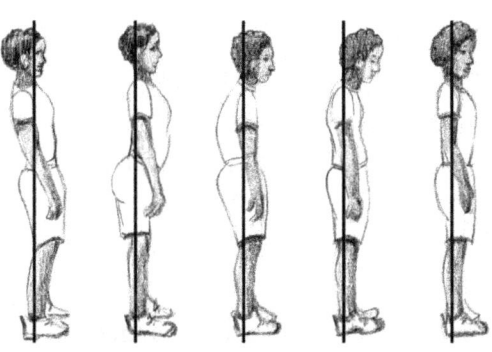

There are many behaviors that people engage in on a daily basis that, unbeknownst to them, is only adding pressure to their already over-stressed spines causing exponential loss of chi. A few of these malpractices are: texting on your phone with your neck flexed forward (called text-neck hunch), carrying an oversized or heavy purse or backpack over one shoulder, long hours of slouching in a computer chair at work, holding your phone between a shoulder and tilted head, sleeping face down on an unsupported mattress or couch, sitting on a thick wallet in one back pocket, and wearing high heels all day long without taking a break. Surely you can identify with one or more of these behaviors that you engage in, and hopefully you take steps to correct them.

While you're thinking, "What does this have to do with sex?" there are actually a lot of supporting activities that can lead to you having better sex immediately. The bad habits that were just listed mold our spines forward into a very unattractive, hunched position (kyphosis), which can also eventually lead to large bends in the length of the spine (scoliosis) causing us to appear shorter, crippled, or even look years older (not so sexy). Some people can even lose lung capacity from forward head postures, caved in chests and tightened pectoral muscles, which can all lead to fatigued states of acidosis. None of this is very good for your sex life, not only because you will not be able to perform to full capacity, but because your energies will not be in sync thanks to the trauma. Because our days are often structured around work, driving or generally moving around in ways that aren't great for our bodies - what we really need is a chance to properly extend our spinal column, which is where the *Kousouli® Method Spinal Stretches (KSS®)* come in. By getting our spines in alignment, which also happens to be the central home for our chakras, we can prepare our body and mind for better sex now through better posture.

As mentioned before, posture is one of the sexiest, healthiest and loudest signals you can send out to potential partners. Standing up straight, walking confidently and having the ability to look young and vibrant are very important aspects of our inborn sexual nature. When we neglect our spines and general posture, we send different messages: unconfident, unhealthy, and unattractive. That's not the energy you want to radiate!

The *Kousouli®Method Spinal Stretches (KSS®)* provide a number of benefits for the body, mind and spirit, which will then be translated into your interactions with your partner(s). A few benefits include:

- Spinae muscle groups become more erect. This improves your posture, making you look young and healthier.
- Stretches improve circulation, which improves stamina and sexual function. (Ex. May lower chances of erectile dysfunction)
- Stretches release tension, which can increase your libido and also improve your interactions on a spiritual level.
- Stretches burn calories, make you leaner and fitter for your sexual partner(s).
- Stretches release endorphins, which improve your mood and therefore the energy you exude when engaging with your partner or seeking a lover(s).
- Stretches increase oxygen flow to brain and lungs, which makes you more alert and aware of your body during sex. This improved breathing also helps with meditation and tantric methods.
- Muscles will be strengthened and stamina will increase, which allows you to be more physical in your sex life.

Some notes before you begin:

- Always consult your doctor before beginning any exercise or stretching program like KSS®.
- If you feel pain when performing any movements - stop immediately.
- Begin your KSS® gently - do not 'jump right in' forcefully. Give yourself time to adapt.
- If you have had a joint replacement or are just coming out of surgery, simply limit, restrict, or avoid major movements.
- KSS® movements and methods may be modified and adapted to suit an individual's age, needs, and abilities. Do the modified versions labeled 'M' if the original stretch is too difficult for you.
- A KSS® program for seniors or arthritis sufferers may be applied slowly, and modified gradually over a period of time, depending on skill level. Move your joints slowly through a full range of motion several times, to help enhance overall circulation, and decrease any stiffness. KSS® may be resumed once tenderness has

diminished and your doctor allows you back to total activity.
- Rest painful, inflamed, or hot joints with a cold ice compress at 15-30 minute intervals, and discontinue for the time being if pain occurs.
- Always breathe deeply down into your diaphragm (not chest), and allow unrestricted flow of your airway while doing KSS® movements.
- Be sure to use a pillow or soft mat for any joints (like the knees) that make constant contact with the ground during modified stretching.
- Practice good technique; do not overextend joints beyond the normal range of motion. Maintain good form and posture.
- Hydrate often throughout the day (A full glass of water per hour awake is recommended.)
- When learning the stretches, consult a more experienced KSS® user for proper form and execution, rather than learning the poses incorrectly.
- Follow your stretching with a cool-down period, including sustaining the end of the stretch to avoid tenderness or stiffness. If soreness or stiffness occurs despite performing a cool-down, reduce your movements and try the modified 'M' version of the stretch.

Instructions on Kousouli® Method Spinal Stretches (KSS®)

Beginning your new KSS® stretching routine is simple! Just pick three stretches (out of the nine provided) to do once in the morning, once in the afternoon, and once in the evening. They can be the same three stretches, but it is recommend that you mix it up in order to get the full advantage of this process. Make sure you that you're paying special attention to your form, and giving these stretches the respect they deserve. They will change your life!

The nine stretches focus on the spinalis, longissimus, and iliocostalis muscles of the back, which form an erect spine. The muscles named semispinalis capitis, semispinalis cervicis, splenius capitis, splenius cervicis, levator scapulae, and rhombodeus major and minor (located in the head, neck, and shoulders) are also a huge focus in KSS®. The Kosouli® Method Spinal Stretches (KSS®) program is a fun and smart program for you that will help you improve your overall spinal health, physical health and sexual ability. The rest of this section will discuss the nine individual stretches at length.

Please note: each stretch can be modified to your individual abilities! There will be a letter "M" next to suggested changes, but feel free to adapt your own until you become stronger or more adept at the stretches.

(A.) HERMES STRETCH

Hermes was a god of the Greek pantheon, designated as messenger to the other gods of Mount Olympus. His symbol was a pair of winged boots. The Hermes stretch is aptly named as it is designed to raise your ankles and feet in the air, pointing them as if you can fly. Hermes is best used as a morning stretch. Start with one arm extended straight up over your shoulder and the knee bent towards your chest. Inhale deeply, and slightly extend your back as you hold the stretch for three seconds. Slowly switch the arms and legs as you exhale. Repeat the stretch on the opposite side. Modified Hermes is done by lying on your back. As you inhale and exhale from your diaphragm, visualize your spiritual body encompassing love and your sexual energies without confinement.

(B.) POSEIDON STRETCH

Poseidon was the Greek God of the Sea, ruling with his trident. The Poseidon stretch is so named because you move from a crouched position into a springing chest expansion, almost as if you are Poseidon leaping from the depths of the sea. To get the best benefits of this stretch, do it in the morning. Crouch on the floor, inhale deeply from your diaphragm and rise up into a standing position with one leg back while extending the spine and pushing the chest out. Keep your arms wide, and hold up your chin. Hold for three seconds, and then exhale as you come back down into a crouched position. Repeat the stretch with the opposite leg. Use this stretch as a meditation to force tensions, resentments or anything blocking you form enjoying your peak sexual experience.

(C.) APHRODITE/EROS STRETCH

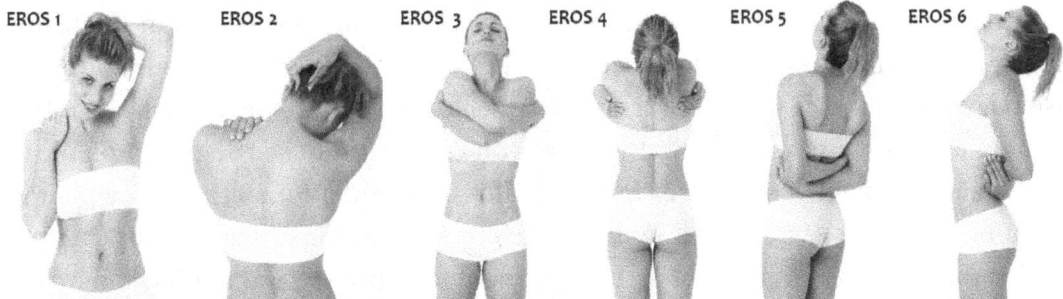

Aphrodite was the Goddess of love, beauty, and desire, a great figure for this book. The Aphrodite stretch is significant because it demonstrates self-love and increasing awareness of your body's sexual energy. Do this stretch in the morning when you shower, or in a bright sunny spot as you start your day. Stand with your left hand on your trapezius and pull the shoulder muscles down and forward. Anchor your fingers from your right hand onto the left posterior inferior occipital ridge (bottom left edge of skull, see picture: Eros2). Gently pull your head forward, down, and to the right with the chin towards your right chest. Inhale and exhale feeling the stretch. Repeat on the opposite side (Eros 1). Next, perform a loving heart hug by wrapping your arms around your chest (Eros 3, 4) as you extend your head back. With a gentle squeeze, try to move your fingers as far back to your spine as possible. Next, wrap your arms around your low back for support. Extend your upper body back gently, feeling the stretch (Eros 5, 6). The modified version of this stretch can be done seated. Use this stretch as a meditation; use the water flowing over you as a sensational experience, or view the golden light from your window as a representation of your inner sex god or goddess.

(D.) APOLLO STRETCH

Apollo was the Greek God of Music and archery, often depicted with his lyre or bow. The Apollo is so named because of the bow-and-arrow motion you make during the stretch. This stretch is a great stretch to engage your muscles during the afternoon humdrum. Start in a standing position, inhale deeply from your diaphragm, arch your spine, and push out your chest as you pull one arm and leg back. Put yourself into an archer position, and hold for a three second count. Exhale as you come back to starting position. Focus on the fluid motion of your body as tension builds upon extension of the back and arms. Repeat on the opposite side. Modify this stretch by kneeling or sitting with legs crossed. Use this as a meditation; aim your arrow and shoot for what you want in life and in love. Visualize it and you shall receive it.

(E.) HEPHAESTUS STRETCH

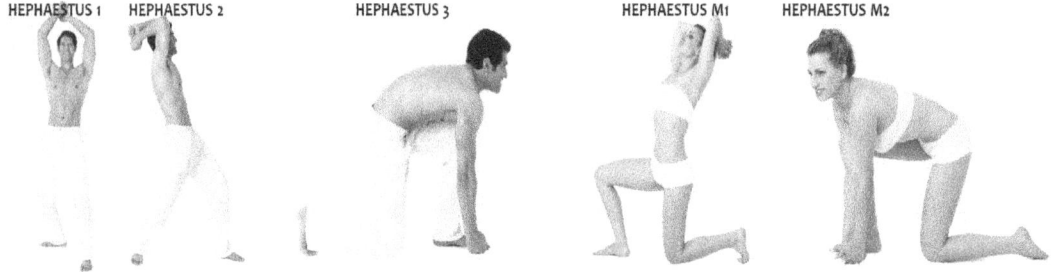

Hephaestus was God of fire and the forge, and his symbols were naturally fire, the anvil, axe, and hammer. This stretch is appropriate of its name, considering the hammer-like motion it consists of. This is a great mid-day stretch to get your body moving after a long day behind a desk. To do the Hephaestus stretch, move from an extended standing position to a crouched forward pose, as if you were wielding a large axe or hammer to the ground. Inhale as you slowly extend a leg and stretch back, hold for three seconds, and then come down gently forward overhead, bending the knees as you exhale. Rotate slightly your upper body through the movement to isolate the abdominals. Go slow and do not overextend your back. Repeat the stretch on the opposite side. Modified version is done by kneeling or sitting with legs crossed. Use this stretch to symbolize your hard labor; with each move of your axe or hammer, you are providing a service to others. When you extend your arms, you can witness your work being transferred into abundance for you and those you love.

(F.) ATHENA STRETCH

Athena was the Greek Goddess of warfare and logic, portrayed by the owl and the olive tree. Athena can be found in the stretch in the "fighting" stance and arm motions. Stand with flexed biceps as if you are holding a large shield in each arm. Extend slightly your spine and inhale deeply. Turn your arms and upper torso to one side and bring up the opposite knee. Tighten your abdominal muscles and hold for three seconds. Exhale and repeat on the other side. As you breathe deep from your diaphragm, perceive yourself as an impenetrable fortress. Use this as a time to reflect on your sexual nature; you are who you are. Outside forces do not influence you, and are deflected off your energy's armor.

(G.) ZEUS STRETCH

Zeus, the Greek god of gods, was the ruler of Mount Olympus and God of the sky and thunder. Naturally, his symbol was the thunderbolt. This night stretch is named after Zeus because it is designed to "throw the thunderbolts" of your day away from you. The stretch should be started with your body crouched and then slowly extend your arms up as you stand into a body X position. Inhale deeply as you slowly stretch to the sky pushing up on your toes. Feel the stretch as you hold for three seconds. Exhale slowly as you descend back into a crouched position. As you descend and exhale, cross your arms as if throwing lightning bolts down to earth from the heavens. Repeat. Focus on the slow fluid motion of your body as tension builds up on the upward motion, and then releases on the downward flow. Modified Zeus stretch can be done kneeling or sitting with legs crossed. Use your downward motion with breathing to let go of any stress you accumulated during your day. Envision any negative energy slide off as it is thrown to the ground, and enter a clear space where you can bring higher vibrations of energy to your lover.

(H.) DIONYSUS STRETCH

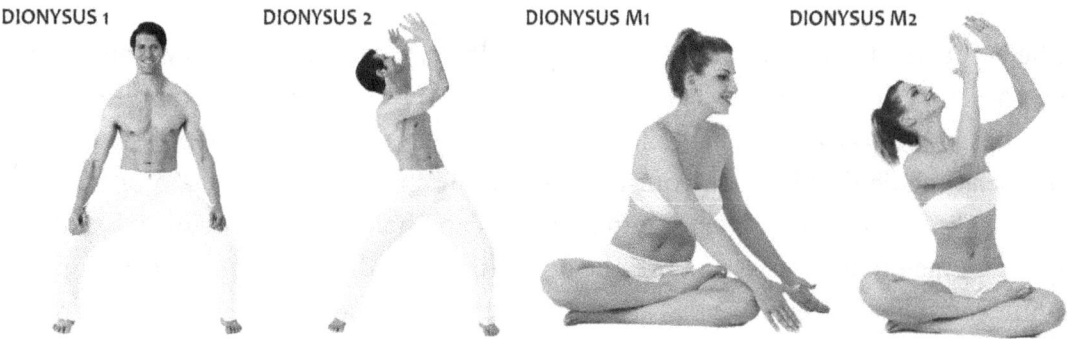

Dionysus was the God of fertility, pleasure and wine, a fantastic godly manifestation for this book. The Dionysus stretch is done standing in a saddle stance. Slowly bring up both arms as if holding an oversized glass of wine. Inhale deeply from your diaphragm, and slowly extend your torso as you rotate to one side. Gently extend your neck and upper back as if you are drinking the wine. Hold for three seconds, and keep your core tight. Return to center as you exhale, and then repeat on the opposite side. Use this stretch to celebrate your vitality and sexuality, and to represent your spirit's excitement for your next encounter with your lover.

(I.) DEMETER STRETCH

Demeter, Goddess of fertility and nature, was also considered the protector of life and death. She was often pictured with corn, her scepter, or a torch. The Demeter stretch is best done at night, and allows us to truly focus on how many cycles we experience. Lay on your back and inhale as you squeeze your knees to your chest; this signifies fertility or pregnancy (new life). Hold for three seconds, and then exhale as you slowly extend your legs down; depicting the seasonal summer/winter cycles. At the completion, slightly arch your cervical (neck) and the lumbar area (low back). Repeat. The modified version is done with hands palms down under the low back or hips for support, and makes the stretch a little easier. Use this stretch to symbolize your day as a cycle; tomorrow begins anew. Your love and sexuality also cycles, and may wax and wane, stretch and contract. Remember that everything starts new when the cycle begins again.

Benefits to the KSS® Stretch Program

KSS® combines a very unique mix of visual meditation, deep breathing and spinal exercise to provide an extremely powerful physical, mental and spiritual exercise. Not only will these stretches become easier as you progress, but you will also come to rely on them to start your day, jumpstart your energy levels in the afternoon, and prepare yourself for bed. All of the stretches are designed to improve your physical condition, which not only improves your health, but also improves your love life. Each stretch is also a form of meditation, embracing your loving nature and focuses on strengthening your sexual chi. Imagine yourself accepting yourself in all regards, and being able to clearly see what you want from yourself and others. Mentally, KSS® allows you to focus on intentions and positive thoughts, which allows you a clear headspace before you interact with a potential partner or current lover. When the mind, body, and spirit work together as they do in these exercises, you will not only feel and look better, but you will exude light and love in all aspects of your life.

Chapter 9:
Attracting the Right Frequency in Partners

"The greatest pleasure isn't sex, but the passion with which it is practiced."
~ Paulo Coelho

The energy you put out in the universe comes back to you in spades. This is a truth many know from their spiritual experiences, or even through learning about the Law of Attraction. But did you know that it also applies to relationships and finding a partner? What personality traits you emphasize, what mood you put off when dating, and even the clothing you wear puts out a message to the universe: I am ready (or not ready) for a partner. When you open yourself up to possibilities, and put your energy into finding like energies, great things will happen.

9.1 Understanding Your Sex Sign

It's now well known in astrology and numerology circles that certain people born at certain times of the year "get" or understand each other better and thus make better pairings with each other. When looking for a lover or a long-term partner, it's fairly obvious that your energies and even your elements can come into play. If you know your astrology sign, you know that you have times of the month or even the year when you are at your most "you."

Each sign has an "element" associated with their star power.

Fire

Fire signs are Aries, Leo and Sagittarius. Fire signs are much more sexually active, as the word "fire" suggests. Aries and Leos tend to be good at showing off their sexual prowess. Sagittarius tends to be very charismatic and sexually appealing. For this group, their abilities are often the highlight of their sexual encounters, and they require a lot of positive praise in order to feel successful.

Earth

Earth signs are much more physical and focused on sensation. Taurus usually enjoys making sex last, focusing on touch and the senses. Virgos are experimenters by nature, but Capricorns may be the ones to get into the "kinky stuff." Things they can touch and taste are very important to them, so wooing an Earth-sign lover may mean more dates, gifts, and public displays of affection.

Air

If the stomach is the way to an Earth-sign's heart, then the brain is the way to an Air-sign's. Air signs are idea people and their minds run a mile a minute. They are much more drawn to intellectual conversations and intelligence. Men and women in this category are much more verbal, and are immediately attracted to a smart, eloquent partner who can clearly communicate feelings and ideas. These signs are Gemini, Libra and Aquarius. Don't even try matching up with Air if you have nothing to offer in the mental category.

Water

Water signs are known for their emotional capacity to care for themselves and others. When it comes to sex, Water signs like Cancer, Pisces and Scorpio tend to find the best sex when there is a strong emotional connection. Cancers tend to want a nurturing relationship that requires a level of dependence. Pisces desire intense romantic passion, while Scorpios need to be wanted.

Astrology Signs: Finding Your Best Mate

If you are looking to have the most momentum behind you when looking for a new lover or relationship, be aware of your star cycle. The time around your birthday is the best time to be bold and make yourself known to the world: Here I am! Adversely, six months past your birthday is when your sign is farthest from its power cycle. While this is not bad, it just means that the full power will not be behind you in your endeavors. Relax, and wait until you feel the power gearing up again. View the astrology chart for a further explanation of your best astrological fits.

You can find your sign's best match, as well as your North and South Nodes in the tables after this section. The North and South nodes represent where the moon falls across the path of the Earth orbiting the Sun, and indicate your present (North) and your past (South). When reading the chart, find your date of birth. Your North node is the "sign" you should be putting your energy towards, whether in your personal interactions or within a potential partner. Your South node is the "sign" that you should be moving away from. Your South node can represent a bad behavior you've acquired or a past event you need to work through. Use your North Node as your compass, and keep moving forward to make a better version of yourself appear so that you can attract a much higher level mate.

If you haven't found Mr. or Mrs. Right, you shouldn't just be looking at your general astrological sign. You must also evaluate your strengths (North) and weaknesses (South) to get accurate match ups. See the North and South Node chart to help you identify your North and South Nodes. There are also plenty of resources in the references section at the end of this book that can help you expand your understanding of your True North. Basic astrology is general at best, while your North and South Nodes let you be much more specific in your readings for love. You can read (but don't worship) the stars; they can provide you with a map to your life. It's your job to ask questions and figure it out.

Questions to Ask Your Lover

While not everyone may buy into the idea of astrological signs affecting sexual compatibility, there are plenty of questions you can ask your partner to make sure you are on the same page. For example:

- ✓ How often do you think about having sex?
- ✓ What is your sexual style? General/usual "vanilla," kinky, etc.
- ✓ How often do you masturbate?
- ✓ Are you a monogamous person or into open-relationships?
- ✓ Do you view sex as a spiritual connection?
- ✓ What are your goals for the future? (Long-term or short-term)
- ✓ Are you seeking commitment or just an activity partner?
- ✓ Have you been with more than one person at a time?
- ✓ Have you been with anyone of the same sex?
- ✓ Have you been sexually safe with all previous partners?
- ✓ Would you get tested with me (together) before having sex?
- ✓ Do you have any past traumas or emotional baggage that we need to address before we get intimately connected?

From this list, we will move directly into the next step, which is attracting partners who match you or answer these questions in whichever way you find preferable. Take a look at the list and find your element on the left. Then follow it to the right to see who you most likely match up best with. Keep in mind that this is very general, and you will have to also take into consideration the North and South nodes (find the range you were born into) when you are making these determinations.

YOUR SIGN	POSSIBLE COMPATIBILITY WITH	SIGNS LESS LIKELY TO MATCH
Aries (Fire)	Air: Gemini, Libra, Aquarius Fire: Aries, Leo, Sagittarius	Earth: Taurus, Virgo, Capricorn Water: Cancer, Scorpio, Pisces
Taurus (Earth)	Water: Cancer, Scorpio, Pisces Earth: Taurus, Virgo, Capricorn	Air: Gemini, Libra, Aquarius Fire: Aries, Leo, Sagittarius
Gemini (Air)	Fire: Aries, Leo, Sagittarius Air: Gemini, Libra, Aquarius	Earth: Taurus, Virgo, Capricorn Water: Cancer, Scorpio, Pisces
Cancer (Water)	Earth: Taurus, Virgo, Capricorn Water: Cancer, Scorpio, Pisces	Air: Gemini, Libra, Aquarius Fire: Aries, Leo, Sagittarius
Leo (Fire)	Air: Gemini, Libra, Aquarius Fire: Aries, Leo, Sagittarius	Earth: Taurus, Virgo, Capricorn Water: Cancer, Scorpio, Pisces
Virgo (Earth)	Water: Cancer, Scorpio, Pisces Earth: Taurus, Virgo, Capricorn	Air: Gemini, Libra, Aquarius Fire: Aries, Leo, Sagittarius
Libra (Air)	Fire: Aries, Leo, Sagittarius Air: Gemini, Libra, Aquarius	Earth: Taurus, Virgo, Capricorn Water: Cancer, Scorpio, Pisces
Scorpio (Water)	Earth: Taurus, Virgo, Capricorn Water: Cancer, Scorpio, Pisces	Air: Gemini, Libra, Aquarius Fire: Aries, Leo, Sagittarius
Sagittarius (Fire)	Air: Gemini, Libra, Aquarius Fire: Aries, Leo, Sagittarius	Earth: Taurus, Virgo, Capricorn Water: Cancer, Scorpio, Pisces
Capricorn (Earth)	Water: Cancer, Scorpio, Pisces Earth: Taurus, Virgo, Capricorn	Air: Gemini, Libra, Aquarius Fire: Aries, Leo, Sagittarius
Aquarius (Air)	Fire: Aries, Leo, Sagittarius Air: Gemini, Libra, Aquarius	Earth: Taurus, Virgo, Capricorn Water: Cancer, Scorpio, Pisces
Pisces (Water)	Earth: Taurus, Virgo, Capricorn Water: Cancer, Scorpio, Pisces	Air: Gemini, Libra, Aquarius Fire: Aries, Leo, Sagittarius

North Node	Dates of Birth	South Node
Virgo	May 25, 1941 – Nov 21, 1942 Dec 16, 1959 – Jun 10, 1961 Jul 6, 1978 – Jan 5, 1980 Jan 26, 1997 – Oct 20, 1998 Nov 12, 2015 – May 9, 2017	Pisces
Leo	Nov 22, 1942 – May 11, 1944 Jun 11, 1961 – Dec 23, 1962 Jan 6, 1980 – Sep 24, 1981 Apr 10, 2000 – Oct 13, 2001	Aquarius
Cancer	May 12, 1944 – Dec 3, 1945 Dec 24, 1962 – Aug 25, 1964 Sep 25, 1981 – Mar 16, 1983 Apr 10, 2000 – Oct 13, 2001	Capricorn
Gemini	Dec 14, 1945 – Aug 2, 1947 Aug 26, 1964 – Feb 19, 1966 Mar 17, 1983 – Sep 11, 1984 Oct 14, 2001 – Apr 14, 2003	Sagittarius
Taurus	Aug 3, 1947 – Jan 26, 1949 Feb 20, 1966 – Aug 19, 1967 Sep 12, 1984 – Apr 6, 1986 Apr 15, 2003 – Dec 26, 2004	Scorpio
Aries	Jan 27, 1949 – Jul 26, 1950 Aug 20, 1967 – Apr 19, 1969 Apr 7, 1986 – Dec 2, 1987 Dec 27, 2004 – Jun 22, 2006	Libra
Pisces	Jul 27, 1950 – Mar 28, 1952 Apr 20, 1969 – Nov 2, 1970 Dec 3, 1987 – May 22, 1989 Jun 23, 2006 – Dec 18, 2007	Virgo
Aquarius	Mar 29, 1952 – Oct 9, 1953 Nov 3, 1970 – Apr 27, 1972 May 23, 1989 – Nov 18, 1990 Dec 19, 2007 – Aug 21, 2009	Leo
Capricorn	Oct 10, 1953 – Apr 2, 1955 Apr 28, 1972 – Oct 27, 1973 Nov 19, 1990 – Aug 1, 1992 Aug 22, 2009 – Mar 3, 2011	Cancer
Sagittarius	Apr 3, 1955 – Oct 4, 1956 Oct 28, 1973 – Jul 9, 1975 Aug 2, 1992 – Feb 1, 1994 Mar 4, 2011 – Aug 29, 2012	Gemini

Scorpio	Oct 5, 1956 – Jun 16, 1958 Jul 10, 1975 – Jan 7, 1977 Feb 2, 1994 – Jul 31, 1995 Aug 30, 2012 – Feb 18, 2014	Taurus
Libra	Jan 1, 1940- May 24, 1941 Jun 17, 1958 – Dec 15, 1959 Jan 8, 1977 – Jul 5, 1978 Aug 1, 1995 – Jan 25, 1997 Feb 19, 2014 – Nov 11, 2015	Aries

9.2 The Right Vibes

Let's be honest for a second: Some guys can be creeps. Most women are familiar with men who, intentionally or unintentionally, put off a creepy vibe or have absolutely no idea how to take "No" for an answer. Because of these unfortunate men, the men who are actually seeking a connection are going to be graded even more heavily against a woman's previous experiences. For this reason, in order to put off the right energy right out of the gates, men need to be aware of this. Since puberty women have been sexually harassed, cat called, picked up, and drooled over more times than they will ever admit, and in some cases it has made them genuinely afraid for their safety. When you want to approach a woman, put yourself in her shoes and consider how best to continue. For most women, complimenting her beauty is the best way to get shut down because you're doing the same thing ALL prior men have done. To look special in her eyes, keep cool, calm, and be polite yet interesting by being different. Instead, ask intriguing questions or bring up interesting information. Avoid creepy opening conversations like, "Have you heard about that guy who killed four people with a spoon in jail?" Don't talk about anything negative, and never go in straight for the kill with a compliment about her looks. Instead, keep it light and humorous.

When you attempt to "hunt" for a date, a hookup, or a long-term relationship, it is important that you know which one you are looking for and keep your search within that group. Your vibes are a result of your intention; a potential mate can pick up on your intentions just as easily as you can pick up on theirs. If a woman is searching for a date rather than a husband, she's going to be a lot friendlier with a lot more people. A man looking for a wife is going to be a little pickier when searching online dating sites or scanning through a crowded room. State your intentions clearly, and your vibes will attract a person with similar intentions.

9.3 The Right Attitude

The number one thing that attracts men to women (and most other combinations of partners) is individual confidence. Guys, the best way to increase your confidence level is to gain skills or characteristics, and embody them in specific ways. For example, if you want a woman to desire you, looking confident in your own skin, in your job, and in your ability to please your future partner are all very important. When you are successful, you are seen as successful. Even if you are hoping to attract a first long-term partner, and have no idea how to even start, let alone maintain, a relationship, showing and possessing confidence is the number one priority. By showing that you are able to take care of a partner (by providing), to love a partner (by being lovable), and to please a partner (by being sexual), you are already halfway there. If you do not exude or illustrate your abilities in any of these areas, you're not showing a woman (or partner) what you have to offer. Ladies, for you to get your dream man, it's an issue of displaying your feminine nature to trigger a man into wanting to nurture and provide for you as a man. If you self-love in a healthy way it will radiate out and men will feel that you have self-worth, therefore feeling you are emotionally stable and a worthy investment for long term love.

Attracting a Lasting Relationship by Loving YOU

The word love is misused so much that it has created difficulty in relationships. Consider a father who says to his child he loves him and that's why he's beating him. This same child grows up thinking love is pain, gets in relationships that are painful so that he can understand the feeling of love. Or a woman may create her current reality in a way that all her personal relationships come to a quick end from self-sabotage; unknown to her from previous events she saw as a young teenager when her single parent mother would repeatedly date abusive men. Unknown to her now, she's set herself up for an emotional loop of repeatedly ruining her own intimacy. Many who get into a relationship end up looking to please others first and end up surprised when they get their feelings hurt. Don't expect to live your illusion looking to find love in others and then think your life will be complete when you find "the one" as that will set you up for failure and continuing the lesson of learning self-appreciation. You cannot attract another to appreciate you unless that same frequency is being emitted by you. Everyone has their own soul and their own body, feelings, thoughts, etc. Each, when used correctly acts accordingly. Achieving the vibration with alignment to that which is our desire without resistance, allows the desire to be fulfilled. When one decides that they are not missing their mate, the mate can appear. We cannot have high hopes for a perfect mate but not be their equivalent in energy. How can someone expect a princess to be their mate if they themselves are still a frog? Fairy tales may have convinced us of this possibility, but a spiritual understanding, and work on oneself is important to enact the law of Attraction so that "like may find like". When we expect that there is no one that's perfect for us, or when we feel "there are no good women or men out there", the Law of Expectation is in effect all the time; especially when one looks for relationships to go their way. If you expect someone to not respect you, you subconsciously bring on more of that disrespect. The key is to maintain as much of your own vibrational frequency and know when that vibrational frequency is overpowered or knocked off its point by you or the surrounding energy. If so, it would be important to get it back onto the proper vibration once more through purifying more of your auric field to that which you are, and removing that which you are not. Kousouli® Method practitioners learn to do this this early in their training.

Do not try to please others without taking care of yourself first. It is not selfish, but a logical necessity for any other virtuous manifestations to unfold. You must be satisfied where you are in your soul development, and remove the thoughts or negative loops that are giving you what you do not desire. The key is to understand you; you first and foremost, before you ever try to share yourself with someone else. If you do not focus on your own soul work first, the energy you attract in another will not match your expectation of the level you really wish to be with, and this almost always ends in disaster.

How Fast or Slow Should I Take my Relationship?

This is a varied question based on intent and scope of the goal you are looking to reach. There is no solid basis for how long you should wait to kiss someone or sleep with them. In an effort to have people know each other really well and have a blessed union between them, religious traditions say you should wait until marriage to have sex. However, waiting until marriage is unrealistic for many and this practice's success rate is ultra-poor. Also, waiting until marriage to have sex doesn't guarantee love or success in the marriage without divorce. So how do we know if we are ready to share ourselves with others?

9.4 Attracting Lovers; Am I Ready? Are They?

Too often a new client will ask me why they attract the same person or romantic/sexual situation into their life, only to find the person they are with now is very similar in many ways to another abusive or incorrect matchup or horror story they have been through before. In actuality, without proper awareness, the relationship they are attracting is exactly the vibration they are emitting into the Universe, thus they are getting exactly what they are *feeling* and *emoting*, not what they are *seeking*. Thus, according to the laws of the Universe - they are *perfectly* matched!

One can only attract the same vibrational frequency one puts out. If you are emitting a frumpy lethargic "level 4" frequency, looking like a mess with your life out of order, and you are seeking a hot sexy vibrantly energetic "level 10" frequency mate with everything going for them, it just won't happen. If it does for some reason happen that you do cross paths, the relationship will not last. If it does last a short while, it will only be because you're naturally trying to increase your frequency. The reason for this dynamic is simple – the same frequencies attract, different ones will repel. It is Universal Law. Ever hear the phrase, "Birds of a feather flock together" or, "Show me who you are spending the most time with, and I will show you who you are." This is vibrational truth and you should heed it. Sorry to break it to you, but fairy-tale "Happily Ever After" sunset scenarios are for the movies. However, you can have a fully mutually satisfying relationship with your mate(s) when you are on the same frequency the majority of the time. Your vibrational frequencies will drop off the path from time to time, bringing you both a challenge to overcome through mutual respect, communication, and understanding, thus bringing you back stronger on the path together; this is very normal and healthy.

In order to help my clients wholeheartedly look at themselves and determine if they are indeed ready for a serious relationship, I have compiled my own list of signs to determine if you are ready for the challenges a relationship presents. If you or your potential mate do not fit the list, it means you should likely stay single to work on yourself spiritually, mentally, and emotionally. This will allow you to vibrate at the higher frequency which you wish to attract. Once you are in the correct frequency, make your intentions clear, and you will enter a relationship that will be mutually beneficial and blessed.

Dr. Kousouli's list - Signs a man is ready to share himself with another individual for a deep spiritual connection leading to commitment:

1. He has mastered bad habits and does not step backwards into repeating old mistakes. He does not obsess about things fanatically whether it is video games, sports teams, or doing illegal drugs. He is not fresh out of a relationship which has just ended, returning to his old girlfriend, or still associated with anyone else romantically. He has taken sufficient time after his last relationship or involvement to assess his growth spiritually, mentally, and emotionally.

2. He gives his word and sticks to it. This shows a commitment to see things through and be there when he says he is. This is a sign of higher masculinity and should be noted as an admirable trait showing the man has outgrown the boy.

3. He takes his time with making choices, evaluating all aspects of the decision - though does not overly analyze choices to death. He goes with his educated decision, knowing that whatever the outcome, he will take responsibility for the fallout and be a better man for it through experience. When you approach him with a challenge, he does not get overly stressed, respond in defense or blame you, but rather takes in all the data to make calm, relaxed choices about what to do. A woman can really tell a lot about a potential mate by evaluating how a man reacts in a crisis situation. This is a very important thing to assess, as relationships bring on many challenges that will be faced by both of you. If he cannot adequately overcome small issues, how can he be ready to take on future challenges of a family or provide emotional support?

4. He gives proper, healthy attention to you and lets you know you matter. A man who is naturally attractive with true charisma from a higher innate inner self worth will emit a frequency of security in himself and those he holds dear to him. A man who is insecure and must win the affection of all in the room sends out a signal that no one is enough and he must have attention from all, which is not a sign of an ascended higher mind. Likewise, if his life is out of balance it will show in him spending more time at work than with you (exceptions may apply). Red flags: If he does not want to see you regularly every week or involve you in his future plans, does not plan ahead or make arrangements to court you, or he continues to woo others in hopes of making you jealous; refrain from further involvement with him, for this connection will not be fruitfully blessed.

5. He likes you enough to introduce you to his friends, family and mentors. A key point of admiration is when a man introduces you to his inner circle, or his "trusted." When a man courts a woman, he is always seeking to establish her role in his kingdom. He qualifies her constantly, seeking to weed out the unserious from the serious. He seeks a woman who will be a partner in his path to greatness and leaves the less than qualified to the wayside. If you are being introduced to friends or family members, you have made some progress through his unspoken list of qualifiers. If you have dated him for over eight months to a year and have not met any of his friends or family, his consideration of you as a potential long-term mate is low.

6. He holds himself to high standards and has a secure financial income that he is happy with and mentors that help him further his success. When a man is fulfilled in his work, he is ready to share this with another in a like state of mind. Financial security and growth in his work is a key component for a man's happiness. Serious minded high level men are always looking to better themselves and those around them. The inventor, humanitarian, physician, teacher, author, director, CEO, and business tycoon minds are about serving the masses and making an impact on the Earth. Their life is about purpose and high intensity work, and making their communities better. Even if the monetary amount isn't in the millions yet, the man who is sought after by high level awareness women is the one making early investments in his schooling, self-growth, skill set, personal connections and spiritual growth. Men who do not do these things are less likely to seek leadership positions and have mates who are likewise on the same path. If a man is not secure in his life purpose and has not yet found his calling, he will have a harder time sharing himself fully with another person, as he will always feel he's not complete in himself, facing his regrets to pursue his full potential until his dying day.

7. He doesn't expect you to change for him or anyone else. He knows you have your path and he has his. Your paths are very similar, but not exact. Exact paths would eventually bring boredom, for they do not give contrast or offer surprises. Your paths should be similar enough to offer interest, but not exact where they become routine. He doesn't change for you, he changes for himself. Alpha males who are sought after are too preoccupied with bettering themselves to worry about another's growth or lack thereof. No one can change him; forget changing any man into what you want to make him be. A man only decides to change himself for the better - or for the worse. If you are with an Alpha male, you will know it because you have to be on your toes to keep up with the ongoing changes. If you are seeking this type of higher level of man, know that he will only be with a woman who is on top of her game, as he is on his. He is ready to take the ride with you into new adventures if, and only if, you are also moving along your path of a better you. No one wants to babysit a boring person who never changes themselves into a better version of themselves every day. If you're not changing as fast as he is, you're going to need to find someone in the Beta or Delta male category.

8. He has a backbone and stands firm in his manhood, not saying whatever needs to be said to please people, but rather speaks the truth- no matter how harsh it may be to hear. He also stands up for you against anyone who may speak ill of you. Women respect a man who calls out bullshit for what it is. They respect a man who is strong when no one else has the cojones (balls) to say what is on his mind. This is always done in a respectful, confident way with strong body language; it's never done in an arrogant or low vibration way. It is difficult for a woman to resist a man who says what he means and means what he says. For some women, this is the ultimate aphrodisiac.

9. His direct communication and honesty of intention with you is stellar. Of all the points on this list, this is the biggest indicator that influences all others. If a man intends to see you only for romantic or sexual advances while still seeing other women, and he is honest about his intentions from the beginning, he can be taken for his word and honored right from the start. You know what you are getting yourself into with him. There are no surprises, as the communication is honest from the start and it is your choice if you wish to mutually share in this adventure or not. If he says to you that he does not want to put labels on the relationship and wants to see how it unfolds, though he wishes to remain in a sexually monogamous relationship with only you, then you can take him at his word. Likewise, if he says he has been with you for some time, worked out the challenges in the relationship with you and you both have a mutual agreement to move into another level of commitment, you can believe him. A man who communicates well will have no reason to lie or play with anyone's emotions, as he states his truth and backs up his words and intention with honest actions. If the actions are not in line with the intention set forth, you are dealing with someone who is not to be trusted.

10. He believes in a higher power than himself. Be it God, his higher self, or whatever he calls it. He does not have all the answers himself and is man enough to seek more spiritual enlightenment for new strength. He humbles his ego and lets his inner wisdom guide his heart to answers.

If a man has acquired ALL of the above for a period of time where he feels fulfilled, he will likely want to share himself with another like-minded partner, and he is a viable candidate to approach if you wish to seek a relationship with this type of man. However, be sure you can provide the same vibrational frequency of mind and body he is presenting. You must match to have true connection.

Dr. Kousouli's list - Signs a woman is ready to share herself with another individual for a deep spiritual connection leading to commitment:

1. She has dropped the drama and no longer attracts the wrong type of men because she has dealt with all old baggage. Everything moving forward is new. She wears her big girl pants and does not blame others for her own mistakes. She is not desperate to fill a void. She does not blame hormones, the time of the month (her PMS), her parents, her boss, her girlfriends, or anyone else. She is over all of her exes. She has reviewed her negative friends and cut them out of her circle. She takes full responsibility for the energy she puts out and receives. She is not partying in clubs, getting wasted, being promiscuous, or sending mixed signals about who she is and how she wants to be treated.

2. She does not look to change anyone but herself. She does not need another to complete her. She knows she needs to love herself enough to not need a partner, but is open to the right partner which will continue to vibrate highly with her own personal happiness. She is not trying to conform to what others tell her she should look like, what she should eat, what she should be wearing, etc. She is not seeking anyone to save her from her loneliness or a bad situation with a current lover. She doesn't seek approval; she is self-approved, confident and knows who she is.

3. She values her independence and spends her time improving her value as a human being. She doesn't feel she "needs to be in a relationship" just to be in one. She doesn't "just want to get married", or "just want kids." She does not spend her time pursuing romantic ideas handed down to her from her parents, friends, or society's programming via movies, television, and women's magazines. Thus, she is not clingy or a nag to anyone she is involved with. She is viewed as a breath of fresh air, (almost) always positive and happy, uplifting everyone around her.

4. She puts importance on interaction with people, not just technological interaction. She would rather talk to you and spend time with you rather than just text you. This is a mature and very important part of courtship, as it allows reading of body language as well as verbal cues, and keeps miscommunication to almost zero. Regardless if calls and texts are returned promptly or not, endless relationships get broken prematurely when one's ego reads the typed text message incorrectly and allows their imagination to run wild with negativity.

5. She introduces you to her parents, friends and acquaintances. If she asks you to meet her parents, siblings or friends, she wants their approval of you. Her parents will be "looking you over" in terms of "fitting into" their family unit as a provider and protector of their precious investment – their daughter. You should maintain who you are and be true to yourself, letting her family know you mean no harm and are looking to be a positive influence both for their daughter and the family.

6. She focuses on the future, continues to educate herself, and seeks to establish her own financial support through a meaningful career; she does not depend on a man for money. This is extremely important in today's society, as the divorce rates continue to skyrocket due to money issues. The financial pressure of raising a family is enormous; being able to pay for food, supplies, housing, healthcare, transportation, clothing, etc. is vital. Thus, to keep financial stress to a minimum, the woman who is educated and intelligent enough to build early skills that feed herself and her children regardless of a man's affection and support is wise. She also puts herself into a solid position of being viewed as a much better suitor for successful men who seek the same fighter and "go-getter" mentality. Together they are much stronger, stable, and have a much more sustainable connection. This is better than having only one stressed, resentful breadwinner supporting the entire family.

7. She has no trust issues, does what she feels is right for her, and is guided by her intuition. She does not listen to stories of her "clock ticking," or the worries and anxieties of her mother and grandmother who fill her mind with insecurities. She meditates, reads, researches, and builds her personal self-worth through curious attention to detail and spiritual enlightenment on a daily basis. She is sure about herself and her life and believes in a higher power. She trusts her partner without fail, because her intuition guides her to her truth.

8. She does not question her sexuality. She may have "experimented" in college or felt certain ways about the same sex, but she is sure she wants the partner she wants, whoever that may be. She possesses a certainty in showing herself as open, honest, available, and true to her partner. She must know who she is and what she wants. Any uncertainty and the relationship is doomed.

9. She does not spend the majority of her time with gossipy girlfriends, her mother or 'guy' friends, returns her calls and texts on time, is never late and shows up on time to dates her man has taken the time to arrange and pay for.

10. She is balanced and has a healthy moderation in her life. She is not fanatical about shopping, flashy cars, travel, or church/religion.

11. She does not put men down and has a great relationship with her father and brothers. Red flag: talking badly on a consistent basis about men they dated or men in their family.

12. She is not interested in material gain or gifts as much as she is interested in spending time with you. Women who are only interested in things a man can give them make a priority to not forget one day out of the year (anniversaries or Valentine's Day) in which they are appreciated, and insist their man make that day special. These women have low self-worth. Women who make every day with their man special (for no reason) and know their man is there with them, regardless of the holiday, have real deep relationships. This woman puts value in *people*, not *things*.

13. She is old enough to have been cultured, traveled, and experienced life. A woman who is too young to get involved in a relationship has nothing to talk about and usually is only looked at for sexual appeal. Women who have seen a little bit of the world, are well read, and over 20 years old (there may be exceptions) have stimulating conversation and more to offer a man of similar vibration.

14. She keeps a man interested by being a pleasure to be around. If she nags him even a little bit or gives him a hard time, a woman is essentially denying him his ability to perform as a man. He will, after several attacks, consider the likelihood that he may be better fulfilled by another female, and the relationship will be in trouble. A man seeks validation, and if he feels in control of his kingdom, he will keep his queen satisfied. If the queen decides to act like a king herself, or weaken her support of her king, the male will rectify his kingdom with action towards re-building a new realm that allows him the peace of mind he seeks.

Re-Learning your Lover

I was first taught hypnosis by assisting my early mentor, the late Dr. Scott Lewis, a respected and renowned hypnotist in Las Vegas who held the longest running stage hypnosis performance on the strip. I was able to see him, within a millisecond, turn a shy person into an outgoing wonder on stage using verbal cues alone. Armed with this knowledge, I started to ask myself, "How could I help my patients change their negative beliefs so that they can mold better personal relationships in their lives?" But even more close to home, how could I develop techniques never shown to me or taught anywhere that enhanced personal relationships in the sexual attraction and fulfillment arena? I decided to explore this field and dove into it, using only trial and error to adapt tactile, verbal, auditory cues, and extrasensory commands. Through my development of these techniques, I was successful in implementing them whenever needed to bring about a happy and healthy outcome to personal, sensual, or relationship challenges I was having with my mate at that time.

In my early thirties I was dating a woman for about three months and although we were intimate for most of our time together, and she was content with our connection, the passion was not at the level I knew it could ascend to and wished it to be. She was a shy natured gal, timid yet curious, with a submerged personal wild streak which I saw only when she drank alcohol at parties. Yet, even in this scenario she was still restricting herself from fully enjoying herself and her sexuality. Much of her repression came from earlier relationships where being uninhibited meant bringing on social backlash and stereotyped name-calling (i.e. slut shaming). She had repressed herself because she now believed subconsciously that being sexual was bad, even though she was in a very safe, private, and free environment with me to be as expressive and as open as she wished to be. In her mind, she believed that if she acted 100% open and freely sexual, she would be in danger of pain, just as she was before in college when she was called a slut by her roommate (after being caught sleeping with a guy she met briefly at a party, and never knew his name.) I knew she would benefit from regaining her freedom of self-expression and wanted to help her (and us) feel a more passionate connection. She needed to finally let go of her limiting beliefs that sex was bad or humiliating, which was still in the dark recesses of her mind. I didn't want her to have to intoxicate herself or put her health in danger to allow herself total pleasure.

Although I thought I already knew her very well, I decided to really study her emotions, her patterns, and her likes/dislikes more intimately. I knew they gave me vital clues about what she held dear in her world that brought her pleasure, and what she avoided because of pain. I started to notice what made her smile, and what made her unhappy. I took notice of the colors she chose to wear, the songs she liked to listen to. I asked her about her mother and father again, looking to go deeper into understanding her parents' way of instilling values and religious dogma, which would affect her thoughts on what was morally right or wrong. I listened when she called me to complain about her day and what set her off and upset her. I got invested, totally invested, in *really* knowing her. I was investing in her, me, and us. The more I listened, really listened – the more I started to feel a psychic connection into knowing the in and outs of her thinking and being. I was connecting to her subconscious wiring, her soul vibration, and it made the relationship so much more exciting in every way. By showing her I really was attentive where no other lover was, and guiding her with some of the techniques shared with you in this book, our vibration naturally improved. She started to let go of her previous reluctance and decided to trust more. Our love making sessions were the best ever experienced together from that point forward. There's big payoff to listening and feeling your lover on a much deeper level.

9.5 Sex, Money, and Men

Sex and money are the two things that couples fight about most in a relationship. Sex is a keystone for any relationship, and when it is not being given freely without strings attached, problems can arise. When sex is used to gain something from a partner, there is an unequal exchange of power, which will either result in an unhealthy relationship or dramatic breakup. Either way, it may not be something you want to experience. For more information, see Chapter Ten, "When Pleasure Becomes Pain."

Long-term relationships (ultimately what most people want) are built on a mutual trust and regard for one another. This mutual trust must be solid. Material comfort in our world needs a constant supply of abundance thinking as family costs grow. This translates into money energy because money is how a person provides for him or herself, as well as their partner or their child(ren). When money becomes tight, or spending, gambling, or debt becomes an issue, it directly translates into how each person energetically relates to one another. It limits freely living the fruitfulness of life, and things which were easy and fun become stressful and difficult. Thoughts on abundance can become unbalanced between the two minds. Many women feel that they are unable to find a man because they make more money than their potential suitors, but men don't necessarily care that you make more money.

Men care that they can still provide something for you. If you are entirely self-sufficient, and don't need him for anything, money is just one reason you are going to fight. If a person is constantly insulted for his or her lower income, or is reminded that he or she holds the higher debt, that person will not feel like part of a team. Equally upsetting is entering a relationship with a specific spending pattern, student loan debt, or just a bad money management system. It can be embarrassing to show your partner the damage you've done to your financial self (which may be a form of hidden self-disrespect or negative thought process involving self-worth), and having that person attack you for your mistakes will make you feel even worse.

The best advice to give here is: There is a way to fix it. Money is, thankfully, something that you can get more of and create a better relationship with. Consider someone who is overweight or obese; they can change their relationship to food and reverse their crash course towards heart disease and diabetes. Couples can do this with money. It is important to note that money is like energy; what you put out sends something back in. The same goes for your relationship; make sure your money and your relationship are on the same energetic flow. Don't sweep the issue of money under the rug. Deal with it head on with love, understanding, and a solution oriented attitude with mutual respect for one another. Help each other grow without adding stress to the situation. Be problem solvers as a couple and build each other up.

9.6 A Note on Gratitude

Think about the last time someone expressed gratitude to you, either for a job well done, for helping them, or for just being yourself. It felt good, right? Now, consider the last time you thanked your partner for all they do for you, or for just being themselves. Can you think of such a time? Why do we, as a society, freely express thanks for things that bring us monetary value or success, but don't express thanks for the love and energy that we have surrounding us in the form of relationships? By addressing your partner, your children, your parents, your friends and telling them that you are so lucky to have their support, so grateful to have their love, you are addressing the energy that connects each of you together. When you address this energy, it becomes stronger, and you become healthier and more attached to the Earth, to the Source, and to each other.

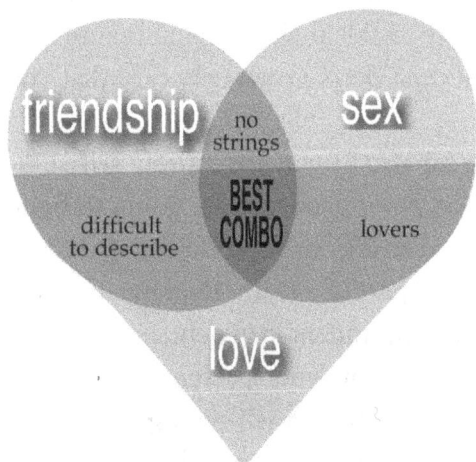

Take a moment next time you see your partner, no matter if you're a new couple or have been together for decades. Look them in the eye and tell them "Thank you," for whatever it may be. "Thanks for doing the dishes last night," or "Thanks for staying up with the baby so I could sleep," or "Thanks for the great sex, you're a rock star. Let's do it again and again and again until we drop from exhaustion." By vocalizing this, you show that you not only love them for doing something, but you noticed. Being noticed for your efforts is half the game when it comes to creating a lasting relationship. You want to know that the other person notices you and respects you. What better way to show that than with a little gratitude?

9.7 Relationships Are Not Easy

Of course, there are any number of things people can do to attract a mate, to hold onto a mate, and to make your love together the best that it can be. A relationship requires work, and a lot of it. Attracting, seducing, acquiring, and maintaining a mate is the largest investment of monetary, emotional, mental, and physical resources anyone will ever make in their lifetime. Home and car purchases pale in comparison. Relationships require a mutual exchange of energy and intention, and it cannot be one-sided. Sometimes, that energy that was once shared and given freely may recede, or one partner may begin requiring more energy than another. When this imbalance occurs, as it does naturally in any relationship, it is up to all parties involved to re-focus on the couple to regain that balance, or to improve upon whatever the issue is. Whether it is a change in the dynamic after a long period of dating, a new baby, or fundamental differences like what you want out of life, politics, or expectations of change, no relationship is ever 100% stable 100% of the time. This is important: Nobody is perfect, not even you. You have to expect some bumps in the road, and you have to be willing to weather the storm together. Relationships are meant to challenge you – they push your limits and grow you into a better stronger version of yourself. If you are not ready for this, you are not ready for a relationship and your energies and intentions are aligned as such. If you are ready for a new level of commitment, your intentions will be shared clearly within your energetic field. You attract most the level you are vibrating, so be honest with yourself.

Sometimes, however, even what we most want doesn't turn out as we always want it to. Sometimes, we give of ourselves too freely, or expect someone to give to us in return, only to be disappointed and find ourselves lonely yet again. In some cases, relationships extend well beyond their expiration date, and both (or all) parties suffer. When you love someone and operate on a plane of the highest vibrations, you experience love. When you neglect this important aspect of love, you experience pain.

Chapter 10:
When Pleasure Becomes Pain

"Everything in the world is about sex except sex.
Sex is about power."
~ Oscar Wilde

10.1 Spiritual, Emotional and Physical Protection

I whole-heartedly agree with Mr. Wilde, though to clarify, power defined in terms of "personal power." Those who know their personal power and are in charge of their power know that this is where your power lies – internally. Energy combined with love causes powerful healthy outcomes, whereas painful emotional forces mixed with lustful intentions results in lower energy and lower vibrations. When there is sex and lust without love or positive intentions, there is no health. The importance is not what you do with your bodies, as sex and physical relationships are natural. No, the importance is in the intention and the direction of your mind, your thoughts, and your energies. If you are merely looking to "get off," with absolutely no regard for the person you are being intimate with, you are not creating positive vibrations that result in divine sharing of energy, health, and happiness. Instead, you are becoming out of sync with your body and your soul, and lowering the vibrations, thus increasing odds of dis-ease. Kousouli® Method shows practitioners how to cultivate, develop, and use one's personal power for success and health. This is also the basis for my own life's fulfillment.

Note this: You may have various sexual experiences and numerous partners; this book is not designed to preach to you about the notches in your bedpost. What matters is the level of interaction you seek through these relationships and intimate union(s). If you are seeking fulfillment, a spiritual connection, and a mutual sense of ecstasy, you will be granted with vibrations of love, gifting you health. If you are seeking selfish needs, a visual or mental acquisition (the hottest girl, the most muscular man, the biggest body parts), or just want to "get off," your energies are not in tune, and you will be susceptible to dis-ease, including STIs and STDs, as well as risking unwanted pregnancy, damage to current or future relationships and more misery. Bacterial infections and viruses, after all, are made up of live frequencies which are attracted through human thought; they will target the individuals afflicted with the same vibratory level of negative frequency.

10.2 BDSM (Bondage, Domination, Sadism, and Masochism) and Demeaning Sexual Interactions

Today's society has become enshrined in a "derogatory sex" movement, whether due to the increasing access to niche category pornography, the loss of a mutually powerful and equal gender and sex roles, or something else entirely. From porn depicting a slight BDSM angle, to mainstream movies and books dubbed "incest porn," to the increased sales of sex toys, the dynamics in sex have changed more to physical pain, sadistic entertainment, and experimentation than focusing on the beauty of the act itself. It has become a sport and an endurance test, rather than a godly interaction.

While BDSM and "rough sex" are not innately bad or good in their own right, people who play with fire and don't know how to control it will get burned. A small percentage of people who are truly committed to this form of self-expression and exploration are using the highest vibrations of energy to engage with others, and are not at risk for dis-ease or repercussions from their actions. Rather, it is when you use these sexual styles as a front for submerged anger, hatred or lust embodied in the savage heart that leads to negative karma and universal whiplash. These negative emotions or traumas, which you bring to sex and use to channel your sexual energy, become infused into the flesh, bringing sickness to those inflicted.

Thanks to proliferate pornography, it is also commonplace for partners to "talk dirty" to one another instead of "talking lovingly." However, there is a line between a little naughty talk and downright demeaning language. If your partner enjoys the verbal tête-a-tête, he or she will let you know, but make sure that you are being respectful and recognizing the divine in them rather than just focusing on their flesh. To each their own, and no judgment is being passed on your sexual style. It is just better to use these sexual activities as an expression of your true highest divine nature, a way to improve the connection between you and your lover, and to experience all that your bodies have to give.

10.3 Troubleshooting for Intentional Sex

As mentioned in previous chapters, the importance of safe sex cannot be underestimated. While "the heat of the moment" can take away some logical functioning, it is important to always enter a sexual relationship or encounter with the right intentions. Without intention or even a conscious understanding of the repercussions of your actions, you may experience a multitude of painful consequences down the road. You may think pulling out a condom kills the mood or shows a lack of trust in your partner. However, it is merely one way to set an intention, to show the Universe that you understand the ramifications of the act you are about to engage in if your thought intention is less than properly aligned. If you would like to enter into a sexual relationship with the highest of intentions for enjoying your lover without risking pregnancy or STI/STDs, here are a few tips:

- ✓ Use a condom that fits your penis well. Magnum condoms are known to help larger men and lowers the rate of a broken condom from friction. (Use polyurethane condoms to prevent a painful reaction if you are latex sensitive)
- ✓ Use a "cock ring" to maintain your erection if condoms are not allowing enough sensation to maintain the erection.
- ✓ Use hypoallergenic lubricant to create a barrier between yourself and the condom to increase sensation and prevent pulling/chafing
- ✓ Make sure the condom does not break, inspect it frequently and replace immediately if it does.
- ✓ Use natural spermicides that do not contain Nonoxynol-9. Nonoxynol-9 (N-9), a common over the counter spermicide, has been known to cause irritation, burning, itching, urinary tract infections, yeast infections, bacterial vaginitis, toxic shock syndrome, and genital lesions with regular use.

Performance Anxiety

Being too much in your head can definitely cause you to ruin the moment and not let you get revved up correctly. When anxious about your involvement in sex, this can set off the "fight or flight" response and surges stress hormones norepinephrine and epinephrine in preparation for fighting off a danger. Since no threat is present, this is confusing and blocks intimacy. Also, this constricts blood flow to the penis, causing loss of erection. Loss of an erection is very normal, and common, among men of any age. For women, this flood of hormones shuts down the ability for the nerves to properly stimulate the brain, leading to an inability to lubricate or reach orgasm. There are a number of reasons this can happen:

- ✓ Fear that you won't last long (premature ejaculation), perform well in bed or satisfy your partner sexually
- ✓ Fighting or arguing in a relationship
- ✓ Concern about how you look nude, especially if overweight, or concerned about penis or breast size

✓ Not putting total focus on the present moment's intimacy

10.4 Pregnancy as a Result of Sex Without Intention

When the male ejaculates in a mechanical unfulfilled way, the creation is disassociated from spiritual connection, his energy dwindles, excited only by more perverse images of sexual stimulation and actions such as forced, non-consensual sex (rape) and other personal frustration in life such as inner loneliness and disassociation from healthy relationships. Likewise the female substitutes her ability to radiate the love she seeks to share with a male by connecting to materialism and finding stimulation in lifeless ob-

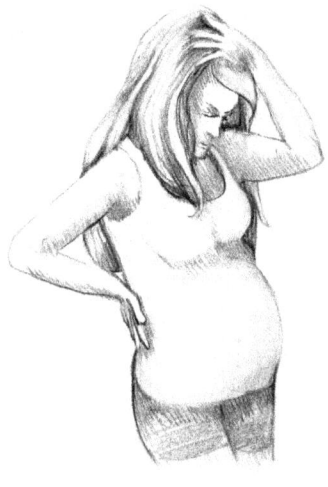

jects, commercial consumption (frivolous money spending), lusting after the latest purse or name brand which needs constant replenishment. She is enslaved by her low level desires, temptations, and the latest fads. Adorned by an external facade of beautiful furs, perfumes, makeup, and the modern clutch, she seeks to attract a male that will deeply appreciate her. This only sends the wrong signal out to the Universe, which reflects her own internal pain, thus attracting to her once again the same previous type of mate, though this will be the "correct" one that matches her low frequency at that time for her. She will still yearn for improved happiness, only to repeat her lesson, until she learns from it and changes her ways to receive a higher-level mate. She must raise her own vibratory frequency by living at a new level of self-respect and personal value, in order to attract her higher equal.

Man impregnates the female, though his masculine responsibility is to give her love and protection from emotional harm to allow the child peaceful entry and growth into this world. The energy signaled into the womb through creation is not to be taken lightly. Spiritual sources claim the soul of the child entering the new vessel greatly depends on the level of thought energy and love enacted by the union. Also, the act of sex makes no man or woman worthy of the creation made, it is only an intention and agreement to create with each and bring another energy being into the world. Together they are a whole in their role as divine male and female union. A woman who receives the sperm energy has the responsibility to bring the child into a world the child can thrive in. Man and woman must equally give of themselves, nurture and cherish each other, for they are ambassadors to the new soul incarnated into this realm.

Effects of Co-Creation Without Intention

How many times have you heard that a couple is "staying together for the kids"? While this is becoming less common with younger generations, many people still believe that a married family is much healthier than a divorced one. The negativity within a home that is not built on love and a higher vibration of positive energy will actually end up affecting a child or children more than having parents living in separate homes. If living together is draining your energy, you have less to give your child. The lack of loving energy within your family dynamic can result in many problems, from behavioral issues to depression to rebellion in children. When parents decide that separating or divorcing is the best scenario, they are able to rebuild their auric fields on their own, providing a better environment of energy for their children than before.

When a child is unintentionally created via low vibrational union, there are karmic repercussions for the parents as well as the child. Consider the lack of high frequency intention and vibrations of love; a child created in a womb that is not engaged in an act of love will not grow in love. While hopefully the child is still wanted, the energies are not present enough to give the child a quality of life that it deserves. The child, already experiencing a dearth of high-energy vibrations, will then be raised in a family unit where love is not present, where spiritual connections are not made. If two people make a child without ever intending to love each other, or care for one another on a higher plane, they are not providing a healthy co-created environment for the child. Because of this, the child was not only born into negative karma, but will be raised in it as well. The child will not learn how to engage with others on a higher vibration, and will only know the dysfunction into which he or she was born.

It is much more desirable to enter a sexual relationship with the intention of play and exploration, with open energies and open hearts. When you hide your true nature, or use sex for unhealthy release, you open yourself up to emotional, mental, physical, and spiritual damage. If you and your partner are open to the possibility of procreation, make that intention known between yourselves and the Universe. Never hide an intention to get pregnant from your partner(s), as that is putting out negative karma. Sex and life go hand in hand, but that doesn't mean you get to sacrifice a great relationship and spiritual connection.

Identity within the Family

In the case of a family where energies are co-mingled in close quarters, family quarrels can be quite frequent when energies of co-creators clash. This is especially true when children growing up are trying to find themselves while maintaining their space, aura, and identity. They have quite a task as they fight off the deceptive mind manipulation of mass marketing through billboards, television, and radio telling them how they should think and act to be happy. It is further challenging to do this when the school system is flawed and home life is overly saturated with the desires and demands of an overbearing parent; one who often lives their life vicariously through their child. For example, an overpowering mother can overtake a growing boy's identity and handicap them later in life when he is an adult by not letting him complete his creation of identity, missing personal energy, which his mother had taken and shaped for years. The mama's boy grows up to be a man with socially awkward tendencies and co-dependency issues. He will subconsciously be trying to find his missing energy, or identity he had as a child by attracting a woman who has similar qualities as his mother. The same is true of women in abusive relationships where an overbearing father disciplined with force or tough love. These women feel in their identity that to be complete or happy in their world, they must be with a male who is a protector through violence, and this is what love is to them. They end up attracting someone like their father, or worse yet, mimic the actions of their father towards their children. The images, thoughts, and ideas in our auric field can multiply and copy to others like a mutated virus through family generations.

The key to loving relationships is the ability to unconditionally love another to the point you allow them to be who they are, and understand they are growing at their own pace within their space. As long as growth is happening with everyone at the same time in a positive manner, the unions can be strong. If one decides to exert pressure through trying to change another, they will most surely be disappointed when the relationship explodes with emotional charge. This is always the case, as one who doesn't grow or feels stuck, repressed, or taken advantage of with pent up anger, resentment, guilt, etc. is sure to make fireworks occur in order to be heard.

Auric spaces in children

A parent-child relationship develops as children without their own complete understanding of the world absorb the energies in the parental auras. The sum of how we act as adults can be attributed to this time in our infancy and childhood, where our spiritual and physical DNA intertwine to develop those characteristics, thoughts, prejudices, quirks, habits, and solutions to the challenges we experience in our worlds. It is this, our interrelationship with

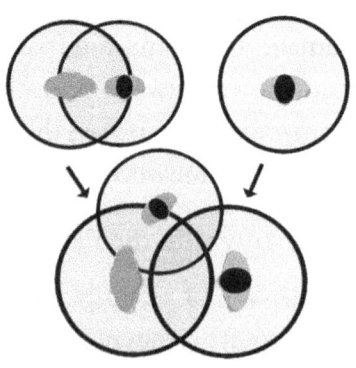

family members, friends, teachers, strangers, or lovers who we allow into our auric space, to give us the illusions we obtain. When parents have unhealthy personal auric fields, or a very unhealthy combination of auric fields between the two, the child is part of that intertwined combination of auras and energy, and those vibrations affect the child's mental, physical, and spiritual development.

10.5 When the Energies Aren't in Sync

Unfortunately, there are situations that prevent a positive sexual experience for a large number of people. Individuals who have had traumatic experiences in the past, ranging from child abuse, rape, to a really bad breakup and anything in between. All of these things shut down our ability to generate positive energy, and therefore we are unable to share that energy with others. It can be a very unhappy situation, and there are many people who never overcome their pasts. What this leads to, sexually, is an inhibited body and mind that are unable to express themselves. In order to get some insight on how to overcome this, see Chapter 11; Sexual Healing through the Kousouli® Method.

There are also other influences on your libido and sex life that don't necessarily involve your past, but involve where you are now. This can mean any conditions that you have, any medications you are taking, or any large life events or stressors present in your life. Medication and medical conditions affect sexual drive more than most people understand. Birth control pills and the Depo-Provera shot have been found to be huge sex drive killers, which is definitely ironic. Even heartburn medications and some antibiotics can kill libido, along with pain meds and illicit drugs like marijuana and opiates. It's important that you know what you're on, and ask your doctor or pharmacist if there are any side effects that you need to be concerned about. If you get diagnosed with a condition, make sure you do your research and understand it fully. Many conditions affect libido for a number of reasons, whether because of the pain you experience or the change in chemicals in the body. Diabetes, depression, alcoholism, fibromyalgia, schizophrenia, Parkinson's disease and even hypertension can lower your sex drive due to the changes within the body. In reality, any disease can decrease your sex drive because your entire body is out of sync and needs major healing. If you notice that you're not feeling well, that your sex drive has been decreased or is almost zero, you should consider medications and disorders as a possible source. You should also see a doctor if you feel the medications you're on are preventing you from leading your life.

10.6 Staying Together When You Shouldn't

There are many reasons a couple stays together, whether it is children, security, sex, or any other ideal situation. However, when the base of that relationship is not built on love and a great connection, those other attachments begin to become toxic. Many women feel that, if they've been with a partner for a while, they've invested too much and have "passed their prime" and are afraid they won't be able to find another partner. Men often stay with or marry a woman because she takes care of him or his children. Even more often, couples stay together because they have amazing sex, but can't stand each other outside of the bedroom. People are also guilty of trying to change one another. "Just give him/her time; he/she will come around." Not only is this not true, but it creates a larger pull of energy, which will either result in a miserable relationship, or one that ends in flames. What happens when you stay with someone for any of these reasons? Your auric field begins to wane, and the relationship becomes unhealthy - creating dis-ease.

10.7 Nagging is Never OK

Society often portrays women as insecure, nagging wives who have little respect for their husbands and even less patience for their manly ineptitudes. While this is a total myth in some cases (not all women are like that), it is a socially accepted way of interacting with a mate for many women. Whatever your relationship looks like, whether male/female, male/male, female/female, or whichever combination you find yourself, nagging is never OK. When you harass your partner over things like laundry or the trash, their debt or spending habits, or anything they do that upsets you, you're sucking the life out of your relationship. Literally, your auric field is pulsating so strongly that you're draining their energy, and you're also going to wear yourself down because you cannot consume that much energy for an extended period of time. The relationship will either end up with you (the instigator) becoming incredibly miserable and taking it out on the other person enough to where you leave, or they leave. Nagging doesn't get you anywhere, it only makes the other person shut down. Stop focusing on every little thing your partner does or does not do. Instead, think about what matters most (socks outside the laundry basket do not warrant a full-scale meltdown), and focus on how you ask for things. After all, you can catch more flies with honey than with vinegar.

Tell your partner, in relatable, calm terms that you would really like something to be done and why it would be helpful. Letting them know that it's important to you will make them more likely to notice and get it done. After that, let him or her be! Don't keep bringing it up, and don't "check their work" to see if they did what you asked. Let them do it in their own way in their own time. Realistically, you should also lower your expectations. If you are a clean freak and your partner is not, you can't anticipate a shiny clean home whenever you walk in the door. Aim for simple things, like dishes or laundry getting done. You love your partner for everything they bring to the table, so don't leverage your love against them when they don't do exactly what you want. Don't put conditional strings on love.

10.8 Why Do People Cheat?

One of those most important things couples need to understand is that sex in a committed relationship is entirely different from sex in a new relationship or sex with a new partner. Long-term relationships are well-known for their sexual dry spells, their lowered libidos, and your physical relationship becomes relegated to snuggling on the couch while you watch rented movies. Now, this is not entirely true of every couple, but given enough time, sex naturally gets placed on the back burner. Life with your partner is full of other things, like social events, children, stressful jobs, family issues, money; the list is literally endless. When you're in the trenches with someone going through all of this together, sex doesn't seem all that sexy. Stretch back to what you learned in the Neurology of Sex chapter, where oxytocin, dopamine, and serotonin levels begin to level out as a couple grows together over an extended period of time. Despite all this, and the growing intimacy you feel knowing your partner's mind and spirit just as well as you know their body, both partners *need* sex. Also, to keep your relationship fresh remember what you did to attract your partner and revisit those actions, feelings, thoughts, and emotions to rekindle those sparks.

Of course, men are known as the ones who need the most sex. For men, sex is a tension reliever, a way to share their emotions without talking, and a way to show their commitment to their partner. As mentioned in the chapter on sexual neurology, men are just wired to need more sex. Evolutionarily speaking, men are designed to "spread their seed, and sow their oats," or whichever idiom you prefer to use. When sex begins to slow in a committed relationship, men may be entirely accepting of it and even be unaware that their body is craving sex at the same level it once was. This is where pornography, masturbation, and even cheating can become an unfortunate issue in a relationship. Men, and especially women, need to both understand that without that physical release and that intimate connection, the body will look for a release in whichever form it can find it. Hormones mixed with ingrained primal animal urges are a powerful force. If a partner cheats, there is always going to be hurt feelings, broken hearts, and lost trust.

What matters most is the understanding that a committed relationship without sex is just as unhealthy as a great sex life without some level of commitment. Sometimes, the relationship may be broken beyond repair and that's ok. But it's also ok to work through the problems, and work towards preventing the same problem from happening again. Society may say that cheating is never ok, and that may be true for you or your partner. Sometimes, thinking something is wrong doesn't mean that it always is inexcusable. People make mistakes, and it may feel like you need to end the relationship on "moral principles," but consider how you feel, and consider what could be done to make the relationship heal. Remember that society can tell you one thing, but as a team, you get to make the rules and final decisions.

10.9 Breakups Can Be Healthy

You know that feeling you get when you leave a stressful situation and get to just breathe? That's how great a breakup can feel after a bad relationship. Your energy has been depleted to the max, your auric field was either diminished or expanded based on your role in the relationship, and you were generally "out of whack." Breaking up can be ugly, and the time before you break up can be nerve-wracking. Most people do not seek to harm their partner during a breakup, so establishing how best to do it can be miserable. However, once it's out there, once you step away, your body, your mind, and your spirit can feel the release that has been holding you back. Don't view breakups as a bad thing; instead, view them as a way to expand yourself and graduate into a better and more well-rounded you that is ready for new adventures with someone who will match your updated level of self-development. It's always a smart move to stay single while you reflect on the "self" for at least four to six months after a breakup, so you may integrate your growth period. This way, you can truly harness the lessons and drop prior bad habits. You will surely vibrate at a higher level and attract a better suited lover.

Chapter 11:
Sexual Healing (Through the Kousouli® Method)

"Your perspective on life comes from the cage you were held captive in."
~ Shannon L. Alder

11.1 Healing Sexual Traumas with the Kousouli® Method

Throughout my many years of working with troubled souls, I have been blessed to witness the intimate connection of the spine, innate energy, and healing of the heart through unconditional forgiveness. The nature of healing sexual trauma starts with the understanding of one's energy and the event(s) that lead up to and come after the trauma. From this, you can begin to understand them as events to grow from. This is easier said than done, as the ego is fragile and very hurt; it cannot see the traumatic event from the higher mind's perspective. Sexual healing - although focused on the lower two chakras, primarily root and sacral (See the Kousouli® Method Master Chart at the end of this chapter) - also requires major healing of the heart chakra. Although this is a subject far deeper than I can address here in this book and dealt with deeply in the seminar discussions, we will discuss briefly how emotions can lodge into the body and create chaos.

11.2 Using the Kousouli® Method to Heal Your Heart

As a hypnotherapist, it's important for me to mention that the subconscious programming that dictates how we relate to unconditional love and pain (lack or the total void of unconditional love) starts in our youth. Healing the heart requires a multidimensional layering of growth, not a linear one-time event. There are many levels, which could be contributing to one's aching heart, that are unseen as the traumatic event(s) take place. For instance, a breakup can bring on feelings of rejection or past memories of failed attempts at courtship in youth, which can lead to feelings of personal unworthiness. This further creates and supports experiences that verify loss, which ultimately ends in heartache and finally physical dis-ease, such as angina or heart attack. Heartbreak is real! However, it can also bring renewed awareness to self, family, life, and passion to become a better person. Many who have beaten major illness attest that they have grown from their painfully traumatic experience and looking back, they now can see how their growth was blessed through it all.

We are continuously being subject to thought form as subliminal impressions, which we translate into our reality. The great thing is that once we use all the aspects of the Kousouli® Method to stop the energy leaks and bring our natural power back into focus, we do not have to be subject to the pain any longer, as our perception once again revitalizes us into wellbeing. By bringing back our power through realigning our chakras, energy bodies, emotions, thoughts, mind and actions with our physical body (spinal alignment), we can overcome pretty much anything that ails us. The mind has everything to do with adding and removing the trauma (which exists at its own frequency or vibration), which depends on deactivating and neutralizing the programming. When the act of sex itself is entangled with negative intent, it can become a portal for unwanted lower vibratory energy forms and frequencies sometimes termed "negative entities", to enter from other dimensions or realms (spiritually speaking).

These entities usually start small, adding to the trauma inflicted in a repetitive cycle, by manipulating its power through thought (looping). When you worry, become anxious, or discuss the trauma with emotion, you give more thought energy to that particular trauma. In turn, without knowing it, you add to the entity's power over you (feeding the monster), you then re-identify yourself as that problem or pain (i.e. continuously saying or proclaiming in mind or in word, "I am a diabetic," "I have cancer," or "I am a rape victim") which then brings this negative thinking into physical manifestation and leads to more dis-ease (thought energy becomes physical matter). For more on entities and the way they may take over your mind and body, please refer to my previous book: *BE A MASTER® OF PSYCHIC ENERGY*.

The Antenna between the Physical and the Spiritual

Right now, you are floating through space on a large piece of rock. Right now, you are being bombarded with radio waves. Right now, microbial organisms and bacteria are crawling all over and inside of you. Right now, the opposite side of the Earth is probably sleeping while you are awake. These are realities outside your immediate perception. Until you focus on them and put them into perspective, you don't acknowledge their presence or effect on your life.

Similarly, you are most likely unaware of the power your spinal system holds (in conjunction with your mind and innate), or the fact that this is the link between your physical world and your unseen spiritual world. Your spine is a highly sophisticated broadcasting station and it is always on the job, even if your present perception is unaware of its workings. You constantly absorb or discharge frequencies that you hold as beliefs. Over time, these frequencies become your core beliefs. These core beliefs become your actions. These actions become your character. Your character then becomes your personality, which defines who you are perceived as - to yourself and others.

In the practice and development of The Kousouli® Method, a clear understanding of the relationship that exists between the physical and the non-physical has been documented. The importance of the spiritual aspect of the human body must be taken into consideration when a healer is seeking answers to a patient's physical problem. The attack on the physical body may stem from an emotional complaint, or a problem with the emotional guiding system itself. However, it is incredibly rare that an illness is not a result of a person's programming; how they think or react to stress due to previous beliefs, experiences in their youth, or previous incarnations. Mental nature is not a physical thing we can touch or perceive in a fourth dimensional reality, and is believed to exist in the fifth dimensional space which is considered a divine aspect of the human being. Thus the answers to physical ailments can be attributed to any realm outside the physical. Ultimately, all surfaces of our perceived reality connect to the energies of which we are composed of on higher dimensional planes. It would be incredibly helpful to understand the work that goes on behind the scenes of the nervous system. The Kousouli® Method works through understanding and applying these energies to provide the most benefit to my clients and you, the reader.

How Do Emotions Affect Your Health?

Our lower frequency emotions of fear, anger, and grief, can all have a long lasting negative effect on our well-being. We occasionally feel sabotaged by negative emotions even long after its original occurrence. When it stays with us for a long time it gets encrypted into our subconscious system, so much so that it jumps into action when we feel a certain way, or undergo a certain stress that triggers us (e.g. relationship breakups, death of a loved one, boss yells at us, etc.).

To further explain, imagine a female walking alone to her car near a dark alley at night. All of a sudden she is attacked and robbed at gunpoint by a large male. She will experience fear for her safety at first; then anger that she was robbed, possibly resentment that she could not do anything about the incident, and then finally revenge as she wishes justice could be served. Her nervous system received strong programming through that incident and responded the way it knew how - according to her previous experiences of danger to keep safe. Now armed with this new and reinforced "programming" her nervous system files it away until it needs to react again to a similar stimulus. However, every time she goes past an alley whether alone or with others now, in bright daylight or at night, she will get a revival of the stored feelings she had from her prior alley encounter, even if there is no attacker or threat present.

There is also a lot of jealousy and insecurity that everyone faces within a relationship, especially at the start. Women and men are jealous of their partner's previous (or current) paramours, people feel too fat or not pretty enough to deserve their mate, and so on. These emotions, while entirely natural, do not serve a higher interaction. In fact, they decrease feel-good hormones that are found in new lovebirds, and can result in a much grander explosion when a couple breaks up. On an energy level, it depletes a person to a state where they have nothing to give or receive from their partner, who is willing and able to share and give their positive energy freely. Jealousy and insecurity should not be acted on, but rather positively channelled.

These responses sometimes serve us by keeping us alert, aware of concerns with your partner, or keep us away from danger and heartbreak. However, if it is negatively affecting us, the loop should be neutralized or "deleted" to allow for newer more useful programming. In the robbery incident, the negativity loop is destructively harbouring the feelings in her nervous system's programming and she'll fail to realize why she is having future relationship difficulties 1) trusting unfamiliar males around her 2) feeling safe in the dark or 3) being physically intimate with a male lover. Without intervention, the negatively programmed loop will be reinforced into the subconscious by any similar trigger with the original incident, and this is forced deeper the longer it goes unresolved. This charged negative energy affects chakra stability and leaking of vital energy occurs over the areas that were weak at the time the incident occurred.

If we happen to be in a destabilized state when heightened states of emotional distress happen due to chemical stress, physical trauma, poor nourishment, or other low frequency emotions, they may lodge deep and take much longer to resolve (or never resolve). Then, years later, we encounter a comparable issue, state, or condition, and the deep-rooted previous emotive reaction kicks in and tries to save the day from any proposed danger or threat. The past event and the present-day situation is connected intimately, without your conscious knowledge. Remember that the emotional reality you hold as 'truth' can radically affect your health.

Parts of our body can hold or express emotional energy too. This is the reason for sweaty palms or cold body extremities before a presentation or an exam. Many emotions plague the bodies of chronic worriers, and these people can end up with stomach ulcers!

I have developed a technique named Kousouli Neural Emotive Reconditioning or KNER® for short, which is part of a larger healing process; the Kousouli® Method 4R Intervention System. My unique technique utilizes visual imagery, hypnosis, deep diaphragmatic breathing, colour therapy, spinal adjustments, and positive verbal declarations. The therapy identifies and neutralizes negatively stimulated emotional belief or vibratory frequency running wild in the subconscious, chakras, and body organs. It closes energy leaks that are producing unpleasant results in the patient's life so that the loop can be reconditioned positively.

KNER® therapy helps conclude if the present physical and energy bodies are stressed with certain restrictive beliefs associated with current unsettled issues, or previously experienced events. The practitioner helps the patient form an emotional picture of the original initiating event for the negative situation by flashback via hypnosis. The body of the patient assumes a similar emotional state very similar to the way it reacted during the event or previous trauma, and the patient is asked to contact the specific body area or chakra storing the emotion, which would have been identified through the practitioner's prior analysis. As the patient inhales or exhales, the practitioner stimulates the associated energy points with their hands or spinal tool while simultaneously instructing the patient with specific imagery cues and verbal declarations.

When applied effectively, the patient's nervous system releases the lingering stress entity through the spine and energy body. It is not unusual to sometimes find the patient go into an extreme dumping of repressed feelings during the session expressed as heavy tearing, heat, rage or laughter. Success varies per individual patient lifestyle variables; however it's completely safe, quick, and the process utilizes simple muscle testing. Patients often report strong emotional discharge that brings deep peace after the procedure. They report feeling as if a burden (described as a sack of bricks) has been lifted from them. No part of the Kousouli® Method uses psychiatric evaluation and is a totally drug free therapy. KNER® is in the 4th part, Reset, of the Kousouli® Method 4R Intervention System.

You are in Charge of YOU

People forget their power of free will and their ability to choose. This is most evident in those who are in relationships and where children are involved. They often feel trapped or feel that there's no way out because of how they define commitment. Their happiness is sacrificed for others constantly. People stay in abusive relationships or situations and say "I can't get divorced," "I can't leave him/her, I'll have to give her/him 50%," "I can't because of the kids," and so on. These are all excuses that keep them enslaved to their insecurities within that relationship. People choose to make their life miserable by not enacting the positive aspects of the law of free will. They choose not to choose, and in return they become slaves to others who are using the law of free will. Those who live according to their God-given free will are happy, cheerful, clear, and create colorful worlds others envy. All choices have consequences, some more and others less. All consequences also lead to more choices. It never ends, growth always occurs; even if the seemingly wrong choice is chosen at that time. Relationships are a way to massive growth and personal challenge. We help each other reflect aspects of ourselves, which may need growth. We should be in appreciation of all relationships, and to all people we've shared our space intimately with. When we look back with our new perspective on where we were and how far we've come in life, we can see just how we have been transformed into a better version of ourselves. I am eternally blessed and grateful to be able to help people see the brighter sides of life by reflecting back to them a new aspect of their reality which is always there, but they have been ignoring. I do this successfully through my unique health intervention system.

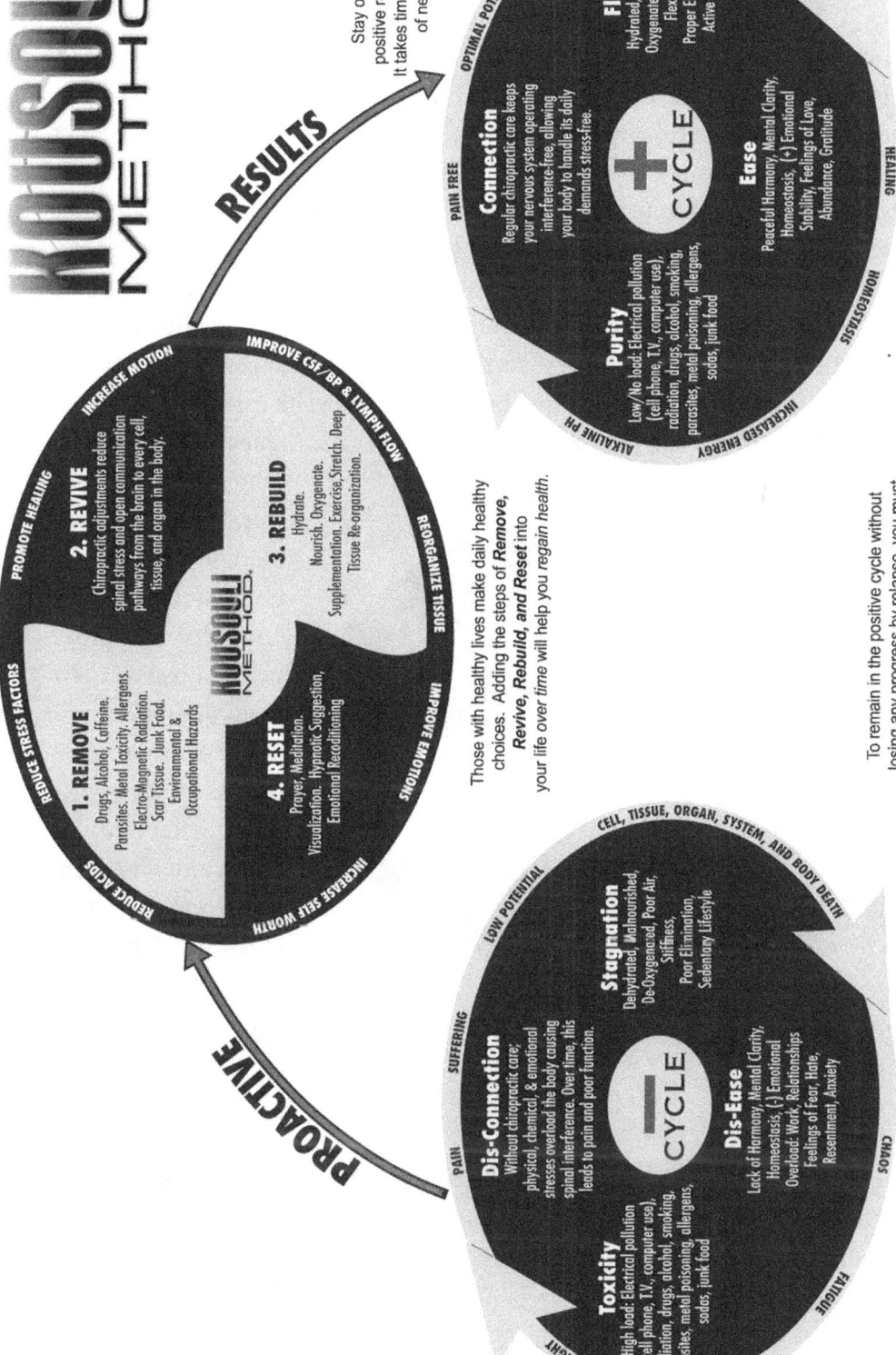

11.3 The Kousouli® Method 4R Intervention System

The 4R Kousouli® Method of Health combines different aspects of chiropractic care, clinical research, energy healing, clairvoyant meditation, and hypnosis. The main goal of the Kousouli® Method is to treat the patient by addressing vital energy loss in 4 main arenas (spiritual, mental, emotional, and physical) utilizing the "antenna" called the nervous system. The nervous system allows us to interact with our internal and external environments and is the master communicator of our health. The Kousouli® Method 4R Intervention System gives patients a daily checklist and simple structure for making sure they are on point to "Rejuvenate the Body, Empower the Mind and Free the Soul."

The diagram has three main circles; two of them are cycle states of health. The first cycle represents the state people are in when they feel ill. Because of accumulated poor lifestyle habits and neglect over time, they feel sick and begin to seek a health care provider to heal the physical body. The first cycle (left side) reflects the negative aspects of health. The center circle represents the **Kousouli® Method 4R Intervention System.** When one becomes proactive and begins utilizing the Kousouli® Method, they complete the 4 steps of **Remove, Revive, Rebuild, and Reset.** This is where change starts, and if maintained during a set care plan over time, favorable results will start to appear. The third circle (right) reflects the positive benefits of health after incorporating the Kousouli® Method. If maintained, the patient stays in this positive cycle until neglect over time pulls the process back to the negative cycle. **The success of the method is due to the focus of the 4R continuous processes:**

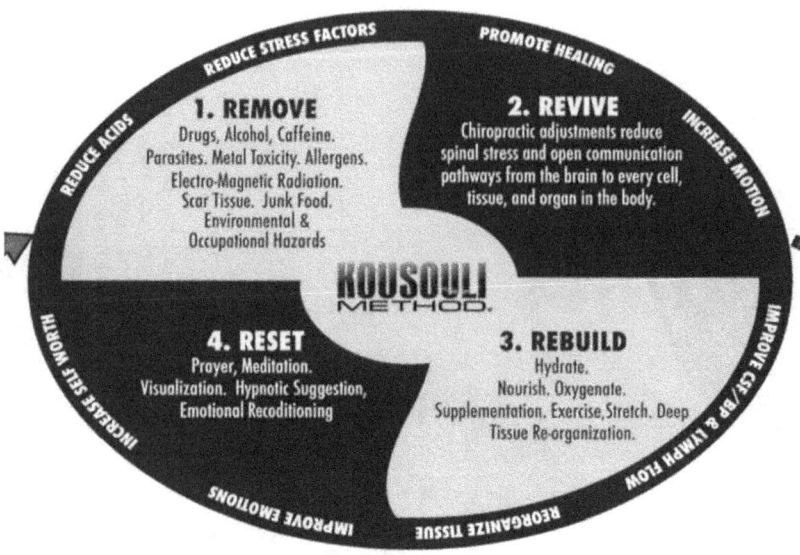

Those with healthy lives make daily healthy choices. Adding the steps of **Remove, Revive, Rebuild, and Reset** into your life *over time* will help you *regain health*.

1. **Remove the toxins.** Cautiously limit or remove drug use, alcohol consumption, caffeine, sodas, smoking, intestinal worms & parasites, heavy metal toxicity, allergens, electro-magnetic radiation, old scar tissue build-up, junk food and fast food, environmental and occupational ergonomic hazards.

2. **Revive the nervous system utilizing correct chiropractic care.** Chiropractic adjustments reduce spinal stress and open vital communication pathways from the brain to every cell, tissue and organ in the body.

3. **Rebuild the body through whole food nutrition and exercise.** Proper hydration, nourishment, oxygenation, supplementation, exercise, stretching, and deep tissue re-organization of spinal muscle attachments.

4. **Reset your thoughts and programming.** Prayer, meditation, visualization, hypnotic suggestion, Kousouli Neural Emotive Reconditioning (KNER®) and proper mind and body rest will ensure that the whole process is perpetuated within yourself and you continue to reap the benefits for the rest of your life.

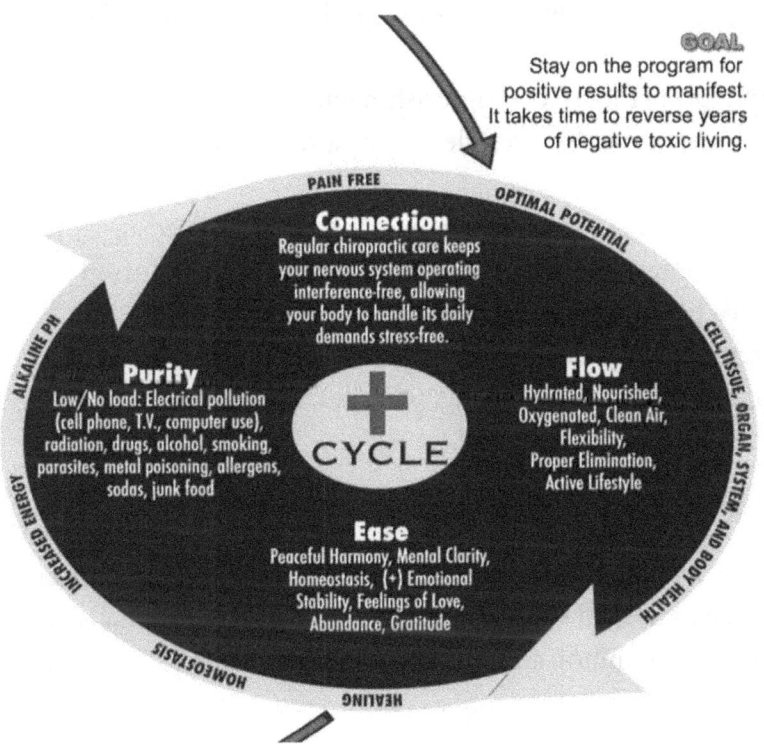

Going through the Kousouli® Method 4R Intervention System will ensure you get the 5th 'R' too; Recovery! Individuals who experience health success make daily healthy choices; benefit from beautiful posture, flexibility, strength, unlimited energy, and lead youthful and healthy lives. Don't delude yourself into thinking that the latest fad diet or work out will help you get healthy. To stay in a positive cycle of health, without relapse, you have to decide that your health is a vital aspect of your daily life. This is not just for a week for a few days; this is a lifestyle change. The Kousouli® Method 4R Intervention System now makes it much easier to keep yourself on track and move toward your health goals. When you remove the toxins and improve the poor status of your body and energy, you can return your health to homeostasis. This also means you can focus your energy and attention on exploring higher states of awareness by yourself or with your partner.

Neglecting to complete these 4 steps of Remove, Revive, Rebuild, and Reset will cause you to fall back into the negative cycle. Choose to be healthy by paying the price of health. The price is dedication and commitment to a new paradigm that maintains your health priorities. Adding the steps of Remove, Revive, Rebuild, and Reset into your life consistently will help you regain and maintain your healthy new perspective. Listed below are the attributes that will help you maintain this positive cycle. There are also lifestyle choices or events that will push you towards the negative cycle provided as well.

Staying in the Positive Cycle

- **Connection:** Regular chiropractic care keeps your nervous system operating in an interference-free fashion, allowing your body to handle its daily demands in a stress-free manner.
- **Flow:** Incorporating proper hydration, nourishment, oxygen, clean air, flexibility, proper elimination and an active lifestyle will ensure a smooth flow of energy within your body.
- **Ease:** Having peaceful purpose, harmony, mental clarity, homeostasis, positive emotional stability, feelings of love, abundance and gratitude for yourself and others will keep you in a positive frame of mind.
- **Purity:** Avoid or remove electrical pollution (cellular phone, televisions, and computers), radiation, drugs, alcohol, smoking, parasites, metal poisoning, allergens, sodas, caffeine overload, junk or fast food.

Reverting Back to the Negative Cycle through Neglect

(i) **Dis-connection:** Irregular, discontinuous or complete lack of chiropractic care; physical, chemical, and emotional stresses all compound spinal overload. Over time, this miscommunication of brain to body leads to pain and poor function.

(ii) **Stagnation:** Staying in a dehydrated condition, receiving improper nutrition, no or low supplementation, poor air or water quality, lymph flow backup, poor elimination, and a sedentary lifestyle are cardinal signs for bringing your health down.

(iii) **Dis-Ease:** Lack of harmony, mental clarity, negative emotional stresses, work or relationship stress overload, feelings of fear, hate, resentment and anxiety all will contribute to disease conditions.

(iv) **Toxicity:** High load of electro-magnetic pollution, radiation, drugs, alcohol, smoking, parasites, heavy metal poisoning, allergens, sodas, and junk food will result in an overall imbalance and a downslide of your health condition.

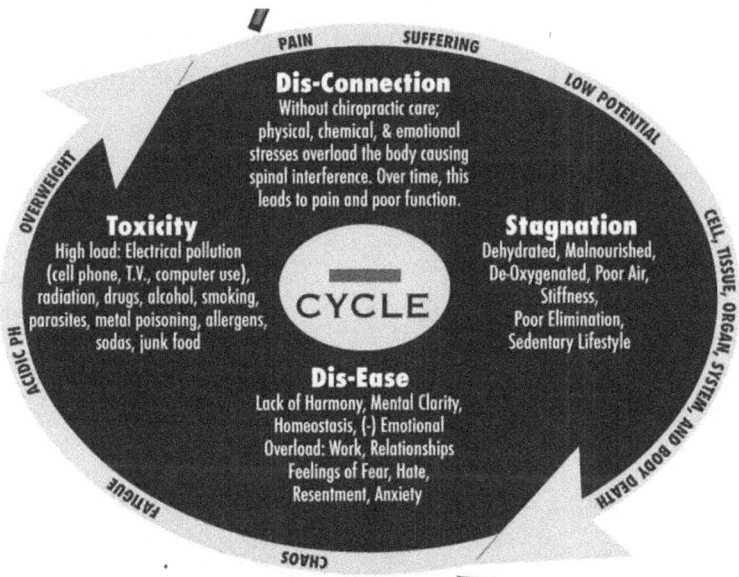

It becomes apparent from the above points that most of your health is a matter of lifestyle choice; being able to regulate your temptations and not allowing yourself to reach a lazier lower vibration path is crucial. Sometimes taking the seemingly tougher route ultimately proves to be wiser, healthier, and perhaps easier than expected. The very same conditions, when done properly, induce and maintain the positive cycle, and a slight imbalance in any aspect can tilt the whole balance towards the negative energy cycle. Consistency is key in maintaining a healthy condition, and the more consistent you are with your good habits and lifestyle choices, the better you will serve your body and spirit. This system is a great guide providing you the ability to keep yourself in check by referring to it often. Ensure you are accommodating all 4 aspects adequately and are maintaining your homeostatic balance. This model will also help remind you if you've been skipping or neglecting yourself; like smoking, eating junk food, forgetting to work out, allowing yourself to become dehydrated, or missing your last chiropractic appointment. All of these behaviors can lead to your regression into the negative cycle.

The Kousouli® Method 4R Intervention System is continuously being developed through clinical application and research. When correctly applied, it has shown successful symptom reduction or elimination of headaches, dizziness, low energy, carpel tunnel, whiplash pains, muscle spasms, joint pains, neck pain, back pain, allergies, depression, hormonal imbalances, fibromyalgia, numbness, limb tingling, IBS, asthma, acid reflux/GERD, arthritis, insomnia and toxicity - just to name a few. The Kousouli® Method through KNER® also takes into account the spiritual, mental, and emotional aspects of health, which usually manifest into the physical plane as pain and dis-ease. By accessing specific energy points and preventing any leaks, the individual can focus their energies into their healing with quicker results.

This system's powerful technique of replenishing health naturally goes beyond the surface scope of this book and is taught privately to interested practitioners at live seminar events. Details can be found at www.DrKousouli.com or www.KousouliMethod.com.

Spiritual	Mental	Emotional	Chakra	Physical - Spinal	Physical - Organs	Function	Malfunction
Trance mediumship, Knowingness, Higher self, Cosmic energy intake	Clarity, Pure awareness, Optimism/Pessimism, Imagination	Peace, Tranquility, Chaos, Blame, Arrogance, Dissatisfaction	Cranial Crown 7	Skull Bones, Cranial nerves	Brain, Pineal gland, CSF ventricles	Cognition, Critical thinking	Mental disorders, Head pain, Dizziness
Clairvoyance, Abstract intuition, Precognition, Inner voice	Trusting, Memory, Intellect, Reasoning, Ignorance	Fear, Pride, Inflexibility, Self conscious, Confusion, Envy, Humiliation	Cranio-Cervical 3rd Eye 6	Occiput, C1 Atlas, C2 Axis, C3-C7 Cervical & Brachial plexus	Brain, Cerebellum, Hypothalamus, Pituitary, Eyes, Ears, Nose, Throat	Brain-body communication, Hearing, Seeing, Smelling, Tasting, Chewing	Head & Neck pain, Dizziness, Eye, Ear, Nose, Throat issues, Migraines, Jaw pains, Sleep disorders
Clairaudience, Telepathy, Pragmatic intuition	Authority, Creative identity, Inner drive	Expressionless, Feeling Stuck, Sadness, Vulnerability, Disgust	Cervical Throat 5	C1-T1 Cervical & Brachial plexus	Thyroid, Vocal cords, Heart, Lungs, Neck & shoulders, Brachial plexus	Brain-body communication, Verbal communication, Hormone regulation	Neck pain, Sore throat, Arm. & Shoulder pain, Stiffness, Hormonal disorders, Sleep disorders
Love Affinity	Self acceptance, Harmony, Equilibrium	Compassion, Love, Tenderness, Joy, Abundance, Heartache, Betrayal, Grief, Rejection, Hatred	Upper Thorax Heart 4	T1-T6 Sympathetic ganglion	Heart, Lungs, Thymus, Liver, Gallbladder	Circulation, Breathing	Chest pain, Breathing issues, Asthma, Heart circulation, Heartburn
Out of body experience, Life force energy distribution, Inner integration	Will Power, Egotism, Restlessness	Paranoia, Anger, Low self esteem, Resentment, Nervousness, Worry, Guilt, Anxiety, Jealousy, Regret	Lower Thorax Solar Plexus 3	T7-T12 Ileocecal valve, Celiac plexus, Pyloric valve	Kidneys, Diaphragm, Liver, Gallbladder, Spleen, Pancreas, Stomach, Adrenals, Large & Small intestine	Breathing, Detoxification, Elimination, Digestion, Assimilation	Kidney Stones, Liver, Pancreatic failure, Gall Stones, Gastric disorders, Sleep disorders, Allergies
Clairsentience	Sexuality, Emotional need, Relationships, Social ambition, Addiction	Enthusiasm, Inner conflict, Peeved off, Frozen will, Fear, Lust, Manipulative	Lumbo-Sacral Naval 2	L1-S1 Lumbar plexus, Celiac plexus, Sciatic nerve	Bladder, Sex organs, Prostate, Uterus, Large intestine, Appendix	Reproduction, Elimination	Low back pain, IBS, Allergies, Sciatica, Kidney & Urinary issues, Constipation
Survival, Material harmony	Safety, Security, Emotional, Physicality, Sense of Lack	Vulnerability, Neediness, Insecurity, Control issues, Obsession, Materialism, Distrust	Sacro-Pelvic Spinal Base 1	S1-S5 Sacral plexus, Sciatic nerve	Rectum, Anus, Colon, Bladder, Sex organs	Reproduction, Elimination	Menstrual pains, Cramping, Sterility, SI pain, Leg circulation, Knee pains, Numbness, Digestive disorders, Allergies
Psychometry, Healing, Telekinesis	—	—	Hands Palm center	Radial, Medial, Ulnar nerves	—	Creative manifestation, Energy transfer	Arthritis, Swelling, Gout, Inflammation, Cramping, Carpel tunnel
Grounding, Earth energy intake	—	—	Feet Foot arch	Tibial, Sural, Peroneal, Plantar, Cutaneous, Saphenous Nerves	—	Transportation, Physical manifestation	Arthritis, Swelling, Gout, Inflammation, Cramping, Tarsal tunnel

Note: Points will cross and may affect multiple chakra sites. This chart displays the most basic relationship between the spiritual, mental, emotional, and physical human planes.

NOUSOULI METHOD
Copyright 2004-2016. All Rights Reserved.

Chapter 12:
The Future of Sex, (Virtual Reality, Artificial Intelligence) and Final Thoughts

"One of the functions of an organization, of any organism, is to anticipate the future, so that those relationships can persist over time."
~ Kevin Kelly

If the first few chapters of this book taught us anything, it is that sexuality is fluid. It changes with cultures, societies, and bends to many different influences. If we were to look at sexuality through time, we would see that where it began and where it is today are two entirely different phenomena. On one hand, you have sex without boundaries, open social norms and a general environment of acceptance. On the other hand, you see strict religious norms dictating what is normal, and social influence forcing people to keep their sexuality a secret. Over time, sex has become something mechanical, and external forces have become so invasive that it is becoming dehumanized and lacking its spiritual spark.

So what is the next frontier? What is the natural progression of these changes? As we've seen with the onset of rampant pornography addiction, many people find themselves more able to express their sexualities in their minds rather than with other people. We are already witnessing a massive change in the use of technology with sex - people can watch whatever kind of porn they want, they can use sex toys that pleasure them better than a mate (they think), and they can explore their darkest desires without ever having to expose themselves or risk ridicule. Is it such a far leap to assume that one day we will entirely remove the human element from sex?

12.1 Robot Sex

You're probably thinking there is no way you're ever going to have sex with a robot. Of course not, human flesh feels too good and you'd be afraid of the potential malfunction that would result in an awkward call to emergency services, right? What if technology had advanced far enough that the sensation of touch, the anatomy, and the robot mechanics had been so smoothly fine-tuned that it became feasible to have a robot sex partner? According to futurist, Dr. Ian Pearson, by 2050 casual sex with humanoid robots will be a regular thing. What about virtual reality simulators that allow you to view a sex tape as though you're the man or woman in the video? Would you buy the futuristic looking simulator goggle piece to view porn and feel like you're really in it? Although the actual life sized robots aren't here yet, the 3D headset technology is available and selling world-wide.

Current Technology

While some of the readers may be familiar with "Real Dolls," some readers may think of a new collection of children's toys. These are not children's toys, and are in fact designed for men and women as high-end sex dolls. "Real Dolls" have been around since 1996, and over the last 20 years they have experienced a dramatic increase in business. To date, the company has developed ever-increasingly complex dolls, and now has both male and female body designs. Their dolls are incredibly, almost freakishly, lifelike and come customizable in just about any way you can think.

Aside from "Real Dolls," there are also virtual reality tools that are designed to be visually appealing enough to make it seem like the real thing. Have you ever been inside a ride simulator, like a rollercoaster or an air raid battle? It's similar to that, using the same technology that has made video games like Halo and Call of Duty so popular; the visuals are so realistic, you get sucked in. Add this technology to the power of the porn industry, and you may have an unstoppable force on your hands (no pun intended). The "Tenga," a Japanese invention designed to simulate a hand job, combines both a robotic arm and pump (where the penis goes) with virtual reality goggles. Place the goggles over your face, the arm and pump over your penis, and you will be placed in a virtual reality where the video and the robotic arm work in tandem to simulate a real experience.

These are just a couple of examples of the vast array of technology already in existence that caters to sex. The outrageous success of the "Real Dolls," whose manufacturers are currently working on a robotic/animatronic version, should be an indicator that robot sex is really not too far flung, and not as far in the future as we once thought. All of this to say: the future is already here, and it looks pretty good for those selling sex.

Upcoming Technology

If you ever follow news releases for an entertainment or electronics exposition, you will know that every year a huge new product is released. The growth of technology in today's world is entirely unencumbered, and the only way to go is up. Because of this, the porn and sex industries take these new inventions and find ways to target them to their (very large) audience. While some may be shy or generally disgusted by the variety of technology available, many more people are intrigued. The reality is that the future of sex technology is appealing to many people, and the industries concerned are definitely going to keep up with demand.

As mentioned before, "Real Dolls" and their manufacturers are attempting to prototype the first ever sex robot. These robots would be controlled wirelessly through a program or app, with preset functions you can adapt to your needs. The doll will be able to move and react similar to a real sexual partner. Let your imagination run wild for a minute here - the options are endless. In addition to this, sex tools such as masturbation devices will only be improved, sex toys will be more customizable and irreplaceable, and so on.

12.2 Benefits of Artificial Intelligence

There's no denying that there will be a massive growth in the sex technology industry - people like their toys. While there are plenty of concerns that go along with this reality, is it also possible that there could be some unexpected benefits? For example, many men and women who have been the pioneers of sex dolls and users of virtual reality interfaces say that they have experienced a positive increase in their overall satisfaction with life. Even more surprising is that most users admit to have an emotional attachment to their sex technology, saying that the dolls or software make them feel less lonely.

Many people in this world feel incredibly demoralized when they are unable to find a mate, or when they suffer from other conditions that affect their mood or ability to socialize (such as a handicap). Maybe sex technology is the best way to provide companionship and a physical outlet for these individuals, and can provide enough security and confidence to help them get through their everyday lives. Scientists have also pondered the physical benefits that a more sexual life would provide many individuals using these technologies. Orgasms are known to increase lifespan and improve overall mood and physical health. Sex itself (whether with a robot or a person) is also a workout, and can result in a longer life as well. If people are frequently reaching climax while having physical sex, maybe it would increase overall health for users.

One unspoken undercurrent of the robot sex phenomenon is that these technologies can aid in social change. If robots are used instead of human prostitutes, society at large could mostly eliminate the sex trade. This could prevent the notorious underground kidnappings and trades made across borders every day. On a smaller scale, robotic sex could prevent adultery or rape, if someone has an outlet like a non-judgmental, programmable robot. Not only this, but it would decrease the prevalence of STIs and STDs, saving lives and promoting public health. Robots can be cleaned, after all.

Still not sold? You're not alone. Apparently only 1 in 5 people polled for a survey admitted that they would have sex with a robot in 2014. While the number is sure to rise, it will most likely be a very hot button issue when fully-functioning sex robots finally hit the scene.

Robots Over Relationships

People who are concerned about the advancement of artificial intelligence cite already lacking human connections as a sticking point for their arguments. Between the Internet, computers, cable and smart phones, humans hardly ever look each other in the eyes as it is. When you replace something as fundamental and connective as sex, you might just be removing humanity entirely. This, of course, is a very legitimate concern especially from the physical and spiritual points of view. Without physical touch, humans are known to become desensitized and less aware of their surroundings. Consider how premature babies can be saved from the brink of death by merely being held by their mother, or how much better you feel after a hug or kiss from a loved one. Scientists and relationship experts alike all agree: we need physical touch.

Many people who support Artificial Intelligence and "sex-bots" believe that the biggest selling point is their ability to provide the perfect relationship. A man or woman can design their robot based on their needs and desires, can purchase the robot, and have it shipped to their house. Little to no care is needed, there are no hurt feelings, and the standards are based on what the owner wants. There are no arguments, no cheating, and most likely no weddings. There will never be children. While this may seem like the ideal arrangement for some, is it not lacking in the human aspect? Don't we need human touch, don't we learn from arguing, don't we want to experience one another?

Just assume, for a moment, that every man and woman has access to a sex robot. How would these individuals interact with real men or women after having purchased one of these "toys"? Would there be mutual love and respect? Would he or she be able to voice their adoration for their partner? Would the fantasies he or she holds be explored with their partner? Or would it simply be about procreation, and the sex robot would be their fall back when they fail to make a human connection? It is possible that humans would fail to interact at all - physically, emotionally, spiritually, or sexually - with access to this technology.

12.3 Spirituality and the Advent of AI

It's fairly easy to assume that, from a spiritual perspective, rampant use of robot sex may dramatically affect the energies and chakras of an individual engaging in this form of intercourse. While physically it may feel the same, the soul will know the difference. After all, what is more intimate about sex than exchanging deep soul-gazing stares with your partner, or feeling the transference of love and adoration from person to person? A robot cannot replenish your yang energy, nor will it ever balance your chakras. Without a well-balanced energy, you will feel constantly dissatisfied and at sea in your life. Robots cannot replace humans, and they certainly cannot replace souls.

As spiritual entities, robot sex is more than mildly concerning. Sorry to be the bearer of bad news, but robots do not have souls and do not produce energy - they merely consume it. Unfortunately, there will probably never be a robot with an aura or chakras, and that would be stretching the limits too far if there ever was. When a human has sex with a robot, or uses a toy to stimulate him or herself to climax, or engages in virtual reality simulation, they are essentially denying their spirit's essence. Your energies connect with nothing, and you are not operating on the highest vibration of interaction in terms of sharing energy with another living person. While there have been some cases (usually men) where a person genuinely cares for their love doll, this is not the same as human love, as that "toy" cannot reciprocate one's feelings for its owner. Could this human interaction void eventually lead to new diseases of the mind and body? Time will tell this tale.

12.4 Mechanics of Sex

Sex robots and sex toys seem like fun additions to your sexual exploration, and they definitely can be. There is nothing wrong with exploring the new frontier, engaging in playful interactions with your lover(s) and these new gadgets. However, as with most things, humans can take things too far or rely too heavily on their technologies in order to get by in daily life. There is nothing inherently wrong with "sexbots" or masturbation gadgets or fancy vibrators or any other thing you can think of. The downside to these new tools does not lie with the tools themselves, but with the user. Humans tend to take the "easy way out," and have shown themselves to be unable to use technology in moderation. Many people today experience addiction-like symptoms towards television, smart phones, cable and technology in general. As mentioned before, nearly 25% of men admit they are concerned about their porn consumption. Many women often admit that they rely on a sex toy to help them reach climax after sex with a partner. What makes humans think they can handle Artificial Intelligence?

We, as humans, have to remember that loving interaction and touch are key components to our health and happiness. Without these things, humans become nearly robot-like themselves: emotionless and mechanical in their daily lives. As beings with a divine spirit within, we also must accept the fact that a robot cannot provide for us what humans can. Technology can be a great addition to our lives, and help us in more ways than we can even fathom. But it can also hurt us if we do not use the tools as they are intended. If society does eventually embrace robot sex, it would have to be under the right conditions where everyone understands the social and personal implications. Maybe, if everyone knew the risks at hand, a lot of damage could be prevented.

Sex is about so much more than just postural mechanics. It's not just about the sensation, the orgasm, or even simply inserting the right parts in to the right holes. Sex is about people and their energies connecting on a level higher than the present plane of existence; sex connects us to the depth and span of the Universe. Without sex, we could not fully love our partner, and we could not create extensions of that love through children. Robots can provide physical stimulation, but they cannot provide for the heart or soul. Humans will come to find, in time, that purely physical sex leads to deterioration in the quality of overall life. Hopefully, society accepts this before fully embracing Artificial Intelligence.

12.5 Conclusion

We are experiencing a rapid social change in regards to sex, one that is constantly moving and evolving. Within the past 40 years or so, we have witnessed sexual revolutions on a massive scale, from women to homosexual and transgendered individuals. Sex is such an integral part of our society, from our television and books to even advertising. Younger and younger children are being educated on the mechanics of sex, and more people are sadly experiencing more STIs and STDs than any other time in history due to poor understanding of sex consciousness. Outside influencers like the Church and Government want to continue enforcement of their "rules" in your bedroom. Science is creating robots capable of sex, as you just read in the previous sections of this chapter. The question is, "Where will our relationship to sex be in 15, 25, 45 years down the road?"

Concerns for Sexuality

While there are most definitely positive advancements in our sexuality, at least in Western culture, there are still many unhealthy views on the subject. Between legislation, religion, and personal beliefs, sexuality is still on the forefront of everyone's mind. Another concern is that sex is often removed from love in our social conversation. While we talk about finding that perfect combination of sex and love, we often believe that sex without love (and love without sex) is a perfectly feasible compromise to make. We have removed the sacred spirit from sex.

The Future of Sex, (Virtual Reality, Artificial Intelligence) and Final Thoughts

In this book, you have evaluated (nearly) everything that there is to know in regards to the spirit, sex, and energy. You've been given an amazing toolkit to enhance your love and sex life, and you've got a better understanding of how your attitude towards sex affects you in more ways than just in the bedroom. If you've found the tips in this book to be helpful, or you've found the information to be applicable to your life or someone else's, please share it! Sexuality is a vital aspect of our humanity and our spirituality. Without a proper healthy respect for it, who knows where we will be in the future.

Love one another.
In the highest vibration of love and light - God bless,

Theodoros Kousouli D.C., CHt.

About the Author

A holistic health care advisor, teacher, speaker, mentor and author who is featured on major networks, Theodoros Kousouli D.C., CHt., is Los Angeles' premier holistic metaphysical energy healer. He is recognized and trusted for effective quick drug-free results, and his remarkable natural, pain-free, holistic healing system, the Kousouli® Method, focuses on getting patients to their top performance levels by unblocking pathways using the body's own repair mechanisms.

His desire to help others stems from his personal journey recovering from semi-paralysis and major heart surgeries, and includes everything he's learned about the optimum wellness techniques that define his practice.

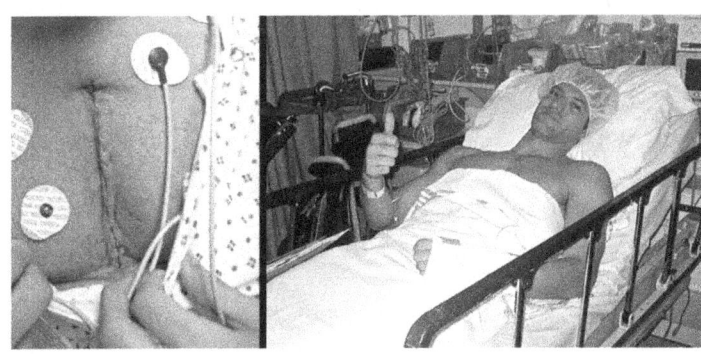

Dr. Theo Kousouli is the author of seven previous books, including *BE A MASTER® of PSYCHIC ENERGY* and *BE A MASTER® of MAXIMUM HEALING*. (www.BeAMaster.com). A personal coach and advisor to entertainers, business leaders, energy healers, and spiritual seekers of all varieties, Dr. Kousouli holds seminars teaching people how to tap into their inner healing and higher level abilities through the use of their nervous systems. Visit **www.KousouliMethod.com** for more information on developing your intuition and personal power to live a more purpose-filled, meaningful, and healthy life. Dr. Kousouli is the ideal speaker for your next event.

To Schedule Dr. Theo Kousouli To Speak At Your Event:
www.DrKousouli.com

Be a Master® of Sex Energy

Life Changing Products · Books · Seminars · Empowerment Audios · Get on the Newsletter!
Connect with Dr. Kousouli, www.DrKousouli.com and on all Social Media Platforms
@DrKousouli #DrKousouli #KousouliMethod
You Will Also Enjoy Dr. Kousouli's Other Published Works Available Now from Major Retailers:

BE A MASTER® OF MAXIMUM HEALING
How to Lead a Healthy Life Without Limits
- Holistic Solutions for over 60 Diseases to Help You and Your Loved Ones Heal!

BE A MASTER® OF PSYCHIC ENERGY
Your Key to Truly Mastering Your Personal Power
- Uncover and Amplify Your Hidden Psychic Abilities to Change Your Life!

BE A MASTER® OF SUCCESS
Dr. Kousouli's 33 Master Secrets to Achieving Your Dreams
- Solid Success Principles You can Apply Right Now to Empower Your Life!

BE A MASTER® OF SELF IMAGE
Dr. Kousouli's 33 Master Secrets to Living Healthier, Happier and Hotter
- Simple Holistic Tips & Tricks for More Weight Loss and Body Benefit to You!

BE A MASTER® OF SELF LOVE
Dr. Kousouli's 33 Master Secrets to Loving Your Extraordinary Life
- Overcome Bullying, Abuse, Depression and Build Massive Self-Esteem & Self-Love!

BE A MASTER® OF YOUR REALITY
Authentically Manifest Your Desires
- Use the Law of Attraction to Radically Transform Your Life!

If you would like to share your story of how Dr. Kousouli's books, audios or seminars have impacted your life for the better, we would love to hear from you! (Messages are screened by staff and forwarded when appropriate.)

For A Free Gift from Dr. Theo Kousouli visit www.FreeGiftFromDrTheo.com

References

Allen, J. (2009). *As a Man Thinketh.* New York: Penguin Books 1903. ISBN: 978-1-58542-739-0.

Allison, S. (2015). *Tickle His Pickle: Your Hands-On Guide to Penis Pleasing.* San Francisco: Tickle Kitty 2004. ISBN: 978-0-9706611-2-8.

Bechtel, S. & Stains, L.R. (1998). *Sex: A Man's Guide.* Emmaus, PA: Rodale Press 1996. ISBN: 0-425-16580-9.

Bering, J. (2010). *An Ode to the Many Evolved Virtues of Human Semen.* Retrieved from http://blogs.scientificamerican.com/bering-in-mind/an-ode-to-the-many-evolved-virtues-of-human-semen/

Berman, L. (2014). *Anatomy of a Climax.* Retrieved from http://www.everydayhealth.com/sexual-health/dr-laura-berman-anatomy-of-an-orgasm.aspx

Bertrand, S. (2012). *Reclaiming Our Wise Blood: The Sacred Power of Menstrual Blood.* Retrieved from http://www.thefountainoflife.org/womb-awakening/sacred-menstruation/sacred-menstruation-reclaiming-our-wise-blood/

Chia, M. & Winn, M. (1984). *Taoist Secrets of Love: Cultivating Male Sexual Energy.* Santa Fe: Aurora Press 1984. ISBN: 0-943358-19-1.

Chia, M. & Carlton-Abrams, R. (2005). *The Multi-Orgasmic Woman: Sexual Secrets Every Woman Should Know.* New York: HarperOne 2005. ISBN: 978-0-06-189807-5.

Cosmopolitan. (2011). *Cosmo's Playbook for Guys: A Guide to Your Best Sex Ever.* New York: Hearst Books 2011. ISBN: 978-1-61837-192-8.

Cox, T. (2003). *Superflirt.* New York: DK Publishing 2003. ISBN: 0-7894-9651-8.

DeLamater, J. (1981). The Social Control of Sexuality. *Annual Review of Sociology, 7,* 263–290.

Driscoll, H. (2015). Sexual Relationships With Robots Could Become Normal in Future. *Huffington Post.* Retrieved from http://www.rdnext.com/Sexual-Relationships-With-Robots-Could-Become-Normal-in-Future-4683661

Dychtwald, K. (1986). *Bodymind.* New York: Pantheon Books 1977. ISBN: 0-87477-375-x.

Easton, D. & Hardy, J. (2009). *The Ethical Slut: A Guide to Polyamory, Open Relationships & Other Adventures.* New York: Random House 1997. ISBN: 978-1-58761-337-1

Edut, T. & Edut, O. (2003). *Astrostyle: Star-studded Advice for Love, Life, and Looking Good.* New York: Fireside 2003. ISBN: 0-7432-4985-2.

Fast, J. (2002). *Body Language.* New York: MJF Books 1970. ISBN: 978-1-56731-636-0.

Fisher, H., et. al. (2002). Defining the Brain Systems of Lust, Romantic Attraction, and Attachment. *Archives of Sexual Behavior,* 31(5), pp. 413-419.

Freeman, S. (2008). *What Happens in the Brain During an Orgasm?* Retrieved from http://health.howstuffworks.com/sexual-health/sexuality/brain-during-orgasm1.htm

Friedlander, J. & Hemsher, G. (2012). *Basic Psychic Development.* San Francisco, CA: Red Wheel/Weiser, LLC 1999. ISBN: 978-1-57863-519-1.

Gardner, A. (2015). *8 Ways Sex Affects Your Brain.* Retrieved from http://www.health.com/health/gallery/0,,20894914,00.html

Genung, M. (2005). *How Many Porn Addicts are in Your Church?* Retrieved from http://www.crosswalk.com/church/pastors-or-leadership/how-many-porn-addicts-are-in-your-church-1336107.html

Grace Diaz. (2014, Jul. 10). *Eating My Vaginal Cream* (video source). Retrieved from https://youtu.be/iI-votStjFM

Grace Diaz. (2013, Sept. 2). *Men's Empowerment: Sperm Retention* (video source). Retrieved from https://www.youtube.com/watch?v=QVm3tHsZr3Q&feature=youtu.be&t=1m3s

Glover, R. (2003). *No More Mr. Nice Guy.* Philadelphia, PA: Running Press Book Publishers 2000. ISBN: 0-7624-1533-9.

Haidt, J. (2005). *The Happiness Hypothesis: Finding Modern Truth in Ancient Wisdom.* New York: Basic Books 2005. ISBN: 978-0-46502-801-6.

Hamilton, L. D., Rellini, A. H., & Meston, C. M. (2008). Cortisol, Sexual Arousal, and Affect in Response to Sexual Stimuli. *The Journal of Sexual Medicine,* 5(9), 2111–2118.

Hanson, H. (2015). Scientists Fear Robots Could Be Bad for Society. *Huffington Post.* Retrieved from http://www.huffingtonpost.com/entry/sex-robots-campaign_55f865bce4b09ecde1d9ef77

Harvey, S. (2012). *Straight Talk, No Chaser.* New York: HarperCollins 2010. ISBN: 978-0-06-172896-9.

Hill, N. (1999). *Think and Grow Rich.* Hollywood, CA: Wilshire Book Company 1999. ISBN: 0-87980-444-0.

Hooper, A. (1994). *Anne Hooper's Kama Sutra.* London: Carroll & Brown Limited 1994. ISBN: 1-56458-649-9.

Infinite Intelligence. (2014, Sept. 7). *Abraham Hicks: Why is Pornography So Appealing to Some?* (video source). Retrieved from https://www.youtube.com/watch?v=GkPcFO0cDWc

Jauregui, A. (2015). 6 NSFW Reasons Why Robots Are The Future Of Sex. *Huffingt0n Post.* http://www.huffingtonpost.com/entry/robot-sex-is-the-future_55c2016de4b0d9b28f04cf76

Joy Happiness. (2015, July 9). *Abraham Hicks: Sex & Self-Pleasure* (video source). Retrieved from https://www.youtube.com/watch?v=-DU3rovgQtA&feature=youtu.be

Kolodny, C. (2015). 9 Things You Didn't Know About American Prostitution. *Huffington Post.* Retrieved from http://www.huffingtonpost.com/2014/03/12/sex-trade-study_n_4951891.html

Kousouli, T. (2014). *Dirty Little Secrets of the Healthcare Indsutry: What Every Patient Should Know.* Indianapolis, IN: Dog Ear Publishing. ISBN: 978-1-4575-2510-0.

Lowndes, L. (1996). *How to Make Anyone Fall in Love with You.* Chicago, IL: Contemporary Books 1996. ISBN: 0-8092-2989-7.

Lyon, A. (2014). *Ancient Egyptian Sexuality.* Retrieved from http://anthropology.msu.edu/anp455-fs14/2014/10/23/ancient-egyptian-sexuality/

Mark, J. (2014). Love, Sex and Marriage in Ancient Mesopotamia. In *Ancient History Encyclopedia.* Retrieved from http://www.ancient.eu/article/688/

Max, T. & Miller, G. (2015). *Mate: Become the Man Women Want.* New York: Little Brown and Company 2015. ISBN: 978-0-316-37536-8.

Mellgard, P. (2015). As Sexbot Technology Advances, Ethical and Legal Questions Linger. *Huffington Post.* Retrieved from http://www.huffingtonpost.com/entry/robot-sex_55f979f2e4b0b-48f670164e9

Michaels, M. (2005). *The Lowdown on Going Down: How to Give Her Mind-Blowing Oral Sex.* New York: Broadway Books 2005. ISBN: 0 7679-1657-3.

Morton, D. (2009). *Sex In The Middle Ages: 10 Titillating Facts You Wanted To Know But Were Afraid to Ask.* Retrieved from http://www.oddee.com/item_96646.aspx

Piver, S. (2004). *The Hard Questions: 100 Essential Questions to Ask Before You Say "I Do."* New York: Penguin Books 2000. ISBN: 1-58542-296-7.

Roman, S. & Packer, D. (2008). *Creating Money: Attracting Abundance.* Tiburon, CA: HJ Kramer Inc. and New World Library 1998. ISBN: 978-1-932073-22-5.

Smith, K. (2015). *Porn Addiction Statistics.* Retrieved from http://www.guystuffcounseling.com/porn-addiction-statistics

ThinkTank. (2012, Sept. 18). *Weird Tradition of... Semen Drinking?* (video source). Retrieved from https://www.youtube.com/watch?v=aUPbCJgoFj4

TomLeykis1. (2012, Jan. 4). *Feminism Was Created to Destabilize Society, Tax Women and Set Up the NWO - Aaron Russo* (video source). Retrieved from https://www.youtube.com/watch?v=zCp-jmvaIgNA

Yuen, I. (2013). *Change from the 1960's-80's.* Retrieved from https://iyuen2013.wordpress.com/

Wikipedia. (2015). *Sexuality in Ancient Rome.* Retrieve from https://en.wikipedia.org/wiki/Sexuality_in_ancient_Rome

Wilson, D.A. (2014). *It's OK to be Spiritual and Wealthy.* Boulder, CO: White Heron Publishing. ISBN: 978-0615962931.

www.ingramcontent.com/pod-product-compliance
Lightning Source LLC
Chambersburg PA
CBHW080541170426
43195CB00016B/2640